SAMURAI

The weapons and spirit of the
Japanese warrior

SAMURAI

The weapons and spirit of the
Japanese warrior

CLIVE SINCLAIRE

THE LYONS PRESS

GUILFORD, CONNECTICUT

An imprint of The Globe Pequot Press

First Lyons Press edition, 2004

Copyright © 2001 by Salamander Books

An imprint of **Chrysalis** Books Group

The Lyons Press is an imprint of The Globe Pequot Press

10 9 8 7 6 5 4 3 2 1

ISBN 1-59228-720-4

Library of Congress Cataloging-in-Publication Data is available on file.

CREDITS
Project Manager: Ray Bonds
Designer: Megra Mitchell, Mitchell Strange
Colour reproduction: Anorax Imaging Ltd.
Printed and bound in China

THE AUTHOR
For over thirty years Clive Sinclaire has been a member of To-ken Society of Great Britain, the oldest club in Europe dedicated to the study and preservation of Japanese swords and armour, of which he is currently the Chairman. For most of this time he has also been a member of the NBTHK (Nihon Bijutsu To-ken Hozon Kyokai), the leading study and preservation society in Japan. He began learning martial arts, specifically *judo*, in the 1960s, and it was this that introduced him to Japanese *samurai* culture and sparked a particular interest in the Japanese sword. He soon realised that a passing interest in such things was not good enough and it was necessary to examine the subject studiously and obsessively. The martial arts, particularly *kendo* in which Clive is 4th Dan, continue to provide a practical complement to his academic study of the Japanese sword and the peculiarly Japanese culture of the *samurai*. Clive has made many trips to Japan over the years with the express intention of studying good swords. This has led to the establishment of many relationships with both the living artisans and swordsmiths in the modern Japanese sword world, many of whom have given freely and generously of their knowledge and experience in this exacting area of study. He has written many articles on various aspects of the Japanese sword and is the editor of the English language magazine on the subject entitled *Nihon-to*.

AUTHOR'S ACKNOWLEDGEMENTS
I would like to thank all those without whose assistance this work would not have been produced. In particular my appreciation goes to Tsuchiko Tamio, Inami Tomihiko, and Iida Yoshihisa in Japan for their generous help with some of the illustrations. Also for the same reason my thanks are due to Victor Harris and Paul Martin of the British Museum, Neil Davey at Sotheby's, Mark Hinton at Christie's, and Roald Knusten, *kendo* teacher, scholar, and artist. My thanks go to my friends who have read my text and made helpful contributions and suggestions. These include both John Anderson and Ian Bottomley, well known armour experts, as well as David Maynard and Rob Warren, fellow sword collectors from To-ken Society of Great Britain. Finally, as always, I am deeply grateful to Mishina Kenji, master polisher of the Honami tradition and chief pupil of the Nakayama Kokan school of polishing for his many introductions and his years of trying to teach me to understand the subtleties of the Japanese sword, both in the UK and Japan.

CONTENTS

Preface 8

CHAPTER 1
What is a Samurai? 10

CHAPTER 2
The Samurai's Armour 26

CHAPTER 3
A Brief History of Japanese Swords 40

CHAPTER 4
The Sword of the Samurai (Nihon-to) 62

CHAPTER 5
Polearms (Yari, Naginata and Nagamaki) . .106

CHAPTER 6
Archery (Yumi and Ya) 120

CHAPTER 7
Guns of the Samurai (Tanegashima) 128

Glossary 138

Bibliography .140

Index 141

PREFACE

For at least the last one thousand years, the history of Japan is largely the history of the elite military class, the *samurai*. Their influence was one that was created by force of arms and it is these arms and armour that we discuss in this book. Although initially influenced in the 7th and 8th centuries AD by mainland Asia, the weaponry quickly developed into styles that were totally Japanese in character, impossible to confuse with those of any other nation and fascinating to the modern collector.

Now, as always, the weapons and armour of the *samurai*, as well as being incredibly efficient in their terrible work, have a beauty of both form and texture that is greatly appreciated throughout the world. Since the end of the Pacific War in 1945, these weapons are no longer used in warfare and now their artistic properties are even more emphasised. However, even those swords, spears and other weapons made today must display their original practical properties (such as being able to cut, to be strong, have a good form, etc.) to have any validity or credibility.

Japanese Historical Periods Related to Sword Production

Nara	710-794	*Chokuto* (ancient straight swords)
Heian	794-1185)	
Kamakura	1185-1333)	
Nambokucho	1333-1396)	*Koto* (old sword period)
Muromachi	1396-1568)	
Aizuchi-Momoyama	1568-1596))	
Edo or Tokugawa	1596-1780	*Shinto* (new swords period)
Bakamatsu (late Edo period)	1780-1877	*Shinshinto* (very new swords) *
Meiji, Taisho, early Showa	1877-1945	*Gendaito* (modern swords)
Later Showa to Heisei	1945 -	*Shinsakuto* (newly made swords)

* Includes first 8 years of the Meiji period.

Although some examples came to the West as early as the 17th century, mainly as gifts to important personages and heads of state, it was not until the second half of the 19th century that all things Japanese took Europe by storm, at a time when *samurai* still wore their swords. Also at this time a number of large and important collections were put together by collectors of these "exotic weapons" from this "quaint and backward little country". Sadly most of these large collections have now been dispersed but clubs and individuals still meet to study and discuss their precious pieces.

Further, the passion of Japanese martial ways has inspired countless practitioners of modern martial arts or *Budo*, all over the world, transcending the original inspiration of *bushido*, the way of the warrior. These include armed martial arts that train one to use the Japanese sword, such as *iaido* and *kendo*, neither of which has any practical value in today's society. However, as has been known for centuries in Japan, with the hard and painful practice of *kendo* and other martial arts, value is to be found in the personal development, both physical and mental and the ability to form meaningful relationships between individuals and even entire nations.

This makes the study and appreciation of Japanese weapons, swords in particular, an important cultural activity for all those involved. It may be said that this study of Japanese blades is a somewhat academic side of the same coin on which the physical practice of *kendo* is also found. Indeed, fundamentally and essentially, such study is all *kendo,* or the "way of the sword".

The subject is vast; the space is limited. We have confined this book to the main weapons and armour of the *samurai*, ignoring some of the more obscure but undoubtedly effective examples that are mainly derivations from those covered. The text is written to help all those interested in the subject and I apologise to those who might consider it too shallow. It is not intended as an academic work, but I hope there is enough to interest all who find the *samurai* culture more than just a romantic thing from a bygone age.

For most non-Japanese speakers, the subject is difficult in terms of both language and terminology. Even the ordinary Japanese person may not understand many of the esoteric terms used to describe some of the features of Japanese bladed weapons in particular. To this end, wherever possible these words or phrases, shown in italics in the text, are explained when first used and repeated in a glossary. Most Japanese names have followed the native practice of family name first, followed by the personal name.

Clive Sinclaire

脚本・菊島
撮影・宮川
製作・田中

菊島隆三
黒沢隆
宮川一

CHAPTER 1
WHAT IS A SAMURAI?

*"It is said that the warrior's way is the twofold
way of the pen and the sword."*
Miyamoto Musashi – Go Rin No Sho

The popular modern image of the *samurai* in the minds of many Westerners has been created by the films of Kurosawa Akira. In these, Toshiro Mifune portrays the *samurai* Yokimbo or Sanjuro as the lone hero who wanders the country with no family ties, earning his keep with his extraordinary skill with his deadly sword. The steely look and flashing eyes tell us of his inner strength and determination ready to burst out in moments of concentrated energy and awesome violence as another rogue or ruffian is cut down and good again prevails over evil. This same man will also be able to appreciate the beauties of the cherry blossom in spring, the simple pleasure of drinking tea, and the beauty of poetry and graphic art. Such apparent contradictions were the product of centuries of tradition, development and breeding in Japan's feudal society.

The word "*samurai*" is derived from the old Japanese word "*saburai*", which means, literally, "one who serves". It dates back to the eighth century AD. At that time, Japan was ruled directly by the emperor from his imperial court in Nara, just south of Kyoto. The emperor was all-powerful and claimed direct descent from the Sun Goddess, Amaterasu. Originally the imperial family was one of a number of tribes who had come over to the islands of Japan from the Asian mainland. They found themselves constantly at war with the native or aboriginal inhabitants. The first emperor, Jimmu, established some kind of leadership over a number of these tribes, by tradition, in about the year 660 BC. This date in Japan's mythological past marks the founding of the empire and the beginning of the imperial line.

LEFT: Toshiro Mifune as "Yokimbo" – an ideal but fictitious lone *samurai*, whose deadly sword and indomitable spirit right all the wrongs of the oppressed.

RIGHT: The 12th century Minamoto hero Yoshitsune scales the steep cliffs at Ichi-no-tani to surprise the Taira clan. As always, his faithful retainer Benki (with the *naginata*) follows him.

By the eighth century AD, the imperial court was well established, but the court alone could not collect taxes, enforce laws or fight battles. The aboriginal inhabitants of the islands, the Ainu, still disputed ownership of the land and something of a frontier spirit existed outside the capital. The dirty work of suppressing the Ainu and crushing internal dissension was given to several powerful military families. They also protected, by force of arms, the rights and privileges of various powerful temples that had amassed vast landholdings following the introduction of Buddhism in the Nara period (AD 710-794).

The heads of these military families were often related to the imperial family and may have been clans founded by the illegitimate sons of past emperors. There tended to be a lot of these as emperors took many concubines. Keeping these illegitimate offspring around the court was a financial burden and their quarrels disruptive. The solution was to rusticate them. They were given titles and shipped off into the country where they built great mansions. Peasants working the land provided a convenient source of income, usually delivered as a rice tax. The peasants were also expected to provide foot soldiers when required, either to fight the "barbarians" – foreigners – or other restless warlords. Heads of villages had to provide a quota of men, horses and weapons in these circumstances. In return, they were given the nominal protection of the lord. After the emergency was over, the peasants were expected to return to the paddy fields to cultivate the rice – there were still rice taxes to be paid. These farmer-soldiers were the original *saburai*.

The rustication of troublesome warlords was a double-edged sword for the imperial court, which moved from Nara to Kyoto in 794. The immediate effect was to rid the capital of troublemakers and to allow the court to continue with its normal business. While the court dedicated itself to artistic, academic and romantic pursuits, and the finer things in life, the rusticated lords led a much harder warlike life out on the frontier, where they created great military clans.

By the early Heian period (794-1185) the imperial court had handed over many of the responsibilities of government to a mighty and noble family called the Fujiwara. The Fujiwara themselves were nearly as noble as

RIGHT: In their small boats the 13th century *samurai* harass the mighty Mongol fleet of Kublai Khan. The turbulent seas herald the approach of the *kamikaze*.

the imperial family and had huge influence over the emperors as they provided the majority of imperial wives and consorts. In fact, of the seventy-four emperors between 724 AD and 1900 (the birth date of the last emperor Hirohito, or Showa as he is known posthumously), no fewer than fifty-four were born of the daughters of the Fujiwara.

Increasingly, both the emperors and the Fujiwara left the running of military in the hands of the *bushi*, or warriors, believing that the authority and prestige of the court was enough to control them. It was a recipe for discontent, with the court supporting its wealthy and effete lifestyle on the taxes raised by land-owning warlords living far away from the capital. These same lords had the power to raise armies from their farming peasants, the *saburai*. So, if they chose, they had the power to rebel against the authorities in Kyoto.

Towards the end of the Heian period, two great clans, both claiming royal descent, emerged. They were called the Taira or Heiki and the Minamoto or Genji. The Taira persuaded the imperial authorities to declare the Minamoto rebels. After a series of minor skirmishes, open warfare began. This was to last from 1180 to 1185. The resulting series of battles became known as the Gempei Wars, which provided all the classic ingredients of *samurai* legend on a grand scale. Two mighty clans were joined in a headlong clash, a fight to the death. There could only be the one survivor.

Many tales of *samurai* valour and heroic deeds from these days are still recounted. The most famous concerns a young general of the Minamoto named Yoshitsune. In 1185, at the great sea battle of Dannoura, the leader of the Minamoto clan, Yoshitsune's elder brother, Yoritomo, finally annihilated the Taira completely. He coerced the emperor to appoint him as

was titular head of state, Japan was ruled by the *shogun* and his *samurai*. This system would be maintained for almost 700 years, ending only with the restoration of imperial power in 1868. The organisation of the *samurai* under the Kamakura *shogunate* had been established in the early days of fighting on the frontier, when the noble lineage of many of the provincial lords attracted the loyalty of those beneath them. These loyalties continued and were encouraged by the Kamakura administration.

A proficiency in arms was also encouraged in Kamakura, where a martial atmosphere prevailed. During the Kamakura period (1185-1333), the Mongol armies of Genghis Khan's grandson Kublai Khan tried to invade Japan twice. Many of the *samurai* took the opportunity to fight, but their battle tactics were inferior to those of the invaders. While the proud *samurai* favoured single combat between social equals, as they had in the Gempei Wars, the Mongols played by a different rulebook. Fortunately, the *samurai* were not put to the test. On both occasions the Mongol fleet was devastated by sudden typhoons – the so-called divine wind or *kamikaze*.

Facing the Mongol threat was the only time in Japan's history, until the mid-nineteenth century, that the country appears to have had any concept of nationhood. Loyalties, while passionately held, were much narrower concepts. Loyalty to one's immediate superior or clan leader, rather than to the country, was the *samurai*'s aspiration.

In the the fourteenth century there was dispute over the imperial succession and, for nearly sixty years, there were two emperors with two courts. The period between 1336 and 1392 is known as the Namboku-cho period (the period of a northern and a southern court). Meanwhile the cost of preparing to meet the Mongol invasion led to the collapse of the Kamakura *shogun*ate and a bloody civil war ensued. It was from this period that such *samurai* heroes as Niita Yoshisada and Kusonuki Masashige emerged. Niita conquered Kamakura and, briefly, restored imperial rule. Kusonuki headed the army of the Emperor Go-Daigo. But his tactical and strategic advice was ignored and the emperor ordered Kusonuki to certain death in battle against rival general Ashikaga Takauji at a place called Minatogawa. Kusonuki, in a classic example of loyalty to the emperor, decided to die in the battle. Late in the afternoon of a hot July day in 1336, Kusonuki, covered in wounds, committed *seppuku* (ritual suicide, more commonly known as *hara-kiri*). The tragic death by his own hand of this loyal *samurai* assured him of everlasting fame as an icon of loyalty and devotion to the emperor.

By 1396, the succession problem was solved and Ashikaga Takauji took over as *shogun*. Ashikaga had already moved the *shogunate* back from Kamakura to the Muromachi area of Kyoto and the period from 1338 to 1573 is known as the Muromachi (or Ashikaga) *shogunate*.

With the Ashikaga *shoguns* back among the dissolute court life of Kyoto, the arts, the tea ceremony and the more refined things in life began to take precedence over the martial virtues of the *samurai*. Meanwhile out in the country, there were numerous *daimyo*, or feudal lords, many of whom maintained standing armies to protect their lands and interests. The *bushi*, or warriors, who served under them, owed allegiance directly to these clan

shogun (literally, barbarian-suppressing general) and set up his court, not in the capital Kyoto but in the small town of Kamakura, far to the east and away from the soft life of the capital. Yoritomo was a better administrator than warrior, but he was very suspicious by nature. He turned on his brother Yoshitsune, who had given the Minamoto many victories over the Taira. He had him hunted down and slain, although the romantic tale persists that Yoshitsune escaped and decamped to the mainland where he became the great Mongol leader Genghis Khan, whose hordes tried to invade Japan some years later. Other tales tell of Yoshitsune being protected to the end by his faithful retainer, Benki, both of them dying lonely deaths in the wilderness at the hands of Yoritomo's henchmen.

Yoritomo was responsible for governing the country from Kamakura, while the emperor played out his ritual role in Kyoto. So while the emperor lords. They held various degrees of rank within the clan, from generals, administrators and advisors through to lowly *ashiguru* or foot soldiers. But as *samurai* were socially superior to the peasants, merchants and farmers, they were allowed to carry weapons.

By the middle of the fifteenth century, the country was torn by small wars as one *daimyo* fought the next over disputed successions or in petty squabbles over land. This period was to last for the next hundred years and was known as the Sengoku Jidai or the "age of the country at war". Over this period, the lofty moral code of the *samurai*, which included unquestioning loyalty and obedience, was observed more in the breach than the practice. This was a time when father murdered son and son murdered father, when bandits could become powerful landowners overnight and when solemn alliances and treaties were broken without a second thought. Although there were individual acts of bravery and examples of well-organised clans, these were in a distinct minority.

One great clan of the time was the redoubtable Takeda clan, headed by the strong and single-minded *daimyo* Lord Takeda Shingen. From his mountainous home province of Kii in central Japan, he attempted to control the entire country. He was supported by a well-organised clan and ten highly able generals. However, his neighbour, Uesugi Kenshin, was equally strong, ambitious and well organised. These lords fought each other no fewer than six times between 1553 and 1567 at a place called Kawanakajima. It appears that they had a great respect for each other and

the "battles" were fought in something of a leisurely and formal manner. Although indecisive, they proved a good training ground for their troops.

An incident at one of these encounters, known as the "salt incident", indicates that the age of chivalry and the true spirit of *bushido* (the way of the warrior) were not entirely dead. Takeda's province, being inland and mountainous, needed to import salt. This was done via the Hojo family who cut off Takeda's supply during one of the Kawanakajima encounters. When he heard of this, Uesugi, whose domain was on the coast, sent Takeda salt from his own supplies with the message: "I do not fight with salt, but with the sword." However, this behaviour was something of an exception in the general confusion and treachery of the Sengoku Jidai.

The middle of the sixteenth century saw the three great "unifiers" of Japan take the stage. The first was Oda Nobunaga, a minor *daimyo* from Owari province who, while a young man, established himself as a strong ruthless leader and accomplished general. He was one of the first to see the potential of massed firearms, which were introduced into Japan in 1543 by the Portuguese. This was demonstrated when he annihilated the Takeda clan, then led by Shingen's son Katsuyori, at the battle of Nagashino. The image of hundreds of Takeda *samurai* hurling themselves fearlessly into a wall of lead shot and dying in their thousands is indeed a poignant one.

Oda's efforts to unite the country were frustrated by his assassination on 21 June 1582 when he was still only forty-eight. He was murdered by one of his "trusted" generals, Akechi Mitsuhide, using the by now time-

honoured Sengoku Jidai method of advancement. But Akechi lived only a few days to enjoy his new status. By 30 June, Oda's highly talented but lowly born general, Toyotomi Hideyoshi, had avenged the death of his master and taken over his unification mission. Toyotomi's campaigns of unification were largely successful and his armies were kept very busy, but he was also something of a connoisseur. His tastes considerably affected Japanese art in what is known as the Azuchi-Momoyama period (1573-1600), and he was a great patron of the tea ceremony.

At this time it came to be more common for the *samurai* to wear two

LEFT: The armies of Uyesugi Kenshin and Takeda Shingen face each other at a 16th century encounter at Kawanakajima. In the front lines are archers and matchlock men; cavalry are at centre and spearmen on the flanks.

ABOVE: A famous incident at Kawakanajima when Kenshin surprised Shingen who narrowly avoids being cut by deflecting the blow with his iron war fan. Kenshin is dressed in a monk's habit over his armour.

swords – a *dai-to,* or long sword, accompanied by a *sho-to,* or short sword. This pair of swords became known as the *daisho.* To maintain peace, Toyotomi began to disarm the general populace. This was not popular among rebellious and dissident members of society. But Toyotomi was a skilled politician. On one occasion he confiscated the swords of the farmers and peasants to have them melted down to make nails and bolts for the erection of a huge Buddha near Kyoto. This, said Toyotomi, would not only benefit the people in this life, but also in the life hereafter. These confiscations emphasised the *samurai* privilege. They alone were allowed to wear swords. This was the beginning of a social stratification that would be formalised in later years.

With the country largely at peace, the *daimyo* found maintaining their standing armies increasingly expensive and unnecessary. The *samurai* became redundant. No longer bound to their liege lords, they were known as *ronin* – literally, wave men, *samurai* who were free to act on their own behalf as they were no longer retained or had been released from their feudal ties. But they were still passionately devoted to the military arts. With so

丈夫鬼柴田

蓑毛菊のゆうち
はうもえきわらめ
故を
中井きわけよ
山海うきず
柴田勝家

ABOVE: Mori Ranmaru defends Oda Nobunaga against assassins sent by Akechi Mitsuhide.

LEFT: The famous general Shibata Katsuiye who served Toyotomi Hideyoshi. Note the *tachi* on the rack behind him.

many unemployed *ronin* around, there was a huge potential for mischief. So Toyotomi decided to dissipate their energies in an ill-conceived invasion of Korea in 1592. He was to die before any real success was gained and, on the news of his death, the generals in the field concluded a hasty treaty and returned home. It was then that the third of Japan's great "unifiers", Tokugawa Ieyasu, came along

Tokugawa built on the foundations of unity laid by Oda Nobunaga and

Toyotomi Hideyoshi. Of the three great unifiers it is said that Oda piled the rice, Toyotomi kneaded the dough, and Tokugawa ate the cake. A major battle at Sekigahara in 1600 effectively ended opposition to his authority. The side that a *daimyo* found himself on at this pivotal battle at Sekigahara would dictate to a large extent his family's social status for the next 250 years. Tokugawa Ieyasu went on to found a dynasty of *shoguns* and moved the *shogunate* to Edo, a small swampy village in the Kanto area of eastern

Japan that is better known by its modern name, Tokyo. The Tokugawa or Edo *shogunate* lasted from 1603 to 1867.

With Japan now at peace, the *ronin* began looking for some way to employ their skill with weapons. Some decided to live outside the law, while others started martial arts schools or became teachers of other arts and crafts they were qualified in. This was also the time of the great sword pilgrimages, usually conducted by *ronin* sometimes with a retinue of several hundred followers. One of its best known exponents was the amazing Miyamoto Musashi.

Born in 1584, Miyamoto Musashi was descended from the powerful Harima clan in Kyushu (the southernmost of Japan's main islands) and his father, Muninsai, was a competent swordsman. Musashi himself was a *ronin* from the modern Mimasaka area in the west of Japan. As a young man he seems to have been wild and untameable, as well as big and strong. From an early age he was inspired to learn *kendo*, Japanese fencing. At the age of only thirteen, he slew a *samurai*, Arima Kihei, in single combat, and he defeated Tadashima Akiyama at the age of sixteen. For Musashi, it seems it was not enough to be proficient with the sword technically. He sought to pursue

ABOVE: Toyotomi Hideyoshi in his distinctive "sun rays" *kabuto* directs the battle. Honda Tadakatsu may also be seen in his antler-adorned *kabuto*.

RIGHT: A 19th century posed photograph of two *samurai* each wearing a *daisho* and the *kami-shiho* (hemp wings) with *hakama*.

enlightenment (in the Buddhist sense of the word) through the arduous, difficult and often painful practice of *kendo*. He went off on a "warrior's pilgrimage", living a life of great hardship and seldom washing – you could be ambushed in the bath with no weapon to hand. Looking unkempt and wretched, he travelled the country fighting duels and single-mindedly perfecting his fencing skills. Before he was twenty-nine, he had fought over sixty contests, winning every one. He was invincible and found it unnecessary to use real swords any more. As he continued his quest for enlightenment through the understanding of *kendo*, he found wooden swords quite sufficient.

Eventually he achieved enlightenment and became a master of many arts. He was an expert painter, carver, sword-fittings maker, calligrapher and strategist, as well as an unbeatable fencer. To him, after enduring years of great hardship and following the torturous path in search of "the way" in *kendo*, all things were possible. He dictated a book, *Go Rin No Sho* (The Book of Five Rings), to one of his pupils shortly before his death. To this day *Go Rin No Sho* is an inspiration for the *kendo* practitioner, as well as the Japanese businessman planning the strategy for an export drive – in the belief that "business is war".

Tokugawa Ieyasu was a brilliant tactician and organiser. But his regime was a police state and its grip was further tightened by his heirs. The *samurai*, who had brought him to power, were given both rank and privilege. By law they wore the *daisho*, which was seen as the badge of rank of the *samurai* class. Tokugawa strategically allocated the *daimyo*'s fiefdoms so that a trusted ally or relative was given a fiefdom next to one who was less well thought of. These decisions were usually based on which side the *daimyo* had been on at Sekigahara or whether they had supported the Tokugawa family before the battle. Those who had been on the wrong side were the so-called outer, or *tozama*, *daimyo* who, at the fall of the Tokugawa *shogunate* in the mid-nineteenth century, would give armed support to the Emperor Meiji.

The *daimyo* built castles, around which towns sprang up, industries developed and *ronin* gathered, hoping for employment. The lucky *ronin* joined the ranks of the *samurai* retained by the *daimyo* of the castle, while the others made their way as best they could. The *samurai* were expected to keep their fencing, archery and horseback-riding skills finely honed – it was feared that a return to the Sengoku Jidai could happen at any time. Every *samurai* was expected to be ready for mortal combat on behalf of his lord at a moment's notice, even if his position within the clan was only that of a clerk. They were encouraged to think of themselves as "already dead" so that they had nothing to lose in combat, which offered them the opportunity of a glorious death in the service of their lord. There could be no greater honour. Such thinking, which had been essential in the age of wars, was now embodied formally in the moral code of *bushido*.

Treatises were written on the various aspects of *bushido* and guided almost every part of the *samurai*'s life in service. *Hakagure*, a book written by Yamamoto Tsunetomo, a retainer of the Nabeshima clan in Hizen province, became widely known throughout the world and has been

ABOVE: Hideyoshi's Fushimi castle at Momoyama near Kyoto. In fact this is a concrete reproduction that faithfully replicates the 16th century original.

ABOVE RIGHT: *Samurai* guards at the Hakone customs checkpoint on the old Tokaido road. As they are indoors they are wearing only *wakizashi* or short swords.

translated into many languages. Interestingly, when Yamamoto wrote *Hakagure*, Japan had been at peace for many years and Yamamoto had never experienced war.

As a military elite, the *samurai* regarded their honour as supremely important and to affront it was to court death. In law, a *samurai* was allowed to slay one of lesser rank without warning if he believed his own or his lord's honour had been insulted. A famous example of this rigid code took place in 1701 at the *shogun's* court which, to this day, is retold in books, films and *kabuki* plays.

By that time, the *shogun* required all *daimyo* to maintain a residence in Edo and attend court twice a year. This system, known as *sekin kotai*, made

provincial lords' families the virtual hostages of the *shogun*. It was also a costly business from the *daimyos'* perspective and meant that they were nearly always travelling back and forth between Edo and their country estates. On the way, they would have to be attended by a huge, and expensive retinue of *samurai* who formed an armed and haughty escort. Consequently, the *daimyo* had little time or money to plot rebellion.

In 1701, Lord Asano Takumi no Kami, from Aki province (present-day Hiroshima prefecture), was due to attend the *shogun* in his palace at Edo. It was necessary that protocol was strictly adhered to and instruction was given by a court official named Kira Kozuke no Suke. Kira is portrayed as a villainous and corrupt individual who expected to be paid handsomely for

this instruction since, without it, great loss of face might occur. He treated Lord Asano with the contempt he reserved for country bumpkins who did not know how to behave in the sophisticated court of the *shogun*.

It is said that Asano was pushed to the point where he could take no more, drew his short sword and attacked Kira. It was absolutely forbidden to draw a sword in the palace and the Tokugawa police immediately arrested Asano. Even though Kira had survived the attack with only slight injuries, Asano's punishment was fixed. He was ordered to commit *seppuku* (*harakiri*) immediately and the assets of the clan wereseized.

The consternation among his retainers can be imagined. Not only was their beloved master dead, the *samurai* no longer had a lord to serve. They

became *ronin* in a time where service to a clan was the most important aspiration of any *samurai*. Without employment, they led dissolute lives – even appearing drunk in public, an anathema to a good *samurai*.

For two years they behaved in this way, then one snowy December night, forty-seven of the *ronin* gathered and attacked Kira's mansion. They found him, slew him, and after taking his head to the Sengaku-ji temple, where their master was buried, they surrendered to the authorities. While the *shogun* wished to encourage the *samurai* spirit, he had no option but to order them to commit *seppuku*. This they all did. Known thereafter as *Chûshingura* (The League of Loyal Hearts), this was seen as a great example to others of warriors dying for their master, faithful to the precepts of *bushido*.

ABOVE: The loyal forty-seven *ronin* attack Kira's mansion, armed with a variety of weapons including a huge war mallet, known as an *Otsuchi*.

RIGHT: One of the forty-seven, Nakamura Kansuke Tadatoki. The script describes him as an austere and frugal retainer, placid and gentle and an expert in the martial arts, as well as giving details of his participation in the attack.

This incident took place in the Genroku period (1688-1704). This was a time when the *chonin* (commoners) took delight in the distractions of the Yoshiwara district of Edo and other red-light areas. It was a time of high fashion in the towns where the merchant class, although socially inferior to the *samurai* who were taught to disdain the handling of money, was gaining ever more financial muscle. So the *Chûshingura* struck a particular chord, setting a great example of proper *samurai* behaviour.

In the early part of the Tokugawa rule, in the early seventeenth century, Japan was closed to most foreigners and Japanese nationals left the country on pain of death. By the beginning of the nineteenth century, foreign warships increasingly challenged the *shogun's* policy of excluding foreigners. The *tozama daimyo*, still harbouring resentment from the battle of Sekigahara 250 years earlier, championed the emperor against the *shogun*, pointing to his incompetence in handling the "barbarians". In 1853, Commodore Perry led the landing of an American squadron of warships in Edo bay. This brought matters to a head. The *shogunate* realised it was unable to resist the pressure to open up the country for trade. This served to bolster the supporters of the emperor in their fight against the *shogun*. The *tozama* clans of Satsuma, Hizen, Tosa and Choshu were particularly militant, with their *samurai* attacking and sometimes killing foreigners who had established communities in the foreign concession ports of Yokohama and Kobe.

Eventually, in 1867 the *shogunate* was overthrown and the mandate given to the first *shogun*, Minamoto Yoritomo, in the twelfth century, was returned to the emperor. In 1868, the Emperor Meiji became ruler of the country in the so-called Meiji Restoration. Remnants of the *shogun's* supporters fought isolated skirmishes. One such was the so-called battle of Ueno, now part of metropolitan Tokyo. In July 1868, between two and three thousand *ronin*, still loyal to the deposed *shogun*, occupied a temple there. They spent the night shouting insults to provoke officials and the soldiers of the new government. The hill at Ueno was surrounded on 4 July and the overwhelming imperial forces eliminated the "unsubmissive elements". In true *samurai* tradition, the rebels fought to the last man with their swords. This battle is recorded in an emotive lithograph preserved in the Memorial Shrine at Ueno. (Another copy is in the author's collection.)

The transition of power was far from smooth. In 1877, the highly respected and conservative Satsuma *samurai*, Saigo Takamori, rose in armed rebellion against the changes being made and the continued presence of the foreign barbarians on the soil of Japan. A conscript army of peasants crushed the rebellion, as the sword-swinging, armour-clad *samurai* were re-taught the lessons of Nagashino – that bullets beat swords regardless of the rank of the user. Saigo Takamori took his own life in the traditional manner, thus ensuring himself a place of honour in *samurai* history.

LEFT: The "battle" at Ueno in July 1868. The *samurai* wear *hachimaki* around their heads and simple *do*

that are similar to modern *Kendo-do*. In true *samurai* spirit, they fought to the last man.

BELOW: A 19th century photograph of a group of armoured *samurai* with a variety of weapons. At the

left of the front row a *samurai* holds a massive *tetsubo* or war club.

A series of laws were enacted that progressively disarmed the *samurai*. The *daimyo* had to hand their estates over to the state and the *samurai* were eventually disbanded as a class. The army was an obvious home and the *samurai*, with their military mindset, soon filled the ranks of officers. Naval officers mainly came from the Satsuma clan, while Choshu *samurai* largely took over the army's officer corps.

The spirit of *bushido* was to inspire the country in its headlong drive to modernisation. This culminated, of course, in the attack on Pearl Harbor in December 1941, which occurred only sixty-four years after the Satsuma rebellion. It cannot be denied that the futile "*banzai* charges" of Guadacanal,

Iwo Jima and other islands in the Pacific, were often led by a sword-waving officer and inspired by the spirit of the *samurai* of old. During the Pacific War, every Japanese soldier had his chance to be a *samurai* warrior, however briefly.

The spirit of the *samurai* lives on today in the Japanese businessmen, who have adopted the strategies of Musashi and *Go Rin No Sho* when planning export drives. It also lives on in the practitioners of *iaido*, *kendo* and the other martial arts. Japanese swords are still made today and may be seen as another embodiment of the *samurai* ethic. Although they have no practical applications outside of martial arts, the artistic properties inherent in their construction can only be admired.

CHAPTER 2

THE SAMURAI'S ARMOUR

"Miochin armour is unsurpassed and the phrase Kessaku (master-piece) is commonly applied to it. A warrior deficient in courage cannot but become a very paladin with the hope of a Miochin armour as a reward for bravery before his eyes."
Sakakibara Kozan – Chuko Kachu Seisakuben

Brought to Japan by the original Yamato people, an armour with a solid plate construction, known as a *tanko* has been excavated from tombs that date from the 4th century AD. We have also seen how much was imported into Japan from the Asian mainland in the 6th to 8th centuries AD, including the Chinese form of writing, Buddhism, horses and sword making technology. Also in this list of importations are armours known as *keiko*, which are depicted on the terracotta burial effigies of the time, called *haniwa*. These *haniwa* show that the armour's cuirass, or *do* – as it is known in Japanese terminology – was of a lamellae nature and a feature of the helmet, called a *mabizashi bachi*, was that it had a pronounced central ridge line. Such armour was flexible and suitable for use when mounted on horseback. Over the next two to three hundred years the armour developed into distinctly Japanese armour along two main styles.

Of these two styles, one was a light armour used by the foot soldiers and general infantry, which we now know as a *do-maru* (literally – cuirass round the body) and was fastened at the side, but was then called a *haramaki* (literally – stomach wrap). Later in the Muromachi period, another armour, which was fitted at the back, was also called a *haramaki*. The other, the *o-yoroi*, was a more ornate, heavier and altogether more substantial style worn by those of higher rank who were mounted. Both of these comprised of horizontal plates, made from leather or iron lamellae, that formed the *do* and were closely laced together in a style known as *kebiki-odoshi*. The *o-yoroi*, which was richly decorated with printed leather and soft metal mounts, had large shoulder guards (*o-sode*) protecting the wearer and a four-piece box-like skirt arrangement (*kusazuri*) of similar construction gave protection below the waist, while the *kusazuri* of the *do-maru* and *haramaki* usually comprised seven sections. The helmet of the *o-yoroi* was of a relatively simple but solid and heavy construction. Often it would have large standing rivets on the helmet

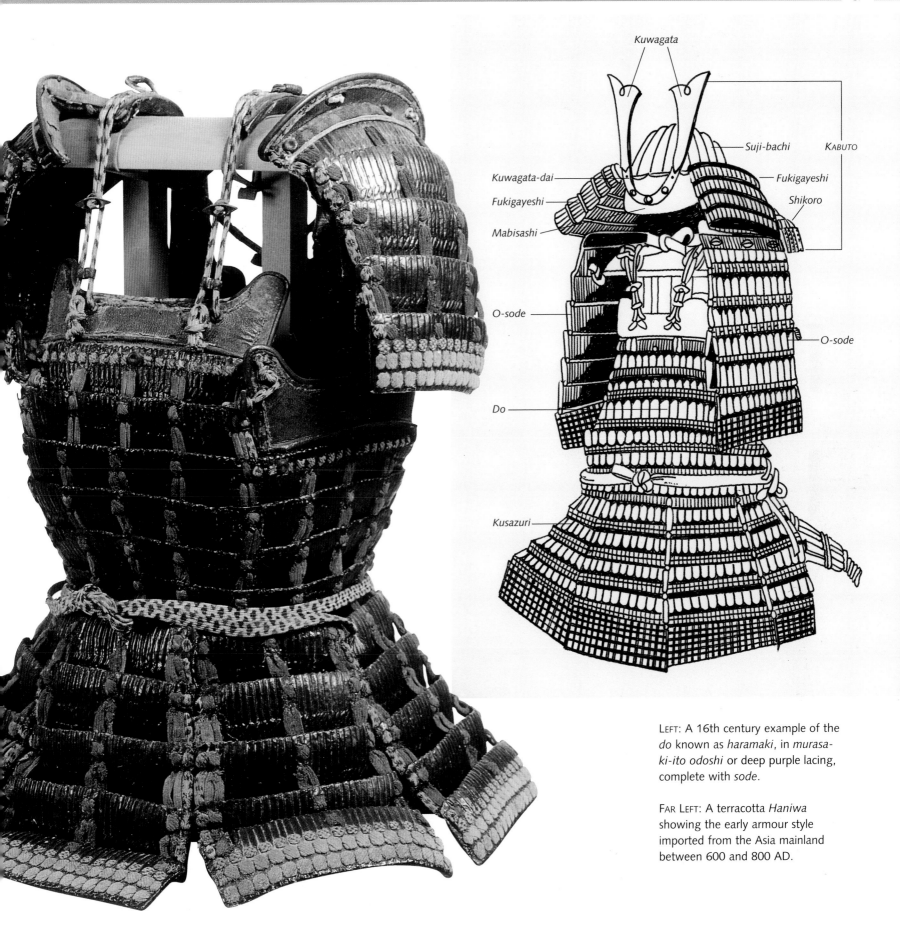

Kuwagata

Kuwagata-dai

Fukigayeshi

Mabisashi

Suji-bachi

Kabuto

Fukigayeshi

Shikoro

O-sode

O-sode

Do

Kusazuri

LEFT: A 16th century example of the *do* known as *haramaki*, in *murasa-ki-ito odoshi* or deep purple lacing, complete with *sode*.

FAR LEFT: A terracotta *Haniwa* showing the early armour style imported from the Asia mainland between 600 and 800 AD.

bowl or *hachi*, which would provide even more protection at relatively little cost in extra weight. A large neck guard called a *shikoro* was attached to the bottom of the bowl and brought forward to the front where it swept back in two large ear-like projections, known as *fukigaeshi*. Both the *shikoro* and *fukigaeshi* would be laced in the manner of the *sode* and other parts of the armour. Both the *sode* and *fukigaeshi* were primarily a defence against arrows, leaving the hands free to use a bow.

On the top of the *hachi* was a ventilation hole called the *tehen*, through which the top of *samurai*'s soft cap might pass. Finally, the peak would often be embellished by two large horn-like protrusions called *kuwagata* whose function may have been to deflect a sword blow but which certainly added a grand and formidable appearance to the armour. Under the *o-yoroi* the wearer would have silk shirt and matching leggings while the shins would be protected and bear fur boots would complete the ensemble. Generally with *o-yoroi*, most of the weight was born by the wearer on his shoulders, which was convenient when riding on horseback.

Until the Kamakura period, and the fighting with the

FAR LEFT: 19th century posed photographs of a *samurai* wearing an ancient styled *o-yoroi*. The large *fukigaiashi*, *shikoro* and *o-sode*, together with the box-like lower defence are clearly shown. He is fully armed with a *tachi*, *tanto*, bow and arrows, including a spare bow string in the circular container by the sword. The *do* is decorated with brocade.

LEFT: A *kon-ito odoshi* (blue laced) *domaru*. This 18th century example is complete with a *kabuto* made of 62 individual plates, the flanges of which are raised in the *suji-bashi* style. The *mempo* has very pro-nounced cheek bones and there is also a large throat defence. The *kutsu* (shoes) are of bear fur.

ABOVE: A modern print from a series depicting "The Field of Battle". This clearly shows the lighter style of armour worn in the Muromachi or Sengoku-Jidai period, as well as the *sashimono* worn on the back as a means of identification. The *mon* on the *sashimono* was common to several families including the Matsudaira.

Mongol invaders and later the imperial squabbles of the Nambokucho period, the *do-maru* remained simpler in construction overall and lacking the *o-sode* or *kabuto* (helmet). However, with the increase of fighting on foot, the lighter *do-maru* where the weight was mainly distributed on the hips, also found favour with the more socially elevated *samurai*. They brought the *o-sode* and *kabuto* from the *o-yoroi* to the *do-maru* and several armours from this period are extant today. At the same time simple rope sandals replaced the less practical bear fur shoes and an armoured apron known as a *haidate* gave extra protection to the thighs.

As the wars of the Sengoku Jidai in the 15th and 16th centuries progressed, huge numbers of warriors required armour and it was necessary for the armourers to produce many munition-quality pieces for the ordinary *ashiguru* or foot soldiers, mirroring the problems of sword production of the time. Both the *do* and *kabuto* were of very simple construction and some, *tatami-do*, were even made collapsible. With so many engaged in battle it became necessary to identify individual units and so flags known as *sashimono* were worn on the backs of these armours while long feather-like banners, similarly attached, were used to identify messengers or couriers. To accommodate the *sashimono* the *shikoro* or neck guard was fitted closer to the back on a simple lightweight, five-plate helmet called a *Hineno-zunari*

kabuto. This was designed and developed from an existing type of helmet by Hineno Hironari and his brother Yajiuemon, both high-ranking *samurai* from Mino province. A large number of helmets made at this time for the use of the common foot soldier are known as *hiyaku-hane-mono* or helmets "for a hundred heads" – that is, not made to special order. The better quality armours of the higher ranks now had armoured arms, mostly of chain mail, and facemasks were introduced.

These facemasks (*mempo* or *mengu*) often had ferocious expressions on their features, sometimes including teeth and moustaches as well as a detachable nose, presumably in an attempt to intimidate the enemy. The inside was usually lacquered a bright red which would reflect on the wearer's face and produce an even more war-like image. However, it is considered that although the *mempo* might have provided some facial protection, the main function was to provide a convenient place to tie off and secure the helmet's cords by means of hook-like projections. In fact, with a *mempo* and *kabuto* secured in place, it would have been almost impossible to open one's mouth and so the shouting of commands must have been quite difficult. A further feature of the *mempo* was a small hole under the chin known as an *asa-nagashi-no-ana* (sweat running hole) whose function is self-explanatory. Attached to the bottom of the *mempo* would be several laced and flexible armoured plates providing a throat defence known as *yodarekake*, replacing the earlier throat guard or *nodowa*.

Variations on the *mempo* included one that had no nosepiece and just protected the cheeks and chin. These half-*mempo* are called *hanbo*, while the full-face masks are known as *somen*, and were probably made mostly in the Edo period. These latter often had a detachable brow piece that, when removed, brought the *somen* back to a standard *mempo* in effect.

Great changes in armour were made in the latter half of 16th century, which reflect the battle conditions of the day. Rather than the fully laced *do* of earlier, full metal *do* of a one-piece construction were introduced. While their main function was to be more bullet proof now that firearms had been introduced into the country, the old *kebiki* or close-laced armours were unsuited to the long continual campaigns of the time. When soaking wet they became very heavy and were difficult to clean and dry, becoming unpleasant in summer and freezing in winter. It has been suggested that in the humid conditions found in Japan the lacing would easily rot and there is no doubt that it was possible that a spear or other weapon could be trapped in the lacing. Even worse, it might become the object of insect infestation, adversely affecting the health of the wearer! The *kebiki*-laced *do*

LEFT: A *somen* or full face armour that dates from the 18th century and is signed Miochin Yoshiyasu. The cheek and brow are deeply wrinkled, while the nose is hinged and detachable and the chin is well formed. The moustache, unfortunately, is no longer present.

was also thought to be weaker because of the large number of holes required in the metal plates to accommodate the close lacing.

These problems were lessened with the one-piece full-metal *do*, some of which were greatly influenced by European armours of the time and some of which were tested to see if they were strong enough to resist musket fire. As most of the foreigners entered the country from the south, they were known as *Nambam* (barbarians from the south) and foreign-influenced armours were given the same name. From this time onwards, the term *tosei gusoku* is applied to armour of the solid plate construction while all the old laced varieties (*o-yoroi*, *do-maru* and *haramaki*) are referred to as *yoroi*.

During the second half of the 16th century the strange phenomenon of *kawari-kabuto* (decorative helmets) emerged among the highest ranked *samurai*, coinciding with the creative outburst in ostentatious sword mounts of the Momoyama period. These *kabuto* had extraordinary designs that were highly individualistic and were very often modelled onto quite simple helmets such as the *Hineno-zunari*, that formed the base. Indeed it was Hineno Hisanori who is credited with first adorning and building a design onto the top of his original helmet creation. *Kawari-kabuto* were spectacular in appearance and, while there is little doubt that wearing one would make recognition on the battlefield relatively easy for both friend and foe, they were at the same time also used to make some kind of personal statement. Both Buddhist and Shinto religious motifs were the most popular and it is understandable that, in battle, the warrior might have felt protected by the divinity as he went about his bloody work, or that the religious device might have been considered as an offering or a prayer for the soul of those he had killed. Symbolic representations of nature, such as waves and mountains, were seen as powerful inspirations to the *samurai* to act with equal majesty and grace. Others, such as long-eared rabbits and hares, expressed virility

FAR LEFT: This *koshozan* (high sided) *suji-bashi* has 62 individual plates and is signed Yoshimichi (working 1521-31); it is considered typical of his work. Each plate has a Buddhist prayer or invocation applied in hard gold lacquer. The *shikoro* of 4 plates is laced in dark blue and constructed of real metal lamellae.

LEFT: This 18th century brown-laced *domaru* is in the style favoured by the Kuroda family of Kyushu. The *kabuto* bowl is *momonari* (peach stone) shaped and lacquered brown, as is the *mempo*, while the horns are gold lacquered. The armour is wearing an elaborate *jimbaori* fashioned from silk and velvet and the crest at the front of the *kabuto* represents a war fan.

BELOW: A *kawari-kabuto*. Based on a simple 6-plate iron bowl, a *shashihoko* or mythical dolphin has been built up in moulded leather. Lacquered black and highlighted in red and gold, the helmet is mounted with silver. (Circa 1600-1650.)

and longevity. Realistically portrayed shellfish, such as crabs or lobsters, were also used, as they too seemed to be wearing invincible armour, while bears and bulls represented ferocious fighters.

Usually the smaller examples were made from thin strips of iron while larger more elaborate forms were carved from wood or bamboo. The majority were built up, sometimes over a wooden frame, with a papier-mâché technique that employed either paper or leather known as *harikake*. Their finish was often spectacularly applied in bright lacquer. A simple metal helmet bowl formed the base, similar to what would have been worn by the foot soldiers of the day. Such helmets, by their very nature, offered little protection should they have been put to the test. The *kawari-kabuto* was designed immediately to show the wealth, position and standing of the wearer as well as to intimidate the enemy. It often flaunted the wearer's wealth by, for instance, being adorned by expensive rare yak hair which could only be imported from Yuan province in China and was therefore reserved only for the highly privileged classes.

The late 16th and early 17th century was the heyday of the *kawari-kabuto*. Such *kabuto* were worn only by the highest of classes. Tokugawa Ieyasu, for instance, on hearing that Hideyoshi had referred to him as the "cow of the Kanto" had a *kabuto* made which had huge horns protruding from its sides and all the plates were covered with cow hide on which the hair was left on. Kuroda Nagamasa fought many battles in a *kabuto* that represented the cliff down which the twelfth-century hero Minamoto Yoshitsune attacked the Taira at Ichi-no-Tani, presumably hoping to emulate Yoshitsune's heroic deeds. Honda Tadakatsu, one of Ieyasu's generals, was immediately recognizable in his impressive antler *kabuto* while the Hosokawa house of Kumamoto adorned their helmets with long pheasant tail feathers. Kato Kiyomasa is often depicted killing a tiger in Korea wearing his *naga-eboshi* (large court hat) shaped *kabuto* which was bright silver with a red sun disc on either side.

It must be stated that the entire area of armourer's birth and working dates, as well as their individual relationships with each other, is full of inconsistencies. Many of the genealogies come from the families themselves and there was always the wish to appear to have old and worthy ancestors. This would give credibility to the present workers, and so the following may be disputed by further research.

During the Muromachi period, there still remained a great demand for more functional helmets. It was in the 15th century that armour makers began to sign their work. The first to do so were members of the Iwai and Haruta families, followed closely by the famous Nobuiye (1504-64) and Yoshimichi (working 1521-31) from two different branches of the famous Miochin family. Nobuiye was previously named Yasuiye, but after allegedly making a helmet for Takeda Harunobu (better known as Takeda Shingen) he was given the character "Nobu" from Harunobu's name as a mark of favour. These latter two differed in the detail of their helmet design but both made *hachi* (helmet bowls) that comprised sixty-two overlapping plates, each of which had a standing flange (*suji*). The bowl was usually left a natural russet iron in colour, which to this day admirably shows the quality

ABOVE: Mr. Ozawa, armour restorer of Tokyo National Museum, shown working on an armour with *eboshi-kabuto*. Few skilled restorers of armour are active today and their skills are much sought after by museums.

LEFT: A blue-laced armour with an *uichidashi* (embossed) *do* and 56-plate iron helmet signed Minamoto Yoshikazu and dated 1851. Yoshikazu was a *samurai* retainer of the *daimyo* of Ueda castle in Shinano.

FAR LEFT: White-laced, this armour is comprised of 5 lacquered plates in the *Sendai* style. The *kabuto* is an *eboshi-kabuto* fashioned to imitate an old court cap. This 18th century armour was made for a young *samurai* boy's *Genpuku* or coming of age ceremony.

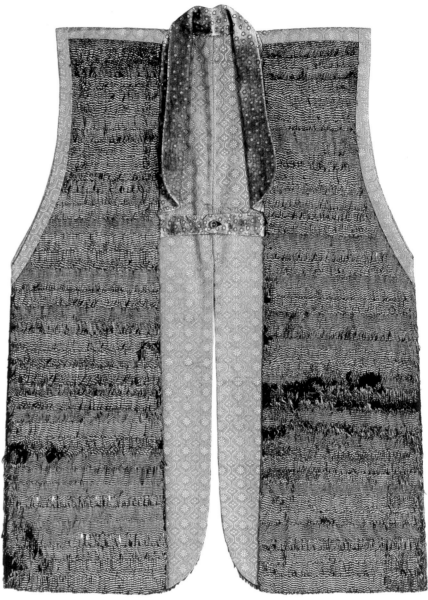

of iron and workmanship. The descendants of Nobuiye and Yoshimichi produced fine helmets, as well as other armour parts such as *mempo* and *uichidashi-do* (embossed metal *do*) for many generations into the 20th century.

Although some authorities believe they were different individuals altogether, the Miochin family made many *tsuba*, many bearing the somewhat dubious signature of Nobuiye. There is evidence that at least some of this famous family of armourers, Nobuiye included, may have made iron *tsuba* as something of a sideline, but especially the Tosa Miochin (from Tosa province, Shikoku Island) may have exclusively made *tsuba*.

Saotome Nobuyasu was allegedly both pupil and son-in-law of Miochin Nobuiye and he may have founded the Saotome branch line. However, there is no mention of him in the Miochin genealogy and he may have been

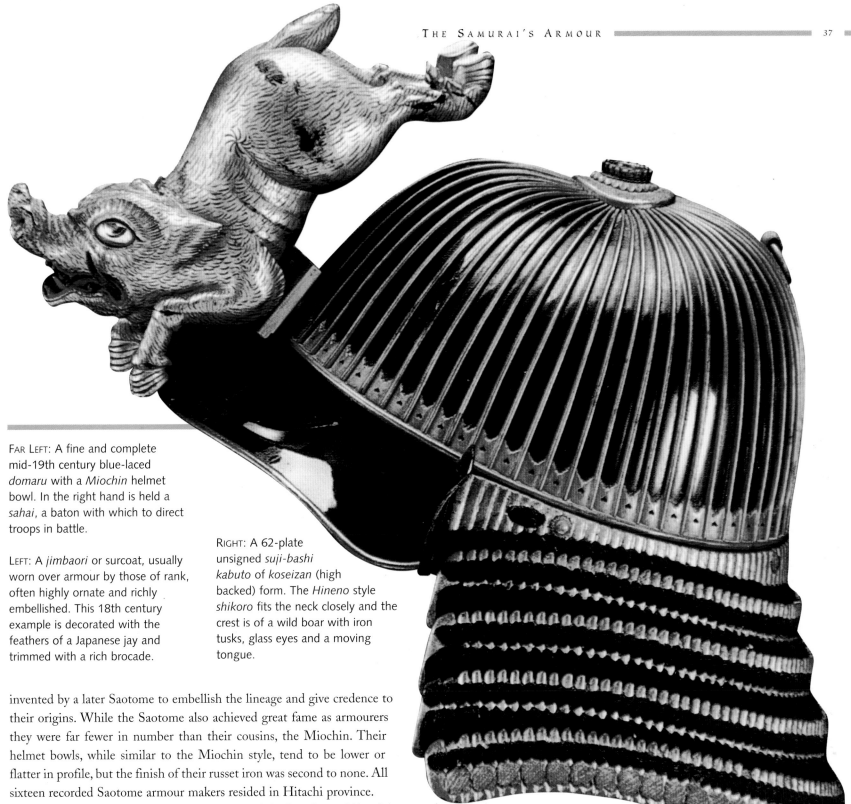

FAR LEFT: A fine and complete mid-19th century blue-laced *domaru* with a *Miochin* helmet bowl. In the right hand is held a *sahai*, a baton with which to direct troops in battle.

LEFT: A *jimbaori* or surcoat, usually worn over armour by those of rank, often highly ornate and richly embellished. This 18th century example is decorated with the feathers of a Japanese jay and trimmed with a rich brocade.

RIGHT: A 62-plate unsigned *suji-bashi kabuto* of *koseizan* (high backed) form. The *Hineno* style *shikoro* fits the neck closely and the crest is of a wild boar with iron tusks, glass eyes and a moving tongue.

invented by a later Saotome to embellish the lineage and give credence to their origins. While the Saotome also achieved great fame as armourers they were far fewer in number than their cousins, the Miochin. Their helmet bowls, while similar to the Miochin style, tend to be lower or flatter in profile, but the finish of their russet iron was second to none. All sixteen recorded Saotome armour makers resided in Hitachi province.

As the Tokugawa peace became firmly established in the middle of the seventeenth century, the need for functional armour diminished. The appearance of the armour gained more importance than practical considerations and generally there was a return to the earlier styles of laced armour. However, this allowed the makers to perfect their skills and, in addition to the Miochin and Saotome, the armour making families of Unkai, Iwai, Haruta and Hori continued to produce excellent workmanship. This was a reflection of what happened to swords as the *shinto* period of swordmaking progressed.

Because the *shogunate* was a military government and the *daimyo*, at least nominally, were military leaders, it is understandable that they and their *samurai* retainers would wish to present a good martial image even though they were now more bureaucrats than active warriors. The *daimyo* needed to appear at their best and especially on

the journeys they made in obedience to the *sankin kotai* system (alternate attendance at the Edo court). They would wish to outshine their peers with their fine armours and martial attitude. Many armours of this time included parts from older suits. It is not unusual to find a fifteenth century helmet bowl completely remounted with *shikoro* and crests in the nineteenth century, as the helmet bowl or *hachi* was virtually indestructible and had every chance of surviving the years, particularly in a time of peace. This applied to other parts of the armour as well and one might encounter a suit made up of several different older and incongruous pieces.

At the same time, fine quality complete armours were being made for these parades, even in very early styles such as *o-yoroi* or *do-maru* and this demand was partly met by Miochin Kunimichi (worked 1624-43) and his son, the 24th master Miochin Munesuke (1688-1735), who is credited with the introduction of the *uichidashi-do* or embossed armour. Although never used on the battlefield, armour was now also being made for horses. Ludicrous masks representing horned dragons placed on the face seem to be the only metal parts, but hard leather scales sown onto fabric covered most of the rest of the animal's body.

Miochin Kunimichi and Munesuke, as well as compiling a dubious genealogy of the Miochin family, also began the practice of issuing certificates of authenticity with armour (*kiwame-fuda*) as the Honami family had been doing for swords over many years. Unlike the Honami family, who appraised and issued certificates for all swords and swordmakers, those of Kunimichi or Munesuke applied only to pieces produced by members of his own Miochin family. Purists frowned upon heavily embossed armours and felt they were not in the true spirit of *bushido* but rather reflected the decline in moral fibre of *samurai* more prepared for tiresome clerical work than war. It was considered that weapons could become entangled or trapped in the complicated designs and the metal was so thin as to cause concern.

By the eighteenth century, embossed armours were at the height of their popularity but a reactions was starting to set in that mirrored Suishinshi Masahide's revival of old sword styles that occurred at the same time. Books such as *Honcho Gunkiko* and *Gun Yo Ki* described the old *o-yoroi* and *do-maru* in detail and, after some experimentation, the later representatives of the Miochin and other families of makers reproduced superb copies of these styles. By then, the *daimyo* and their *samurai* retainers had to impress not only each other, but also the foreigners breaking the isolation policy of the Tokugawa *shoguns*. The last time that armour was worn in combat was during the unsuccessful Satsuma rebellion of 1877. Many fine armours and swords were sold as curios to antique shops by impoverished *samurai* ill-equipped to make a living in the changing times. They were snapped up by shrewd foreigners at a fraction of their true value. After the disturbances of the Meiji Restoration, little armour was made other than for special presentations and only a few artisans managed to make a living restoring old pieces for museums and the shrines that owned them. Mostly that ended by 1945 and now only a handful of talented armour restorers are active in Japan.

LEFT: A white-laced *domaru* of 18th century manufacture. The 62-plate *suji-bachi* is signed Saotome Iehisa who was working in the mid-17th century and lived in Hitachi. The gold-coloured crest is in the form of a *ken* or ancient straight sword, with a *vraja* hilt. The Saotome are thought to be related to the Miochin.

RIGHT: This unusual brick red armour is laced in blue. The helmet shape represents the cap worn by priests of the Nicheren sect of Buddhism. The *maedate* (fore crest) is in the form of a copper *oni* or devil. The *Hotoke-do* (saint's breast) is iron that has been smoothly lacquered and had a Buddhist mantra lacquered on it in gold. The *kabuto* is signed Nagasone Masanori (working 1673-70) and the iron *mempo* is by Miochin Muneyasu (working 1833-38).

CHAPTER 3
A BRIEF HISTORY OF JAPANESE SWORDS

"The way of the warrior is to master the virtue of his weapons."
Miyamoto Musashi – Go Rin No Sho

RIGHT: An elegant *ko-Bizen tachi* blade by Yoshikane (approx. 1030 AD) with its transitional and distinctive curvature at the base and straightening towards the small point.

FAR RIGHT: Several battles were fought at the Uji river during the Gempei wars. This scene depicts the warrior Sasaki Takatsuna, wearing *o-yoroi* and brandishing his sword, winning the race to cross the river and be the first to join in battle with the enemy. Great honour was to be had by being the first into battle and, by his feat, Sasaki was assured of immortality in the legends of the *samurai*.

In time of war, advances in technology move ahead at a greatly increased pace. This is certainly the case with the arms and armour of the *samurai*, so the evolution of the Japanese sword, the main weapon of the *samurai*, together with Japanese weaponry generally, must be set in historical context. In this brief history I have used the broad periods into which Japanese swords are classified for the sake of convenience.

It was only on 6 August 1945 – the day of the "black rain" when the atomic bomb was dropped on Hiroshima – that the Japanese sword finally lost all claim to be a decisive weapon of war. A long and glorious history of sword making for practical use on the battlefield, dating back over one thousand years, ended with the mushroom cloud over that city in western Japan.

KOTO (old swords, before 1596)

The earliest Japanese swords were in fact, not Japanese at all. Along with Buddhism, armour and the Chinese style of writing, they were imported from the Asian mainland before and during the Nara period (719 to 794). These swords were straight and flat (*hira-zukuri*) and, although they had a cutting edge, they were far better suited to a stabbing action rather than cutting or slashing. Eventually, possibly indicating a change in the style of fighting, a ridgeline appeared on one side, near to the cutting edge, giving a more effective cutting edge. This style of blade, known as *katakiri-zukuri*, belonged to what were probably the first swords made in Japan. These swords had a tempered or hardened edge, for which the Japanese sword was to become renowned. Many of these swords were made in the Yamato area, around Nara, and the swordmaking tradition of *Yamato-den* is considered as the oldest in Japan.

The most common weapon at this time was the bow and arrow, which

was accorded high status among the nobility. And we know about the style of early armour of this period from terracotta models known as *haniwa*, dating from the time. They show the laminated structure of the *do* (cuirass), while the helmet has a high-standing ridgeline as its central feature.

We know that the change from a stabbing style of sword to a cutting one was deliberate. The action of cutting efficiently requires curvature so that, in the action, the sharp edge stays in contact long enough to do its job. Over the next three or four hundred years we see the gradual introduction of curvature, or *sori*, to Japanese swords. Firstly this curvature was only to be found in the *nakago* − that is, the tang of the sword which fits into the handle. The rest of the blade remained straight. But gradually it was introduced in the blade itself, at first just above the *nakago* producing the so-called *koshi-zori*. There are a number of swords like this extant, including *warabite-tachi*, *kenuki-gata-tachi* and *ko-garsu-maru* (a very famous double-edged sword made by Munechika, currently in the imperial collection but previously a long-time heirloom of the Taira clan). These all demonstrate the transition to strong curvature near or on the *nakago* itself. The use of curvature was a direct result of the mounted style of warfare employed at that time. This rendered stabbing almost impossible while making a cutting action with one hand while seated on a horse's back relatively easy. These swords are considered invaluable examples of the early transitional style between straight swords and the fully curved Japanese sword and, as such,

are officially designated "National Treasures" and "Important Cultural Objects" by the Japanese government.

By the late Heian period (second half of the twelfth century), the Japanese sword was fully developed and not dissimilar to those still made today. These early swords had a slender, graceful shape and a small point. At this time, the bow was still the primary weapon and the sword was considered to be of secondary importance in battle. Exchanges of arrows preceded battles and grappling and the use of the *tanto* or dagger may, as suggested by Stephen Turnbull in his 1990 book *The Lone Samurai*, have decided close combat. In this case the long sword might only have been used against the lower-ranking foot soldiers. Casting some doubt on this theory is the fact that relatively few *tanto* have been preserved from this early time, while there are many more longer *tachi* blades in existence.

By this time the laminate armour had developed into the large laced variety known as *o-yoroi* or great armour that was completely Japanese in style. This came with a heavy helmet, constructed of a few plates. These helmets have a neck guard and large horn-like decorations on the front called *kuwagata*. Spectacularly laced in bright colours, this armour was supposed to inspired the wearers to great and heroic deeds in battle. A number of examples of the *o-yoroi* are extant, mainly in shrines and museums in Japan.

Even in these early days, the sword was supposed to be a beautiful work

of art. It was thought to be imbued with a spirit of its own in keeping with the ancient Japanese religion of *Shinto* which attributed a spiritual property to everything – animals, trees, rocks and mountains. This spirit, or *kami* in Japanese, was also present in human beings and its highest form was to be found in the highest form of person, namely the emperor. This made it easy for the Showa Emperor (Hirohito) to deny to the Japanese people that he was a "living God" under the orders of General MacArthur at the end of World War II, as everyone knew exactly what his *kami* status was and no words could change it.

The sword was made of three of the basic elements – earth, in the form of iron ore; fire, in which it was forged; and water in which it was quenched – each of which has its own *kami*, so the sword, by definition, also has its own spiritual properties. Consequently *Shinto* shrines were often the centres of sword making. Right up to modern times, swords were made as votive gifts for these shrines and they own some of the best swords existing today. The making of a sword was almost a religious act with the smith undergoing purification ceremonies before starting to produce a blade, so it is easy to see how the Japanese sword blade was considered something rather special by the ancient *samurai* warrior.

The Japanese have a way of turning even the humblest of utilitarian objects into works of art. The knack of combining the practical with the

artistic extends to many things that Western society has come to appreciate as fine art. These include *netsuke* (toggles used for securing an object into a sash), tea cups as used in the traditional tea ceremony, screens and *inro* (lacquered boxes which carry medicines and potions). The sword is thought to be the highest form of this practical art expression. Its beautiful lines, the exquisite forging patterns and the intricate patterns (*hataraki*) found in its *hamon* or quenched and hardened edge, combined with its deadly efficiency, make it poetry sculpted in steel and an awesome cutting weapon.

The spear had not really come into its own at this time, but the *naginata* or halberd was popular with both the *samurai* and the *sohei* or warrior priests. These formidable weapons were made by the swordsmiths of the time who developed them from agricultural implements, mounting the blades on long poles. Skill with the *naginata* was apparently difficult to acquire but once acquired the user became almost invincible in close combat. Many screens and paintings of the wars of the late twelfth century show warriors armed with both swords and *naginata*.

By the end of the twelfth century, the emperor no longer ruled the country directly. Nominally he appointed a military dictator or *shogun* from the military class to do the job for him, while he retired to Kyoto to pursue artistic and courtly activities, including much plotting and scheming. This could loosely be compared to the Queen of England, who is titular head of state and who commands respect and performs many ritual functions but has no real executive power, which is held by the government and embodied by the prime minister. To further confuse matters, an emperor would often abdicate in favour of a young heir, sometimes only a child. Unencumbered by tiresome ritual and ceremonies, he could concentrate full-time on planning, plotting and scheming while maintaining control by manipulating the heir. When this happened, he would be referred to as a "cloistered emperor", one who ruled from "behind a curtain".

To a certain extent this system was also operated by some of the *shoguns*. For example, the Kamakura *shoguns* allowed the Hojo family to act as regents after ruling directly for only three generations, a relatively short time. This kind of cloistering of power is a very Japanese characteristic, even today. Nothing is quite what it seems and nothing should be taken at its face value. There is often a hidden agenda or somebody else pulling the strings from "behind the curtain".

The *shogunate* attempted to rule and control the *samurai* or warrior class and much of the history of Japan is about rival war lords competing for control of land, rice and the property and estates of other war lords. These were known as *daimyo* – literally: great-names. With such an intensely military government and so much warfare taking place, it is hardly surprising that great importance was placed on weapons and the ability to use them. The sword and the bow were the preferred weapons of the gentleman, but it was the sword that soon gained a lofty status while swordsmiths attracted fame and respect, sometimes nation-wide. By the end of the twelfth century, swordsmiths began signing their names on the *nakago* or tang of the blade, usually with just the two characters of their names. Rather than helping today's collector trying to ascertain the authenticity of these swords, signatures have become a distraction as so many forgeries exist.

The early Heian period sword contains all of the characteristics of much later swords, even those made before the Pacific War in the twentieth century. However, both the sword and armour continued to develop and change in subtle ways throughout the years. These changes were either forced on swordsmiths by changing battle tactics or later on by the influence of *kendo* and *iaido* (martial arts of the Japanese sword) techniques. Sword manufacturing was developed in particular areas of the country where the raw materials were available and customers could be found. This led to rural groupings of swordsmiths who tended to produce work that looked similar. Often these groups are referred to as "schools", but more correctly they should be called basic "traditions" or even styles of swordmaking.

The first three of these were situated in Yamato, Yamashiro and Bizen provinces. The Yamato group, centred around the Yoshino area near Nara city, grew up in response to the demand for weaponry from the militant warrior monks of the Heian period, known as *sohei*, who were attached to the great Buddhist temple estates of the area. These fearsome warrior monks were often recruited into armies, since their martial prowess was famous. As Nara was Japan's most ancient capital, swords in the style of Yamato (*Yamato-den*) are the oldest of all Japanese swords. *Yamato-den* is

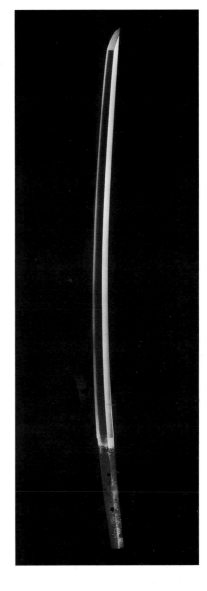

RIGHT: A *suriage Yamato-den* blade attributed to Norinaga of the Shikkake school. The blade dates from the 14th century.

LEFT: Kusonuki Masashige prepares to do battle for the imperial cause. Behind, his helmet and standard bearers attend him.

sub-divided into five schools or groups of swordsmiths, each of which were either affiliated to or had close associations with various of the powerful temples. The Hosho school, for example, was connected to the Taima temple, while the Shikkake school was connected to the Kokukuji temple and the Tegai school to the Todaji temple. To protect their property and their privileges, these great temples were guarded by heavily armed men who provided a ready market for the Yamato swordsmiths, many of whom did not sign their works.

The second group, in Yamashiro province, owed its existence to the imperial capital city of Kyoto, which had been moved there from Nara at the end of the eighth century. The most refined and sophisticated swords of the Heian period, reflecting the influence of the imperial court, were to be found in the Yamashiro tradition (*Yamashiro-den*).

The third of these very early styles or traditions was to be found in Bizen province, which is the present day Okayama prefecture. This area has an abundance of the raw materials needed for sword manufacture and *Bizen-den* continued its tradition of gorgeous and flamboyant workmanship for centuries. Early Bizen works are known as *ko-Bizen* – Old Bizen. Although things may be changing, it is the Bizen school that most influenced the swordsmiths of the latter half of the twentieth century.

After annihilating all competition in a series of bloody wars that are now part of the folk history of Japan, the first *shogun*, Minamoto Yoritomo, established his court, known as the *bakufu* or "military camp", in the late twelfth century, as far away as possible from the effete and corrupting influence of the imperial court at Kyoto. His capital was far to the east in

Kamakura, close to present-day Tokyo, where it was easier to maintain a martial atmosphere. During the Kamakura period (1180-1333), the military atmosphere there naturally attracted many swordsmiths.

A major achievement of the Kamakura *bakufu* was defining the position of the *samurai* in a legal code called *Goseibai shikimoku* that had previously only recognised the roles of civil and priestly aristocracy. Not surprisingly, the imperial court objected strongly to what it saw a usurpation of its powers by the military. The retired Emperor Gotoba set up his own court in Kyoto and called disenchanted warriors to his banner with the aim of restoring imperial rule. He waited until the death of the first *shogun*, Yoritomo, which threw Kamakura into a state of confusion and panic. In 1221 Gotoba rose in armed rebellion against the *shogunate* in what is known as the Jokyu Disturbance. The disturbance, however, was soon crushed by the rapidly reorganised Kamakura troops and Gotoba was put firmly back behind the "curtain".

Gotoba is of particular interest from the perspective of the Japanese sword. Today, a number of swords exist in Japan that have no signature. Instead they have a sixteen-petal chrysanthemum, or *kiku*, the imperial crest, engraved high on their *nakago*. These are known as *kiku-gyusaku* swords. It is said that the Emperor Gotoba, who was a great lover of swords and a keen amateur swordsmith himself, made these swords as he plotted his revenge on the Kamakura *shogunate*. It is also said that the dark, brooding character of Gotoba can be seen in these swords. Many of the best swordsmiths of the day, now known collectively as the *goban-kaji*, taught him swordmaking. They took it in turn to teach him, each taking a month of the year. However, it is thought most likely that he only performed the *yaki-ire* process (the quenching of the hardened edge) rather than the physically demanding forging and hammer work. But there is no doubt that he had great knowledge of the Japanese sword and gave imperial patronage to the profession of sword-making, even if his plans for revenge came to nothing. I have studied one of these blades first hand. It was made in the *Awataguchi* style – a sub-school within *Yamashiro-den* – and I can certainly attest to the fine quality of the workmanship, if not the broody character of Gotoba. Such swords are of course, of great historical value.

Sources differ slightly about who the *goban-kaji* actually were, but an ancient document called the *Showa Mei Zukushi* from the Showa era (1312-1317), now preserved in the Kanchin Temple, lists the following swordsmiths:

January: Norimune (Bizen province, Ichimonji school)
February: Sadatsugu (Bitchu province, Aoe school)
March: Nobufusa (Bizen province, Ichimonji school)
April: Kuniyasu (Yamashiro province - Kyoto, Awataguchi school)
May: Tsunetsugu (Bitchu province, Aoe school)
June: Kunitomo (Yamashiro province - Kyoto, Awataguchi school)
July: Muneyoshi (Bizen province, Ichimonji school)
August: Tsuguie(Bitchu province, Aoe school)
September: Sukemune(Bizen province, Ichimonji school)
October: Yukikuni(Bizen province, Ichimonji school)

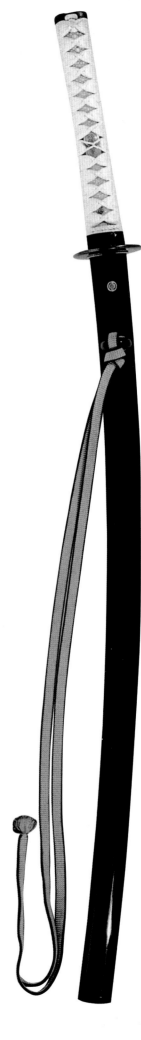

BELOW AND RIGHT: A *tachi* blade by a swordsmith from the famous Bizen Ichimonji school who signed with the simple character "Ichi" – number one. The *nakago* has been shortened several times and the redundant holes have been plugged. Dating from the Kamakura period, it has been mounted later in the restrained *katana koshirae* shown.

November: Sukenari (Bizen province, Ichimonji school)

December: Sukenobu (Bizen province, Ichimonji school)

(Seven months Bizen swordsmiths, three months Bitchu province swordsmiths and two months Yamashiro swordsmiths.)

I think that this well illustrates the overwhelming popularity of the Bizen Ichimonji swordsmiths in the early part of the Kamakura period. Swords up until this time were made of a one-piece construction, but the *goban-kaji* are credited by some sources with the innovation of inserting a core of softer steel called *shingane* into the blade, thereby greatly increasing its flexibility and durability.

The Kamakura *shogunate* faced a far greater threat than could be mustered by Gotoba, which also precipitated a major change in swords styles. This was the attempted invasion of Japan by the Mongols in 1274 and 1281 as part of the great Kublai Khan's plan for world domination. These formidable invaders did not play by the knightly rules established by the *samurai* in the internal warfare over the previous couple of centuries. The *samurai* would ride out announcing their lineage and request combat against an opponent of equal rank. Instead, the Mongols would attack with flaming missiles, concentrated archery and massed spearmen.

The Mongols' tactics, weapons and armour caused the Japanese many problems, not the least of which was that their beautiful swords became chipped or broken on the Mongol leather armour and were totally irreparable. This put pressure on the swordsmiths of the day to come up with a solution. With the Mongols threatening a full-scale invasion, panic set in. The priests and other holy persons worked overtime praying to the gods for divine intervention. These prayers seem to have been miraculously answered. On the two occasions that the Mongol hordes tried to invade Japan, their fleets were wrecked by timely typhoons, known thereafter as the "divine wind" or *kamikaze*. This was the inspiration for the World War II suicide pilots some seven hundred years later, although they were somewhat less effective.

Although the invasions were repelled, there was no guarantee that Kublai Khan would not try again. For many years afterwards, Japan stayed on a war footing, and the pressure remained on the sword-makers to come up with a way to mend chipped and damaged swords. The result was a much broader sword with a longer point and wider quenched edge that could be repaired and reshaped after having been chipped. Other technical innovations were made and a fourth distinct tradition was born. The name most closely associated with this new tradition – and the most famous name in Japanese sword production – was that of Masamune, although he did not sign his work since he was essentially a government employee. He perfected and refined changes already developed by his father, Kunimitsu, and his teacher, Yukimitsu. He produced the most wonderful swords, a number of which are extant today and considered priceless. They are a great artistic achievement as well as artefacts of historical importance. Such is the fame of Masamune even today among the ordinary Japanese that *kabuki* films and TV shows have all featured him. He had also been given the highest honour of all – a premium blend of *sake* is named *Kiku Masamune*.

Another effect of the Mongols' attempted invasions appears to have been the increased production of *tanto* or daggers. Many scrolls and pictures of the fighting show very close quarters action, which might well account for this. One famous scroll shows a *samurai* in full armour, kneeling on an Mongol's back and sawing off his head with a *tanto*. A high proportion of the blades existing from this time are *tanto*.

When a swordsmith attained great fame and status within his own lifetime, many students were attracted to him. They flocked to Masamune's forge from all over the country and it was Masamune and his ten great pupils, known collectively as the Masamune *jutetsu*, spread the style of Masamune throughout the country. As this school's style and characteristics were so different from those of *Yamato-den*, *Bizen-den* and *Yamashiro-den*, it was soon recognised as a fourth tradition. Masamune and his students centred themselves on Kamakura in Soshu province, where the *shogun's* court generated plenty of eager customers, so this fourth tradition became known as *Soshu-den*.

Swords of that period lost the slim and graceful style of the Heian and early Kamakura periods and became broader bodied and altogether more robust, while points were longer and the quenched *hamon* (hardened edge) was generally wider. *Soshu* blades are also characterised by larger *nie* (martensite crystals which form the *hamon*) and the activities associated with *nie*, such as *inazuma* (bright lines like lightning) and *kinsuji* (similar to *inazuma* but golden) within the *hamon*. This shows that Masamune was quenching blades at a much higher temperature than had been done before, resulting in a far harder *hamon*. The larger *jihada* (wood-grain like pattern on the body of the sword) would also include activities such as fine *chikei*, which are strings of *nie*. Only a few swordsmiths resisted the changes and continued to make swords in the courtly and graceful style of the old Heian period.

RIGHT: A *kakemono* (hanging scroll) by Honami Chokon depicting three great swordsmiths from the Kamakura period: Awataguchi Yoshimitsu, Go Yoshihiro and Masamune, all important smiths associated with *Soshu-den*.

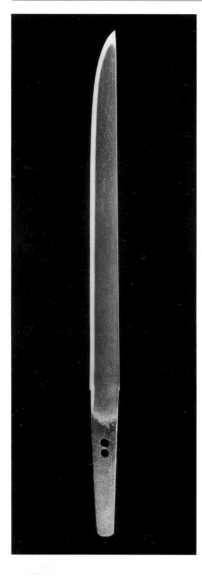

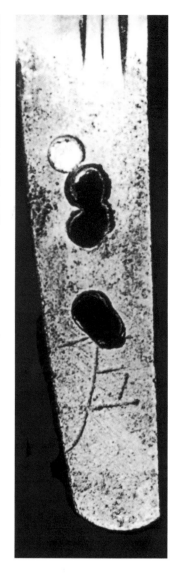

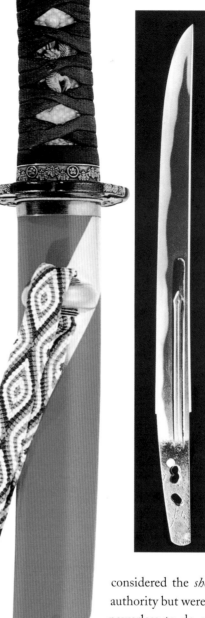

LEFT: A *hira-zukuri tanto* blade, 13th century, by Shintogo Kunimitsu who was the father or teacher of the famous Masamune and highly influential in the founding of *Soshu-den*. The *jihada* is characterised by beautiful swirling grain with fine *nie* activities. The *hamon* is also formed of *nie* in *suguha*.

RIGHT: The blade of this *tanto* was made by Sa of Chikuzen province and dates from the 14th century. It has been altered at least four times and has a *horimono* of a straight sword or *su-ken*. The mounts of the sword reflect the ostentatious taste of the Momoyama period with a brightly coloured and striped *saya*.

Masamune's famous pupils, according to Inami Hakusui, were:
• Hasabe Kunishige and Rai Kunitsugu, from Yamashiro province (Kyoto).
• Shizu Saburo Kaneuji from Kinju, Yamato province.
• Go Yoshihiro and Sakei Norishige, from Etchu province.
• Kanemitsu and Nagayoshi from Osafune, in Bizen province.
• Naotsuna from Iwami province.
• Sa from Chikuzen province.

In addition, there was Sadamune who was Masamune's chief student and assistant and had famous pupils of his own. His skill and fame are almost on a par with those of Masamune.

The reputation and popularity of *Soshu-den* spread throughout the late thirteenth and fourteenth century Japan, largely at the expense of *Yamato-den* and *Yamashiro-den* – although the *Bizen-den* remained popular. Particularly favoured were the swords from the town of Osafune, which appears to have been entirely populated by swordsmiths for hundreds of years.

As the threat of a third Mongol invasion receded, the imperial line returned to its favourite pastime of intrigue and plotting. The emperors considered the *shoguns* to be usurpers of imperial authority but were usually financially and politically powerless to do anything about it. But a plot to overthrow the *shoguns* and return the country to imperial rule by the Emperor Go-Daigo (1319-38) met with a degree of success. At the time the *shogunate* had been financially weakened by its preparations to meet the Mongol threat. Go-Daigo's initial supporters were mainly anti-*shogunate* warrior monks. They attacked Kamakura and overthrew the Hojo regents who were ruling on behalf of the Minamoto *shoguns*. Many *samurai* were persuaded to join the cause for imperial restoration. They were dissatisfied with the *shogunate*. They felt they deserved some reward when the invaders were thwarted. In domestic warfare, they were usually given land taken from the defeated party, but in this case, as no land was taken, so the *shogun* had none to grant.

LEFT: A *tachi* blade with its *ito-maki tachi koshirae*. Made at the village of Osafune in Bizen province by the talented swordsmith Kagemitsu, it is dated 1325. The blade has a full length *bo-hi* or straight groove, while the *koshirae* carries a family *mon* or crest both on the *saya* and the metal mounts.

BELOW: The classic *daisho*, the badge of rank of the Tokugawa period *samurai*, with fine but restrained black lacquered *saya*, while the metal mounts and accessories are all made of the alloy, *shakudo*. It is seldom that *koshirae* in such good condition are earlier than 19th century, although blades may be.

The 1333 imperial restoration is known as the Kemmu Restoration, or *Kemmu no Chuko*. However, it was not long before the *samurai* Ashikaga Takauji rebelled and Go-Daigo left Kyoto to form a court at Yoshino in Kii province to the south, while another, Ashikaga-supported puppet emperor remained in Kyoto. In 1336, there were two imperial courts in Japan, the Hoko-cho or northern court in Kyoto and Go-Daigo's southern court, the Nan-cho. Both courts claimed to be the rightful rulers of Japan, but Go-Daigo argued that, as he had physical possession of the imperial regalia, he had the better claim to the title of emperor. (Six hundred years later, during the troubled militaristic Showa period before World War II, the muted opposition to the rule of Hirohito contested his imperial right as he was a descendant of the northern emperor.)

The two courts ran side by side for nearly sixty years. In sword history this is known as the Namboku-cho period (1336-1392), or the period of the northern and southern courts. Many *samurai*, previously employed by the Kamakura *shogunate* and often of relatively lowly status, joined whichever side they felt had the best chances of winning in the hope of advancing their careers. However, some of the imperial supporters are folk heroes in Japan to this day. Kusonuki Masashige and Nitta Yoshisada are seen as paragons of the *samurai* ideal, loyal to the

imperial cause, even to death. Although in the first few years the two courts had some power and influence, the warfare quickly degenerated into a power struggle between the powerful *samurai* or *bushi* armies, whose influence increased greatly. The country became embroiled in a bloody conflict often fought in difficult and mountainous terrain. However, for our purposes, there was a bright side to this conflict – there was a great demand for Japanese swords.

The swordsmiths of the day were kept busy fulfilling the enormous demand for blades. But confusingly they dated them in both the different systems used by the northern and southern courts. The *tachi* blades of the late Kamakura period, developed by Masamune and his *Soshu* artists, were larger than the blades of previous times. These larger proportions were further exaggerated during the Namboku-cho period for reasons that are not fully understood. There may have been a degree of sabre rattling involved, although a very large sword was a great advantage in bringing down a horse if the *samurai* was on foot. Some swords of the Namboku-cho period were so big they had to be worn slung over the shoulder – in a style known as *seoi-tachi* or *odachi* – rather than in the normal slung position at the waist. *Soshu-den* and *Bizen-den* were both popular at this time and a hybrid of the two, *Soden*, was produced by such smiths as Kanemitsu and Motoshige from Osafune in Bizen province.

At about this time, a swordsmith named Shizu Saburo Kaneuji, who had studied under Masamune but had originally worked in the Yamato tradition, moved to Mino province. The *Soshu-den* teachings of Masamune and his previous *Yamato-den* influence established a new tradition in Mino province, known as *Mino-den*. This style of sword became very popular about a hundred years later and *Mino-den* became the fifth of the five great

LEFT: A beautifully shaped *tachi* blade from the Kamakura period. Although unsigned, it is attributed to Kunitoshi of the Rai school from Yamashiro province. It has been remounted into *katana koshirae*.

RIGHT: This fine *ito-maki tachi koshirae* has a gold lacquered *saya* on which is the *mon* of the Tsuchiya family. The *mon* is repeated on all the metal mounts, which are in *shakudo-nanako*.

FAR RIGHT: A *hira-zukuri tanto* of the 16th century made by Kanefusa of Mino province. This shows the typical work of Mino province and Kanefusa in particular. The *hamon* is in *nioi* and the colour of the metal has a whitish hue. The *saki-zori* is a distinctive feature of Muromachi period blades.

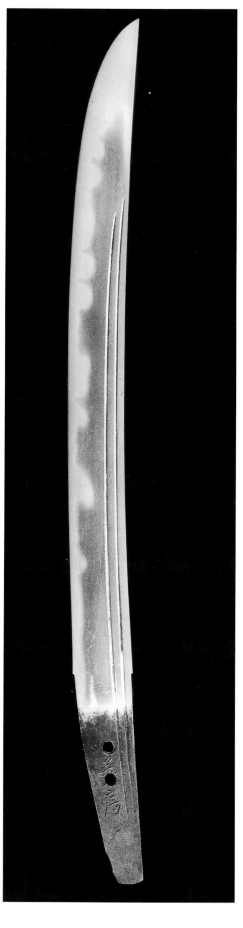

koto period traditions of swordmaking, known collectively as the *gokkaden* – although this classification of swords seems to be a definition not widely used until the early twentieth century. Classifying swords into their correct division of the *gokkaden* is a fundamental guide to judging both age and style when appraising a sword.

The imperial dispute was finally settled in 1392 by the unification of the two courts at Kyoto. The Ashikaga family were still the ruling *shogunate* family in the person of Yoshimitsu, now no longer resident in Kamakura. His court was situated in the Muromachi district of Kyoto and the next two hundred years or so are known as the Muromachi period (1392-1573) in sword history. The *shogunate*, however, did not control a great military force and the real power lay with certain great feudal lords or *daimyo*. The old question of the imperial succession solved, rivalries broke out both between the *shogunate* and the great *daimyo's* clans. Within these great clans, the *samurai* retainer's influence was also growing and they too became involved in these struggles for power. In this highly charged atmosphere, the *shogunate* ran into its own succession problems and the country split into two armed camps. In the first year of the Onin period (1467) open warfare broke out in the streets of the Kyoto, devastating the capital and swiftly engulfing the entire country. During this disruptive and cruel period of civil war, the Sengoku Jidai or "the age of the country at war", which was to last for another one hundred years, sword and armour production was increased to cope with the demand. Armour became lighter and more flexible as more fighting took place on foot – the *o-yoroi* worn previously was more suitable to mounted combat.

This was not exactly the most glorious time in Japanese history. It was full of assassinations and family feuds. Power struggles occurred between the *shogun* and his *daimyo*, the *daimyo* and their *samurai* retainers, and the *samurai* and everyone else. Bandits were able to overthrow old established families. Finally, the long-suffering peasants, whose taxes and farming kept the warring factions fed, revolted. Warfare, killing and treachery became Japan's almost exclusive pastime. In this terrible time of dog eat dog, the lower classes discovered that the easiest to make progress in life was by killing the upper classes. When they became landed gentry themselves, their underlings followed their example and dispatched them. This replacement of the higher orders by their social inferiors, known as *gekokujo*, was commonplace. It was Darwinism on a human scale. Shifting alliances and unreliable loyalties were the order of the day. The lofty ideals of *bushido* appear to have been abandoned for practical purposes and wounded and defenceless *samurai* were stripped of their swords and armour and murdered by peasants for profit.

At the same time the imperial court was facing economic catastrophe. One emperor lay unburied for twenty years since there was not enough money to inter him; another was forced to sell calligraphy on the streets of Kyoto.

Huge armies, sometimes numbering hundreds of thousands, fought for the Sengoku *daimyo* throughout the length and breadth of the land. Every one of them needed to be equipped with swords. The swordsmiths of Bizen and Mino took up the challenge and were soon making swords on what was virtually a production line. Teams of artisans would co-operate in sword-making, often skimping on raw materials in their haste to fulfil orders. The popularity of *Soshu-den* declined, while the towns of Seki in Mino and Osafune in Bizen seemed to be totally geared-up for sword production and little else as vast numbers of blades were made to meet the demand. It was impossible to maintain the quality of blades made during the Kamakura period, which can be truly called a golden age of sword production. Rather, these mass-produced blades of the Muromachi era, or *kazu-uichi-mono* as they have become known, were made for purely practical purposes and have little artistic merit. However, it is unlikely that this was of great concern to anyone about to have his head removed by a sharp and efficient *kazu-uichi-mono*. Similarly, simple lightweight and utilitarian armour for the common foot soldier was produced in vast quantities. The few good swords that were made were usually ordered specially by wealthy patrons and can be identified by their superior quality and, often, a personalised signature. But these were in the minority.

With more fighting conducted on foot that in previous periods, the *uichi-gatana* or *katana* became popular. Previously mainly worn by lower-class warriors and foot soldiers (*ashiguru*) who were unmounted, this sword was worn thrust through the belt with the cutting edge uppermost. That way, it was far more convenient to draw when on foot. Closely related to this development, another interesting phenomenon that helps identify blades from the Muromachi period is known as *saki-zori*. This is a noticeable curvature (*zori*) close to the point (*kissaki*) of the blade. This development is usually attributed to the start of the practice of *iai-jutsu*, a martial discipline that involves drawing the sword and making an initial and pre-emptive cut on an opponent in a single action. The *zori* near the *kissaki* makes this initial draw (*nukitsuki*) easier with obvious advantages to the user. This is yet another example of how practical use and battlefield tactics have changed the Japanese sword. By the end of the Muromachi period, the *uichi-gatana* had fully replaced the *tachi* on the battlefield, while the *tachi* was mostly reserved for ceremonial and formal occasions. At the same time, thousands of spearmen were employed by the Sengoku *daimyo* to great effect.

In the mid-sixteenth century, roving Portuguese adventurers introduced firearms to Japan. Soon after them came Jesuit missionaries on a crusade of conversion, but the state of chaos and inter-clan warfare in the country continued. Eventually, a strong but minor *daimyo* from Owari province, named Oda Nobunaga, came onto the scene and set about pacifying the country. He was a beneficiary of *gekokujo* and from the age of seventeen began to make moves to take over the whole of Owari province. Before long, he controlled three provinces. Oda Nobunaga fully appreciated the potential of mass musket fire, which he used at the decisive battle of Nagashino to defeat the powerful Takeda clan. Some readers may recall seeing this battle admirably depicted in Akira Kurosawa's magnificent movie *Kagemusha*. The use of firearms led to the development of much stronger armour, which was able to withstand gunfire. Much of it was influenced by foreign armour. However, the use of spearmen continued to be an important element of strategy. At the same time, weird and

LEFT AND FAR LEFT: An early 16th century *hira-zukuri tanto* by Muramasa who had a sinister reputation and whose blades were said to have a bloodthirsty character. They were especially unlucky for members of the Tokugawa family.

wonderfully decorated helmets known as *kuwari kabuto* were fashionable among the top ranks of *samurai*.

With his brilliant general Toyotomi Hideyoshi, Oda was able to bring about an uneasy peace after the battle of Nagashino. But before he was able to complete the job of unification he was treacherously murdered by one of his own generals, Akechi Mitsuhide. Within days, Toyotomi avenged him and Akechi is now mocked by the nickname of "The Thirteen Day *Shogun*". Toyotomi carried on with the good work of unification and was greatly aided by another of his allies, the redoubtable Tokugawa Ieyasu.

In political history, the Muromachi period ended with the downfall of the Ashikaga *shogunate*, which limped on to the first year of Tensho (1573). But, for convenience, in sword history the Muromachi period extends up to the end of the Bunroku period (1592-1596). As peace had broken out everywhere, Toyotomi sent many of his now redundant *samurai* off on his ill-advised military expedition to Korea. This gave these restless fellows someone else to fight for a while, leaving Toyotomi in control at home. Most of the emerging *daimyo* who had survived the Sengoku Jidai were now subject to Toyotomi's rule.

Toyotomi attempted to prevent further *gekokujo*, by disarming the lower orders. In his famous "sword hunt", all the lower classes and peasants were ordered to surrender their swords. However, the sword hunt emphasised the *samuari's* privilege of wearing the sword.

Following Toyotomi's death and the abrupt recall of the Korean invasion forces, Tokugawa Ieyasu assumed control and, in 1600, fought the decisive battle of Sekigahara that finally brought lasting peace to the country under his new Tokugawa *shogunate*. In political history, the period from the death of the Ashikaga *shogun* in the first year of Tensho (1573) to the battle of Sekigahara in 5th Year of Keicho (1600) is known as the Azuchi-Momoyama period. This time of relative peace, after over a hundred years of fierce civil war, saw a great renaissance in artistry and creative work. Some of the most magnificent Japanese screens and paintings come from this time. The same creativity was applied to sword-making, now that the pressure to produce huge quantities of low quality *kazu-uichi-mono* was lifted. The long, cumbersome blades of the *Namboku-cho* were shortened and mounted in *uichi-gatana* mounts to be worn in the appropriate manner. Such swords were quite wide in the body and had little tapering towards the quite extended point, but were now at least manageable. At the same time, swordsmiths such as Kiyomitsu, who was still in Osafune in Bizen province, started to make swords that were of a similar shape to these shortened *Namboku-cho* pieces and created a noticeable improvement in the quality of production.

The end of Momoyama period marks the end of the seven- to eight-hundred-year *koto* period in Japanese sword history, during which both the very best and arguably some of the worst swords were made. Those at the end of the Muromachi and of the Momoyama period are known as *sue* (late) *koto*. This period was to be followed by the so-called *shinto* (new swords) period, which is usually dated as starting in the first year of the Keicho period (1596).

SHINTO (*new swords, 1596–1780*)

Tokugawa Ieyasu became *shogun* and set up his capital in Edo (present-day Tokyo), reverting to the strategy of keeping the *shogunate* as far away from the corrupting influence of the imperial court at Kyoto as possible. The *bakufu* or *shogunate* system that Tokugawa Ieyasu inaugurated was a system of strict order that was built to last – it survived for over two hundred years. However, peace and social order were bought at the price of an oppressive military dictatorship.

The first priority was to control the *daimyo* who still had their personal armies. They were a potential source of revolt that could plunge the country back into another *Sengoku Jidai*. This was done by the allocation of fiefdoms tactically, so that a *daimyo* loyal to Tokugawa would be placed adjacent to a potential troublemaker. Social order was further strengthened by marriage alliances and the policy of *sekin kotai*, which required regular attendance at the *shogun's* court in Edo. *Sekin kotai* ensured that *daimyo* had to keep travelling backwards and forwards from their fiefdoms to Edo, as well as maintaining expensive residences in the capital where their families were required to live as virtual hostages of the Tokugawa. This involved huge costs and left little time or money to plan revolution. The system, at first optional, was made compulsory by Ieyasu's descendant, the third *shogun*, Iemitsu.

All foreigners, except for a handful of Dutch traders in Nagasaki, were banned from the country on pain of death. At the same time, Japanese were forbidden to leave. Christianity was proscribed and Christians persecuted. The last resistance to Tokugawa Ieyasu's enforced peace took place at Osaka castle during the Winter Campaign of 1614 and the Summer Campaign of 1615, by troops loyal to the memory of Toyotomi Hideyoshi. This is important in sword history because many fine and ancient blades were damaged by fire in the siege. However, others survived unharmed. Indeed, hostilities were actually halted while certain swords, whose importance were thought to transcend that of the fighting, were lowered from the walls of Osaka castle and given to the enemy for safe-keeping. Later, skilled swordsmiths were kept busy re-quenching many of these damaged swords and giving them new *hamon*, although usually their past glory could not be recaptured.

The Tokugawa government improved the communications throughout the country, so swordsmiths were able to buy their raw materials from central sources rather than smelt their iron ore locally as in *koto* times. From

LEFT: A *wakizashi* by Ikkanshi Tadatsuna of the Osaka *shinto* school, dated 1698. Tadatsuna was particularly known for his *horimono* of dragons, which have a "humorous expression" on their faces. The sword has a strong looking appearance and a wide and active *hamon*.

THIS PAGE: This *Osaka-shinto wakizashi* is signed Tsuda Echizen (no) Kami Sukehiro and is dated 1669. It is a broad and powerful blade with a wide undulating *hamon* that is typical of *Osaka-shinto*.

a collector's point of view, this might be considered a somewhat retrograde step as the identifiable local characteristics of the *koto* blade were now largely lost. Some influences of the five old *koto* traditions persisted but effectively the swords from this new period formed a sixth tradition called *shinto tokuden*. One of the major differences was the development of more flamboyant and even picturesque *hamon*, as well as more intricate and decorative *horimono* (carvings on the blade).

Beginning in the Momoyama period, the necessity for huge numbers of swords had diminished and the sword-makers were able to experiment and concentrate on the artistic aspects of Japanese swords. At first the style of the period was known as the *Keicho-shinto sugata*, meaning the shape of swords of the Keicho period (1596-1624). They have a fairly broad blade with little tapering towards the medium length point and with shallow curvature. Such a shape was derived from the shortened swords from the Namboku-cho period and were now custom-made as *katana*. The *shogunate* ordained that the *samurai* should wear a *daisho*. These were a pair of swords with matching mounts and sometimes, but not necessarily, with matching blades. The *daisho* became the badge of rank of the *samurai*, immediately distinguishing them from the *chonin* or common folk.

In the early Tokugawa or Edo period, sword-makers could be found in three main cities: Osaka, the commercial and business centre of the country; Edo in Musashi province, the *shogunate* capital and administrative centre; and Kyoto, still the imperial capital. Outside these centres, some of the best swordsmiths were directly retained by the more affluent *daimyo*, where they found secure employment, often for many generations. Among such patrons were the Tokugawa *shogun*s themselves who favoured the Yasutsugu swordsmiths from Echizen province and honoured them by allowing the Tokugawa *aoi-mon* (their heraldic crest) to be engraved on the *nakago* above their signature.

A good example of a retained swordsmith is that set by the Nabeshima clan in Saga in the province of Hizen, northern Kyushu. The Nabeshima family appear to have been both shrewd and enlightened as they brought many Korean potters and ceramic workers back to their fiefdom after the abortive Korean invasion and did good business exporting their wares to other provinces. In 1596, the *daimyo* Nabeshima Naoshige recognised the potential in a young swordsmith named Hashimoto Shinsaemon. He sent the young man to Kyoto to study under the legendary Umetada Myoju who brought out the best in Hashimoto. When Hashimoto returned to Saga, he took the sword-making name of Tadayoshi, the "Tada" character having been given to him by his teacher Umetada. Tadayoshi founded a sword-making dynasty that remained in the employ of the Nabeshima for nine generations. Tadayoshi's swords are known as *Hizen-to* and they became well known throughout the country.

Different branches of the Nabeshima clan employed cousins of Tadayoshi – Masahiro, Yukihiro and Tadakuni – who were also talented swordsmiths, and their offspring for many generations. The sale of their work was as lucrative as the clan's business in pottery and ceramics. It is interesting to note that, for both potters and swordsmiths, skilled control of heat in a furnace was fundamental.

As the Nabeshima clan was a *tozama* clan, far away from the great metropolis of Osaka, Kyoto and Edo, *Hizen-to* tended to be rather conservative, especially those made by the mainline Tadayoshi family. This means that swords made by, say, the eighth-generation Tadayoshi, who died in 1853, have much in common, in terms of workmanship, with those of the first generation, who died in 1632. A similar retained relationship existed between the Kunikane swordsmiths and the Date clan at Sendai, on the

BELOW: A *katana* by the top *shinto* swordsmith, Nagasone Kotetsu. The shallow curvature is typical of the middle period Edo blades. This sword has a gold inlaid inscription stating that it was tested by Yamano Kanjuro Hisahide in 1668 and cut through three bodies. In 1946 the sword was surrendered in Sumatra.

other side of Japan, where at least ten generations of swordsmiths worked.

It should be noted that many swordsmiths claimed fanciful lineages going back many generations. In many cases, especially when these go back into the early *koto* period, they should be taken with a pinch of salt. But doubtlessly it lent credibility to their sword-making. Also, it is a common practice in Japan to adopt into the family if no male heir is born or if he does not wish to continue the family business. So, even if there are nine generations, each is not necessarily succeeded by a natural heir. This still happens in Japan today and such adoptees are considered equal to natural heirs.

The creativity that came with the peace spread to many arts. In the field of sword production, one home of this was the studio Tadayoshi's teacher, Umetada Myoju, opened in Kyoto. Umetada's genius was famed in his own time. He was highly skilled at many things including the making of *tsuba* (hand guards), blade-making and the carving of designs onto sword blades (*horimono*). He is known as the "father of the *shinto* period" and attracted many students who spread his teachings throughout the country. His best student was named Kunihiro. A *samurai* retainer of the Ito clan in Kyushu, Kunihiro travelled around the country after the clan's downfall. He eventually became a resident of the Horikawa district of Kyoto where, in turn, he taught many of the great swordsmiths of the time. Kyoto was the cradle of the *shinto* period, but the new styles were quickly taken up in other areas as students of both Umetada and Kunihiro dispersed around the country. However, the Kunihiro school was somewhat overshadowed in Kyoto itself by swordsmiths who migrated from Mino province – in particular Kanemichi, who brought his four sons with him to Kyoto. All of them were highly skilled swordsmiths and gained such fame that, along with another Kanemichi student, they became known as the *Kyoto gokaji*, or the "five famous swordsmiths of Kyoto".

The prolific swordsmiths from Seki in Mino province also took their trade to various other parts of the country. Their influence on the new *shinto tokuden* was great and schools known as Owari Seki and Echizen Seki reflect this. It is interesting that the equally prolific swordsmiths of Osafune in Bizen province were unable to follow this example to any marked degree. It was said that a series of great floods in the late sixteenth century halted production in Osafune and virtually destroyed the village. Another theory is that the Bizen smiths from western Japan were responsible for arming the Toyotomi forces while those from Mino were supplying the Tokugawa forces. Such political reasons may have favoured the Mino smiths in *shinto* times.

Another feature of *shinto* swordsmiths was the increasing use of honorary titles in their signatures, some granted to them by the *shogunate* and others by the imperial court. Examples of this are Tamba (no) Kami for Yoshimichi in Kyoto, Harima Daijo for Tadakuni in Hizen province and Kawachi (no) Kami for Kunisuke in Osaka. These titles gave status to many swordsmiths and helped them obtain better prices for the products, but they became debased in later years and some refused to accept them. One particular family of Kyoto swordsmiths, the Kinimichi – descendants of Kanemichi – were in charge of recommending the names of those to whom titles should be awarded for many generations. This became a very profitable sideline to their main business of sword-making.

Experimentation with foreign steel was a fashion of the time. The fact that *nambam tetsu* (literally iron from the barbarians from the south) was used was often recorded in inscriptions on the *nakago*. *Horimono* (carvings on the blade) also became more ornate and subjects other than strictly religious motives, such as flowering branches, were depicted.

Although both swords and armour had always been exchanged as presents between *shoguns* and *daimyo*, during the Tokugawa period this became more common. As feudal boundaries were now set and mostly unchangeable, the old reward for meritorious service, a gift of land, was no longer an option. However, swords by the great Kamakura swordsmiths such as Masamune and Sadamune were considered every bit as valuable as a gift of land and therefore a worthy reward. Unfortunately there were not really enough of these genuine blades to go around, so the wily Tokugawa Ieyasu had some more made. He retained a skilled swordsmith from the Echizen Shimosaka school, named Yasatsugu, to make copies for him. Yasatsugu made very beautiful swords and making copies of old blades for the *shogun* was continued by his ancestors for many generations. No one complained. After all, if you were a *daimyo* and had just been given a blade the *shogun* said was a Masamune, you were not going to argue.

The main sword-producing centre moved from Kyoto to Osaka and Edo. These cities had two distinct types of workmanship and the characters of their places of manufacture can be seen in their swords. Osaka, which for many years had been a commercial port near Kyoto, produced sophisticated blades with flamboyant *hamon* the like of which had never been seen before and reflected the continuing peace. These novel *hamon* had evocative names such as *toran midare* (irregular breaking waves) and *kikusui* (chrysanthemum on the water), or might depict Mount Fuji. As well as this ostentation, masters of the so-called *Osaka-shinto*, such as Sukehiro and Shinkai, showed their true skill when producing the technically difficult *suguha* (straight) *hamon*, which had a thick *nie* (martensite crystal) structure. *Katana* and *wakizashi* (the short sword that accompanied the long sword in the *daisho*) were popular and few *tanto* (daggers) are seen from this time.

Somewhat in contrast to Osaka blades, the sturdy *Edo-shinto* swords represented the martial spirit of the new city's *samurai*, who were expected to live the simple life according to the precepts of *bushido*. Nagasone Kotetsu, originally an armour maker, and Yamato Kami Yasusada were the famous swordsmiths of *Edo-shinto* in the Kanbun era (1661-72).

As the peace continued, almost uninterrupted, it was necessary for the *samurai* to maintain their martial prowess by practising *kendo*. *Kendo* (literally, the way of the sword) allowed practice of sword fighting without the bloody consequences of using real blades. Instead wooden ones were used and a certain amount of padding was worn to prevent serious injury. The Nakandashi Itto Ryu school designed the first *kendo* armour, which was essentially the same as that worn today, in the early eighteenth century. The wooden blades were either *bokkoto* (solid wood and shaped like a sword) or *shinai*, straight and made of bamboo. Today, the latter are used for free-fighting practice while the former is used in pre-arranged forms known as *kendo-no-kata*. As this was a time of peace, the spiritual aspects of *kendo* and the quest for enlightenment through vigorous, disciplined and punishing practice, were emphasised. Likewise in sword-making, the artistic properties were emphasised over the practical aspects of a blade.

By the Kanbun period (1661-72), especially in the city of Edo, *kendo* had become pretty formalised and the swords that were made became almost straight, copying the style of the bamboo *shinai*. By this time there were few alive that had experienced actual warfare. The continuing peace was eroding the martial fervour of the *samurai* and it is said that a straighter sword meant that you did not have too get so close to an antagonist, with all the dangers that might bring. The Kanbun-*shinto* blade has almost no curvature and tapers noticeably towards the small stubby point. Personally, I do not find this a particularly pleasing or graceful *sugata* (shape or form). However, some very good and effective swords were made in this shape, particularly by the two Edo swordsmiths, Kotetsu and Yasusada.

Throughout the years of peace, the *samurai*, particularly those in Edo, were still nominally warriors who were prepared to die at a moment's notice in accord with the precepts of *bushido*, so an interest in the sword was still maintained, and obviously swords whose cutting ability had been put to the test were preferred. This led to the terrible practice of *tameshigiri* where swords were tested on human bodies. *Tameshigiri* had been practised occasionally in earlier times but, as with many other things, it became structured and formalised under the Tokugawa *shogunate*. The Yamano family – Yamano Kaemon, Yamano Kanjuro and Yamano Aseomon – were

the official testers and they were allowed to test swords on the bodies of convicted criminals. The result of the test would be inscribed, usually in gold characters, on the *nakago* of the blade and this added greatly to the value of the sword. A *saidan mei*, or cutting attestation, might typically give the date of the test, the name and monogram of the tester, and the result – for example, *mitsu do saidan*, "cut three bodies through the trunk".

As such swords fetched much higher prices, there was much faking of tests and test results. Indeed, the swords of master craftsmen were often faked. Swords made by the famous Edo period swordsmith, Kotetsu, for instance, often carry a *tameshigiri* inscription. His swords were faked even while he was still alive and working in the seventeenth century. A two-hundred-year-old fake can easily deceive even the experienced collector. It is said that Kotetsu's swords with *suguha hamon* (straight quenched edge) may have been especially made for *tameshigiri*, as swords with *suguha hamon* cut the best.

Swords were then classified by sharpness with the sharpest being known as *saijo wazamono* or "supremely sharp". These gradings were laid out in a book written by Yamano Aseomon Yoshitoshi in 1815, entitled *Kaiho Kenjaku*.

There are many stories of the cutting prowess of Japanese swords, the majority of which are most probably rather fanciful. One appears in the book *Sword and Same*. It concerns a puppet showman from Dewa province who performed with his puppets during the day and was a robber at night. When he was caught, he was sentenced to death by the local *daimyo*. The criminal was a powerfully built man and a certain *tsuba* maker named Shoami Dennosuke was ordered to perform *tameshigiri* on him. He was

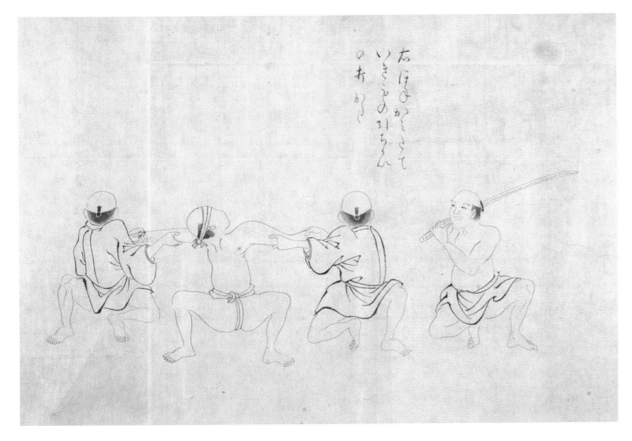

LEFT: Part of a secret hand scroll written by Yamada Satake Asaemon, being a manual describing the Yamada's cuts and the positioning of bodies when testing swords on human beings.

ordered to use the *kesagiri* cut, which begins at the left shoulder and cuts diagonally downwards to exit at the right hip – a particularly difficult cut, I am told. The thief was tied into the stocks and the following dialogue is said to have taken place:

Robber: "Is it you that will cut me down?"

Shoami: "Yes, you must be ready to be cut alive as you are sentenced."

Robber: "In what way will you cut me?"

Shoami: "I shall cut you in the *kesa* style."

Robber: "It is too cruel to be cut through alive."

Shoami: "It is all the same, before or after death."

Robber: "If I had known it before I would have swallowed a couple of big stones to spoil your sword!"

This is a good example of the gallows humour often encountered in such tales. We assume the test proceeded according to plan.

Not all cutting tests were carried out in such an official manner and not all were carried out on convicted criminals. It seems almost anything, including sheets of metal, old helmets and bundles of straw might have been used to test a blade. And it was certainly not unknown for the less reputable to lurk on street corners and wait for a suitable passer-by on which to carry out a test. A very famous and highly skilled swordsmith named Shigetaka, more commonly known as Hankei, is said to have been found dead in an Edo street, cut from shoulder to hip by the *kesagiri* technique, a victim of *tameshigiri*.

The modern-day swordsmith Yoshihara Yoshindo had one of his swords tested on an old helmet a couple of years ago for precisely the same reasons as these old *samurai*. He wanted to know whether the sword was an efficient tool for cutting or just looked good. These days, cutting tests are rare, but it was not unknown in twentieth century to test swords on a soaked straw bale, which is said to have the consistency of flesh and bone.

As the Tokugawa peace continued, the martial spirit of the *samurai* flagged and the demand for new swords diminished. Few swordsmiths were active after the Genroku period (1688-1703). Armour of good quality but with decorative considerations rather than practical requirements uppermost were made for the more affluent *samurai* of the day. At the same time, the merchant class was growing in both prosperity and influence. They were permitted to wear short swords and became the best customers of the few swordsmiths that were still active. These short swords, while technically sound, would often be highly decorative with very fancy *hamon*. The intricate carvings on them, rather than simple religious designs, reflected the tastes of these *nouveau-riche* gentlemen. However, it was the merchant class who, in some cases, commissioned the sword-fittings makers to produce some of their most skilful and intricate metalwork.

The *samurai* culture strongly disapproved of the handling of money and disdained the idea of doing business to maintain their life-styles. No social security existed and the *samurai* increasingly found themselves in debt to the despised merchant class. Those *samurai* fortunate enough to have enough to be able to afford it indulged in un-warrior like pursuits such as visiting the *kabuki* theatres or frequenting the Yoshiwara pleasure district in Edo or

LEFT AND BELOW: The long point and wide construction indicate that this *katana* is of *shinshinto* manufacture. The inscription states that it was made by Nobutaka, the 10th generation of this name, and he had the title Hoki (no) Kami. The blade is dated 1869 and has a sober *koshirae*.

other red-light districts. A significant number lived in great luxury, rather than the austere and simple ideal lifestyle expected of them. It was left to the swordsmiths retained by *daimyo*, usually living far away from the temptations of the big cities, to perpetuate the art of sword-making and maintain high standards. Only the more provincial swordsmiths, such as the Tadayoshi family still retained by the great and powerful Nabeshima clan, maintained the purity of their art, generally refusing to follow current styles and fashions in sword-making.

The eighth Tokugawa *shogun*, Yoshimune, realised the dangers of running a military government at a time when military morale was low. In the second year of Kyoho (1720), he tried to revive sword-making as an expression of the *samurai* ethic. He invited a number of swordsmiths to make swords at his castle in Edo. Among these, two swordsmiths from distant Satsuma province, right at the southernmost tip of Kyushu island, excelled. They were Mondo (no) Sho Masakiyo and Ichinohira Yasuyo. They worked in the old-style tradition of *Soshu-den*. They were honoured by the *shogun* and were allowed to carve the *shogun's* crest on their blades.

For a short while, Yoshimune's efforts were effective and there was a temporary increase in the demand for Japanese swords, but the revival of the ideal of the *samurai* leading a simple life and having a healthy and moral outlook did not last very long. At the end of the *shinto* period sword-making was again in a period of decline.

SHINSHINTO (*New New swords*)

By the latter half of the eighteenth century, pressure was being put onto the *shogunate*, both from within the country and from outside it. After the death of Tokugawa Yoshimune, a series of reforms failed to stabilise the economy. The *samurai*, whose philosophy disdained money and financial matters, were finding themselves in severe economic difficulties. Traditionally, their stipend came in the form of a rice allowance and they were completely at a loss in the new money economy. The increasingly influential merchant class had them tied up in mortgages. Further, the moral climate was degenerating with *shunga* (erotica art), *ukioye* (woodblock prints) and *kabuki*. These were the arts of the common people and often satirised the government and the *samurai* class. Earthquakes and crop failures added to the problems, and the *shogunate's* policy of excluding all foreigners was being increasingly tested by western seafarers looking for trade.

A number of *tozama* (outer) *daimyo* from clans in the west of the country, many of whom were historically antagonistic to the Tokugawa, attempted to implement economic reforms within their own fiefdoms. Some of these met with a certain amount of success. Their resentment of the *shogunate* was a fertile ground in which revolutionary ideas might germinate and these *tozama daimyo* would become the driving force behind the restoration of the emperor to direct rule – in the Meiji Restoration – a few years later.

The industrial revolution was in full swing and major world powers – Britain, America, Russia, Germany and France – all had enormous wealth and power, built on foreign trade and colonialism. By contrast Japan, because of its 250-year-old policy of isolation, did not even have any ocean-going ships. The appearance of gunboats demanding trading rights at a number of Japanese ports threw the administration into total confusion. The *shogunate* had no idea how to handle the situation. Public opinion was divided between those progressives, who felt the country should be opened up for trade, and the conservatives, who felt the seclusion policy should be enforced. Either way, it seemed to many that conflict was inevitable. Anti-government feelings grew stronger. At the same time royalist feelings gathered momentum among the more reactionary clans. The threat of an inevitable clash of arms rekindled the forges of the swordsmiths again and preparation for the coming conflict resulted in an upturn in business.

The stirring of martial fervour was to be accompanied by a great revival in the making of Japanese swords. This period became known as the *shinshinto* – "new new swords" – period, running from about 1781 to 1876. A retainer of the Akimoto clan of Uzen province named Kawabe Hachiro Masahide led this revival. Together with another swordsmith named Tomotaka from Tosa province, Masahide advocated a return to the styles of the golden age of Japanese sword manufacture in the Kamakura and Namboku-cho periods. This was fraught with difficulties. As there had been so few swordsmiths around since the seventeenth century, the manufacturing secrets had largely been lost and it was especially difficult to know how the swords from the *koto* period, with all their regional differences and characteristics, were made. Masahide, arguably a better theoretician than maker of swords, wrote a book expounding his theories, entitled *Fukkoto*. This seems to have inspired many would-be swordsmiths who flocked to Masahide's forge. He ended up with over a hundred students. Meanwhile Masahide had moved to Edo, which soon became the centre of sword manufacture again. He made swords in the style of Osaka-*shinto* and old Bizen, but he is probably better known for his theories and the talented students he taught than for his own production and expertise.

Although there are masterpieces from this time, many of the swords are not very well made as the old techniques had been lost and the raw materials used were not the same. Understandably, when compared to swords of the Kamakura and Namboku-cho period, both *shinto* and *shinshinto* appear brash, bright and generally new looking, without the subtleties that come with great workmanship and age. Typically, a *shinshinto* blade has a wide body, a long *kissaki* (point) and feels rather heavy and clumsy in the hand. The *jigane* (steel) was forged in tighter than previously and the fashion was to polish the *jihada* (body of the sword) so that no grain or other features could be seen. The preference was for a mirror-like finish (*muji-hada*), leaving only the *hamon* visible.

No *samurai* alive at this time had been involved in warfare and, at most, might have fought the odd duel. The *samurai* were faced with the prospect of having to go to war and needed confidence in the sword that they were wearing. Some wanted a heavy sword: if they were unable to cut anyone with it, at least they stood a chance of clubbing an enemy to death. Nevertheless, Masahide's school, known as the Suishinshi school, prospered and produced many blades. After his death his more talented star pupil, Naotane, carried on the school.

Swordsmiths who produced the various *koto*-revival styles of the time include Koyama Munetsugu, who worked in the Bizen style. There was the eighth-generation Tadayoshi from Hizen, who continued in the Yamashiro style of his forebears. The later Kanesada line practised in *Mino-den*, while the later generations of Kunikane from Sendai City preserved the straight grain (*masame-hada*) of the old Hosho-Yamato style. A number of this new generation of swordsmiths were also skilled at making *yari* and *naginata*.

Generally considered to be the best swordsmith of the *shinshinto* period was a complicated character named Kiyomaro. He had a habit of changing his name several times, but is most commonly known firstly as Minamoto Masayuki and later as Kiyomaro. In 1835, he moved from Shinano province to Edo. There, his talent was recognised by Kobuta Sagane, a *hatamoto* or direct vassal to the *shogun*, who became his patron. Even so, Kiyomaro managed to get himself into trouble. Kobuta Sagane secured an order for a hundred blades, but only one seems to have been completed when Kiyomaro ran away to Choshu province. After a while he was persuaded to return and settled in the Yotsuya area of Edo. He changed his name to Kiyomaro in 1846 and was nicknamed Yotsuya Masamune (the Masamune of Yotsuya), indicating that his talent was recognised at the time. Although trained in the Bizen style of sword-making, he was also able to master that of *Soshu-den*, but he sees to have been a tormented genius and took his own life in 1854 at the young age of forty-one. His popularity seems to have greatly increased during the Showa period (1926-89) mostly because of promotion by the Fujishiro brothers (a family of sword appraisers and polishers) and his work is highly sought after. As a result there are many fakes of Kiyomaro swords around today.

Following the gunboat diplomacy of Commodore Perry in 1853, Japan's seclusion policy was at an end and the credibility of the *shogunate* was in tatters. The anti-Tokugawa forces in the land, the *tozama daimyo*, increasingly pressed for the *shogun's* rule to be replaced by that of the emperor in Kyoto. Overwhelming pressure for trading agreements from Britain, France, Germany, Russia and the USA forced the *shogun* to open up several ports. Ports such as Yokohama and Kobe became foreign concessions where foreigners lived and "extraterritorial rights" were maintained – that is, Japanese law was suspended and replaced by the law of the concession country. Manifestly unfair treaties were forced on the *shogunate* and were deeply unpopular. The royalists seized on the encroachment of the barbarians on Japanese soil as a *cause célèbre*. Numerous unpleasant incidents occurred when disenchanted *samurai* or *ronin* encountered foreigners, sometimes with bloody or even fatal results. They were often *samurai* of the *tozama daimyo* from Hizen, Satsuma, Tosa or Choshu provinces, who would play a large part in the final return of direct rule to the emperor a few years later. Many of them wore large *han-dachi-katana* (half-*tachi*) known as *kinno-to* or "loyalist swords". Others carried blades made by Muramasa of Ise, a swordsmith from the late *koto* period, who was considered to be very unlucky for the Tokugawa family.

In 1867, after a number of assassinations, political manoeuvrings and bloody incidents, the last Tokugawa *shogun*, Yoshinobu, unable to resist the twin cries of "expel the barbarians and revere the Emperor", handed back the commission nominally handed to his illustrious forebear Ieyasu over 250 years before. The fifteen-year-old Emperor Mutsuhito, using the reign name Meiji, assumed direct rule of the country in 1868. The Meiji Restoration was completed when the emperor moved from Kyoto and evicted the ex-*shogun* from his castle at Edo, which was then renamed Tokyo. In 1869 the *daimyo* were reduced to government-appointed governors of their fiefdoms and had to hand their lands over to the state, as personified by the emperor. Isolated skirmishes, such as the so-called "Battle of Ueno", meant that the restoration was not entirely bloodless.

The new government soon realised that the cry to "expel the barbarians" was totally impractical as the enormous technological advances of the previous 250 years had by-passed Japan in her isolation. However good and deadly the Japanese sword might be, especially combined with the powerful *samurai* spirit, it was no match for modern firearms and Western armies and navies. Some stubborn *samurai* tried to cling onto their privileges and way of life, but they were taught a lesson in the new realities by the resounding defeat of the Satsuma rebels and the *seppuku* of their leader, Saigo Takemori. These heroic but anachronistic *samurai*, complete with their traditional swords, *naginata*, spears and armour, were decisively beaten, in 1877, by a conscript army of peasants, armed with modern rifles. The *samurai* and their swords were simply out of date and out of step with modern warfare. The lesson learnt, Japan began a headlong rush to modernise and to adopt everything they could from the West.

The bloody birth of modern Japan had been a boom time for the swordsmiths of the day and the *shinshinto* period was very productive. However, a rush of imperial edicts began to limit the use of Japanese swords. In 1871, the law that insisted the *samurai* must wear the *daisho* was revoked. Then in 1876 the wearing of swords was banned. This brought an end to the *shinshinto* period and, along with it, the history of the Japanese sword as worn and used by the feudal *samurai*.

It was thought that the Hito-rei edict of 1876, banning the wearing of the Japanese sword by the *samurai*, would effectively finish off the manufacture of the traditional Japanese sword. However, the Japanese sword, in its ever-evolving styles, has proved durable in the face of both government control and thermo-nuclear fission.

GENDAITO and SHINSAKUTO (1876 to date)

While the *samurai* as a social and military class were no longer recognised, these same people, with the single-mindedness and devotion to duty learned from *bushido*, now took Japan into the modern world. Japanese swords of the Meiji period, following the restoration, and the first half of the twentieth century are known as *gendaito* or modern swords. They have had a checkered history. In the very early years, very few swordsmiths could earn a living exclusively forging blades, and the few that did usually made copies of *koto* blades for the collectors of the time. Leading swordsmiths, such as Kasama Ikkansai Shigetsugu and his pupil Okimasa among others, were reported to have engaged in this rather dubious activity.

Okimasa was particularly noted for his skill in reproducing the work of Kiyomaro. So good were some these copies that it is thought, even today, that some swords considered to be the genuine article may indeed be fakes. Other swordsmiths were forced to make mirrors, cutlery or whatever they could turn their hands to.

As Japan adopted Western military ways, for much of the Meiji period, the sword was seen as out-dated and redundant by most people. However, the Emperor Meiji, himself, was an avid collector of swords and many old family heirlooms found their way into the imperial collection at this time. He became a patron of sword-makers and promoted Gassan Sadakazu and Miyamoto Kanenori to the status of *Teishisu Gigei*, the equivalent of today's *Juyo Mukei Bunkazai Hojisha* or *Ningen Kokuho* – which roughly translates as "Living National Treasure". But there were very few orders for swords from other sources until the militarists began to take hold of Japan in the Showa period.

Revolutionary changes in polishing, pioneered by the Honami school, allowed far better appreciation of the *jihada* (the wood-grain pattern of the metal of body of the sword) especially. Up until this time, little attention had been paid to this feature and its emphasis led greatly to the sword being appreciated from an artistic point of view, now that the sword had lost its role as a weapon. This appreciation also widened the appeal of the sword to the more general population rather than being confined to just the old *samurai* class.

With the overseas military adventures against China and Russia in the Meiji period, interest in the Japanese sword was revived for a while. It was not until the early Showa period (1926-1989) however, as Japan descended into the *kuro taniwa*, the dark valley of military fascism, was this interest sustained. It was then that the *gunto* (army sword) and *kai-gunto* (naval swords), whose dimensions were generally regulated to about 2 *shaku* 2 *sun*, became popular.

The swords of the Nihon To Tanren Kai (Japanese Sword Forging Society) of the Yasukuni Shrine in Tokyo, together with the swords of the Nihon Tanren Denshujo (Japanese Sword Forging Institute, founded by Kurihara Hikosaburo or Akihide, in which Kasama Shigetsugu was the chief instructor for a while) and those of Horii Toshihide of Muroran are among the best and most representative of the pre-Pacific War Showa period, 1926-41. Their traditionally forged and water-quenched blades are also known as *gendaito* (modern swords) and they continued to maintain the tradition of fine sword production. These are really the last swords made by sword-makers who believed that they stood a good chance of actually being used in combat. Some say that this is why post-World War II swords have so far generally failed to reach the pre-war standards. Interestingly, the qualities of *gendaito* appear to be more appreciated in the West than in Japan, whose collectors are only recently beginning to consider the merits of such swords.

Also in this period and throughout the Pacific War, poor quality swords were mass-produced as weapons for the Imperial Japanese Army and Navy. All officers were required to carry a sword as part of their uniform and to inspire in them a sense of the *bushido*. But, as always in Japanese history when there had been a massive demand for swords, quality was the first casualty. These swords were often made by hastily recruited blacksmiths who appeared "like the sprouting of bamboo shoots after the rain" with only a rudimentary knowledge of sword-making. Unlike the *gendaito*, their swords lack any artistic merit. They usually carry a stamp, *Kanji SHO* (for Showa), or *Kanji SEKI* after one of the main production centres in Gifu prefecture, continuing the Seki tradition of old Mino province. Other stamps are also found and their significance is the topic of much discussion among Western collectors, though they are generally agreed as being Imperial Army or Navy acceptance markings. These swords were only occasionally made in the traditional manner using proper materials. These often carry a star-shaped stamp (*hosho kokuin*).

The mass-produced Showato blades are usually signed in a very loose and unattractive manner and the *nakago* are generally poorly finished. The imitation *hamon* is often quenched in oil (*abura-ire*) rather than with water in the traditional method (*yaki-ire*). This allows the process to be carried out at a far lower temperature and avoids the risks of cracking, inherent in proper *yaki-ire*. An imitation *hamon* is produced in this manner, but it will appear flat and lifeless and, as no *nie* or *nioi* (martensite crystals) are produced, it cannot reflect the light the way a proper water-quenched sword does. With the lack of proper materials and short cuts in the forging process, it is difficult to call these Showato blades true Japanese swords. In Japan these swords are usually considered as illegal weapons rather than "art swords". They are destroyed when found. This can be compared to finding something quite ordinary like a cup or plate that bears a Nazi swastika – we think of such an item as Nazi first and only secondly as a well-designed cup. In the same way, in Japan, swords with a *Kanji SHO* or *Kanji SEKI* stamp are primarily associated with the war and the militaristic history of the early Showa. Most Japanese people have no desire be reminded of those times and such swords are often collected by those whose interest lies in the military history and militaria of the period.

When the occupying forces came to the Japanese homeland in 1945, the making of Japanese swords, as well as the practice of the martial arts, was banned in an attempt to democratise Japan and remove the militaristic influences of the recent past. Many outstanding and important swords were either confiscated by the occupation forces or destroyed at this time. No distinction was made between those swords with artistic and historical merit and Showato, so valuable and historic swords were lost. However, as in previous "sword hunts", many owners hid their treasures away under the floorboards until the heat died down.

It was not until 1949 that there was any easing of this ban. The occasion was a special dedication at the Ise Grand Shrine, which had taken place every twenty-five years for the preceding thousand years. The authorities gave permission for about sixty swords to be made by selected smiths for this ceremony. These swords were not the normal curved swords. Instead they were made in the ancient style known as *kiriha-zukuri chokuto* and some measured from 31 to 38 inches (80 to 96cm) long. Making these swords was a great honour for the swordsmiths who were allowed to resume their craft for this special occasion. They included Miyaguchi Toshihiro and Sakai Shigemasa (both Kasama Shigetsugu's pupils), Takahashi Sadatsugu and Miyari Akihira (who were subsequently made "Living National Treasures"), Ishi Akifusa, Nigara Kunitoshi and Endo Mitsuoki. Sato Kanzan Sensei stated that the 1949 ceremony was the first important stimulus given to the swordsmiths of Japan in the post-war period.

In 1953, a new law allowed the resumption of sword-making and, in Showa thirtieth year (1955), the first post-war competition and exhibition of *shinsakuto* (newly made swords) was held. Apparently the quality of pieces submitted was, understandably, not particularly good. In 1960, the Nihon Bijutsu To-ken Hoson Kyokai (the Japanese Art Sword Preservation Society, commonly abbreviated as the NBTHK) was formed. By then the crisis had passed and the Japanese sword was saved from complete destruction. Today the NBTHK does much important work, which includes the operation of a smelter or *tatara* that produces the raw material for forging a sword (*tamahagane*). They also run the Japanese Sword Museum in Tokyo and organise the various artisans' annual competitions. They are well known for conducting regular *shinsa* or sword judging and appraisal sessions, for which they issue certificates of authenticity and quality. Another important function of the NBTHK is to foster communication between various artisans of the Japanese sword. This is quite a turnaround from earlier times when schools of swordsmiths jealously guarded their manufacturing secrets, but after World War II virtually an entire generation of swordsmiths had been lost and the survivors had to communicate with each other in order for sword-making to survive.

One annual contest organised by the NBTHK covers many aspects of the art of the Japanese sword, including sword-making, blade polishing, scabbard-making and metalworking. These competitions, as well as giving swordsmiths something to strive for, serve to give the Japanese collector or other sword buyer the confidence of having instant provenance from a recognised and successful artist.

When blades are entered for the annual competition all of them are ranked, from the top to the bottom. This ranking is very important as it gives relative values to each smith's work for the next year. When a swordsmith has consistently ranked in the top few, he is awarded the title of *Mukansa*. This means that a *Mukansa*'s work, although entered into the competition, is not subject to being judged. Above the rank of *Mukansa* is that of *Ningen Kokuho* (Living National Treasure). In 1998, there were only two living swordsmiths, who held *Ningen Kokuho* rank, Osumi Yoshitsugu and Amada Akitsugu. Examples of their work and other *Mukansa* swordsmiths were exhibited in London in 1993. The late Gassan Sadaichi was also a *Mukansa* at the time of his death in 1996, as was Sumitani Masamine. The next *Ningen Kokuho* will be drawn from the ranks of the existing *Ningen Kokuho* swordsmiths, and in 1998 Nagayama Kokan, a fine Honami style polisher, was also raised to this level for his work in sword polishing.

Outside of the martial arts, the Japanese sword now has no practical purpose. Consequently, a sword's artistic properties, which had always been appreciated by the knowledgeable and educated Japanese, rather than its practical uses, are increasingly emphasised. However, most of the properties of a good sword may be traced back to the sword's traditional role as a weapon. A sword must be of good shape and balance, be made of good steel, have flexibility and a sharp edge, as well as being attractive to look at in detail. The annual competitions, as well as shows put on by various commercial and retail outlets such as Ohnishi Token, have helped to greatly improve the standard of *shinsakuto* since 1954. However, I believe that few present-day swordsmiths have attained the standards reached by the best of the early Showa period when swords were still being taken to war. The removal of a practical purpose seems to detract somewhat from the quality of the sword production. However, as a distinct move away from the dominance of *Bizen-den*-style blades and a move towards *Soshu-den*-influenced styles seems to be under way, even this situation may be changing.

Swordsmiths are licensed by the Japanese government and are mostly members of the Japan Swordsmiths Association. They are allowed by law to make no more than two long swords a month. This number was arrived at by observing the swordsmith Miyari Akihira, who apparently was a slow and methodical worker. Many swordsmiths and artisans that I have spoken to believe that this figure is too low and many present-day swordsmiths would be quite capable of producing more. However, this rule is also designed to prevent the manufacture of cheap weapons with no artistic value and, as such, I believe it is well founded.

There are other rules that regulate current swordsmiths:

1. Only a licensed swordsmith can produce a Japanese sword (defined as any cutting instrument with a blade over 6 inches (15cm), a *hamon*, and a rivet hole in the tang). Edged weapons less than 6 inches in length and lacking a rivet hole are considered knives, or *ko-gatana*, and are not subject to regulation. A licence may be obtained only by serving an apprenticeship under a licensed swordsmith for a minimum of five years.

2. A licensed swordsmith may produce a maximum of two long swords (over 2 feet/61cm) or three short swords (less than 2 feet in length) a month.

3. All swords must be registered with the Agency of Cultural Affairs.

Today, most *shinsakuto* are sent straight to the polisher, *habaki* maker and *shira-saya* maker, although some are mounted in modern *koshirae*. Many swords are now made in the Bizen style, which is popular with the Japanese collectors. Sumitani Masamine's Ichimonji *utsushi* (copy) was put on show in London a few years ago. This sword had a very flamboyant *choji midare hamon* in the style of the Kamakura period Fukuoka Ichimonji school and it may be that this National Treasure swordsmith's skill in *Bizen-den* has influenced many other younger swordsmiths. When looking at such swords we may search for and sometimes actually see *utsuri* (a kind of shadow above the *hamon*, which is a feature of good old blades, particularly those in *Bizen-den*). It seems that, in the attempt to equal the swords of bygone days, the quest to reproduce *utsuri* is very important. Although a kind of *utsuri* may sometimes be found, to me this resembles the *shirakke utsuri* (a foggy shadow) of Muromachi period Kaga province or *sue-Seki* blades and I have not seen a convincing Bizen *midare utsuri*, for instance. Recently some swordsmiths have been experimenting in *Soshu-den* which is a completely different style and manufacturing process from *Bizen-den*. A number are also producing their own *tamahagane* (raw materials), rather than rely on NBTHK sources exclusively and this may have far-reaching consequences on *jihada* especially.

This post-war period has been compared to the renaissance of Japanese swords that heralded the advent of the *shinshinto* period in the late eighteenth century. There are some valid comparisons. Both periods followed a decline in Japanese sword production and both periods seek to recapture past glorious ages of Japanese sword-making as well as making great innovations in production methods. I think the current changes in sword-making are at least as drastic as those earlier changes and possibly more significant. I hope they will not be accompanied by the same eventual decline and that today's artists manage to train sufficiently skilful students who will be able to preserve and continue the arts.

The Japanese sword establishment is still a very conservative body. I think that many of the older generation believe it is impossible for foreigners to really appreciate the Japanese sword. When I started collecting swords in the mid-1960s, very little information was available to foreigners who could not read Japanese. There was also a feeling that those few who appeared to have any knowledge would jealously guard it. An unhealthy and secretive attitude pervaded.

Fortunately today, in the younger generation of sword collectors from Japan, many of whom have travelled abroad and been exposed to Western collectors, there is a far less conservative attitude. A great deal of information is available through useful and informative translations. The 1993 Shinsaku-to Exhibition in London demonstrated that Japanese friends could co-operate with foreigners to bring the beauty of the Japanese sword to a wider audience. And the "Swords of the *Samurai*" exhibition at the British Museum provided convincing evidence that even large institutions could handle such cross-cultural ventures.

RIGHT: The master swordsmith Amada Akitsugu at his forge. Amada Akitsugu has been designated "Ningen Kokuho", a "Living National Treasure" in the field of swordmaking.

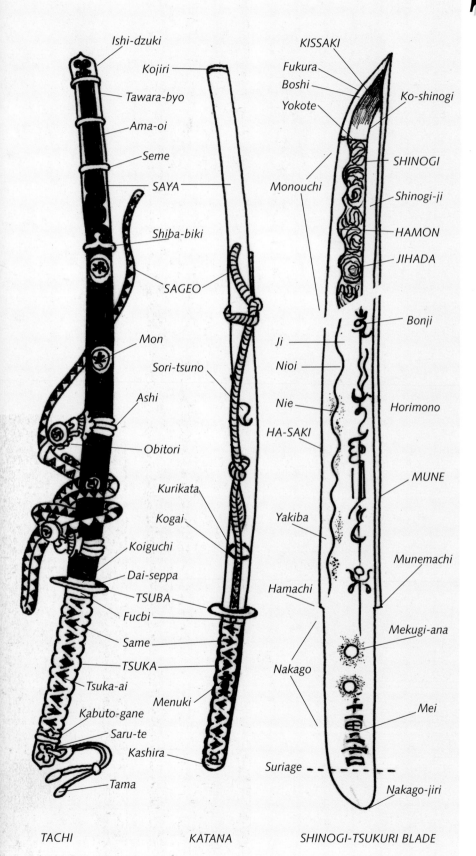

Ishi-dzuki
Kojiri
Tawara-byo
Ama-oi
Seme
SAYA
Shiba-biki
SAGEO
Mon
Sori-tsuno
Ashi
Obitori
Kurikata
Kogai
Koiguchi
Dai-seppa
TSUBA
Fucbi
Same
TSUKA
Tsuka-ai
Menuki
Kabuto-gane
Saru-te
Kashira
Tama

KISSAKI
Fukura
Boshi
Yokote
Ko-shinogi
Monouchi
SHINOGI
Shinogi-ji
HAMON
JIHADA
Ji
Bonji
Nioi
Nie
Horimono
HA-SAKI
Yakiba
MUNE
Munemachi
Hamachi
Mekugi-ana
Nakago
Mei
Suriage
Nakago-jiri

TACHI   KATANA   SHINOGI-TSUKURI BLADE

CHAPTER 4
THE SWORD
OF THE
SAMURAI
(Nihon-To)

"The true way of strategy is revealed in the long sword."
Miyamoto Musashi – Go Rin No Sho

It has often said been said the "the sword is the soul of the *samurai*". If this is true then the blade is certainly the soul of the sword, while the mounts are the clothes and protectors of the blade.

CONSTRUCTION OF THE BLADE

If we take claims that the Japanese sword is the finest cutting weapon ever made at face value, what makes it so? Essentially the Japanese sword blade is a curved, single edged blade with a ridge running down the middle of its body. Like a sabre, such a blade is made for cutting or slashing rather than stabbing. Outside Japan, swords were either sharp and made of very hard but brittle steel, which was liable to break, or they were of much softer steel, heavy and unable to hold a sharp edge. The seemingly insurmountable problem of combining the two features was solved early in Japanese sword history. This was to make the *samurai* sword unique. A hard – high carbon – edge that could be finely sharpened was combined with a lower carbon body that provided both weight and flexibility. A further refinement was to insert a low-carbon steel core into the blade, adding to the durability and providing certain shock-absorbing properties. The quenched and hardened edge, known as the *hamon*, is the most distinctive part of the Japanese sword. Without a proper *hamon*, a sword cannot be classified as *Nihon-to*, or a true Japanese sword.

A Japanese sword is made from a substance known as *tamahagane*, which is obtained from smelting the natural sand-iron ore, *satetsu*, found in riverbeds and on seashores in Japan. Before starting to make a blade a swordsmith might fast, abstain from sex and undergo other purification rites. The making of a sword is almost a religious act. Selected *tamahagane* is forged into the blade by the swordsmith hammering and folding a billet of high-carbon steel. It is seldom folded more than fifteen times, as the steel will begin to deteriorate and lose carbon after that. The swordsmith will

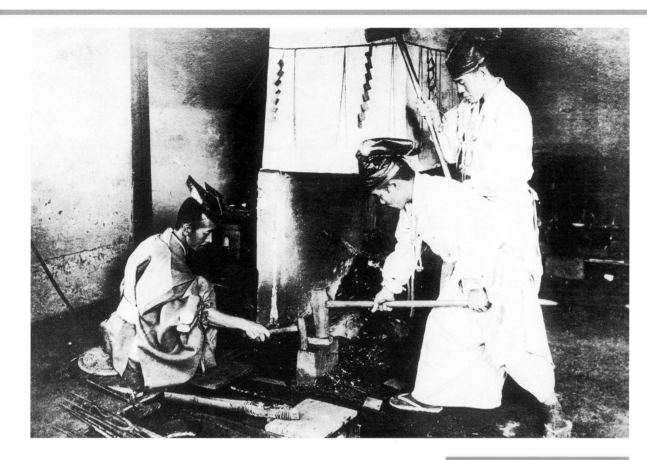

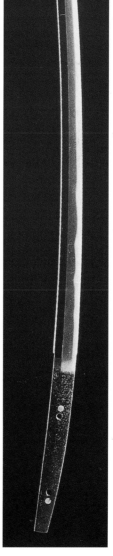

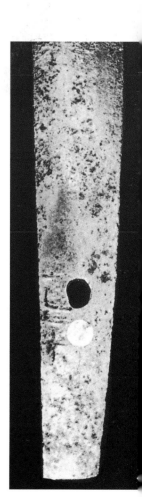

then work in the same way on another billet of low-carbon steel. This is inserted into the first billet by hammering the high-carbon billet into a "V" shape and inserting the low-carbon billet into it, providing a core for the blade. These are then welded together and beaten out into the rough shape of the sword, with an allowance made for the *nakago* or tang. The swordsmith's forge was a dimly lit place as he was only able to control the heat and to judge the temperature of the blade by the colour of the glow of the red hot metal. All work was done by hand and the swordsmith might employ two assistant hammermen (*sakite*) wielding heavy hammers in this forging process. These days, though, a power hammer often replaces the *sakite*.

After drawing out the sword blank, called a *sunobe*, the swordsmith begins to form the *kissaki* (the point) and the *mune* (back edge), followed by shaping the *ha-saki* (the cutting edge) and the *shinogi* (ridgeline). He leaves the cutting edge quite thick as this is soon to be exposed to great stress. In a process known as *yaki-ire*, the hardened edge is to be formed. The swordsmith applies a coating of clay – each has his own secret recipe for this – over the entire blade in a process known as *tsuchi-dori*. He makes it thicker near the back and thinner towards the cutting edge. He then shapes the *hamon* and re-heats the blade until it is red hot or glowing "like the moon in February or August". At precisely the right moment, he plunges it horizontally into a trough of water. This is where the effect of the varying thickness of the clay comes into its own. Where the clay is thin, the steel will cool more quickly than where it has been applied more thickly. Where it is thin near the edge, the fast cooling produces martensite crystals of

ABOVE: The master swordsmith Ikkansai Kasama Shigetsugu forging a blade in about 1920. Two unidentified *sakite* or hammermen assist him.

RIGHT: A shortened *tachi* blade by Kanehira, that retains its signature. Kanehira was a famous swordsmith of the Ko-Bizen school who worked in the Heian period (12th Century). One particularly well known sword by Kanehira, known as *O-Kanehira*, has National Treasure status in Japan. It is incredible that such swords have been preserved for such a long time.

varying sizes, making much harder steel than where it has cooled more slowly. This is the most critical stage of blade making as the rapid change in temperature create huge stresses and strains in the steel, to the point where the whole blade may crack. If this happens the sword must be scrapped and the swordsmith must start again.

The dividing line between the *hamon* and the body of the sword, the *jitetsu*, where the martensite crystals have formed, is known as the *habuchi*. These martensite crystals are variously known as *nie*, *ko-nie* or *nioi*, depending on their size. The word *nie* translates as "bubbles" or "boiling". Their appearance is exactly that, while the smaller nioi, appear more misty, like "the stars in the milky way". The swordsmith might now make a few adjustments to the shape of the blade with a coarse polishing stone and will

check it for any flaws or faults. If all is well, he will finish off the *nakago* or tang and make a hole in it (the *mekugi-ana*) that will be used to secure the blade into the handle of the sword. He may also sign the *nakago*, date it and inscribe other information about the sword on the *nakago* if he is satisfied with his work. The sword will then go off to a professional polisher, and a scabbard and *habaki* (collar for the blade) maker.

Originally a polisher's job was only to sharpen the blade. Now additionally, his skill is used make all the workmanship of the forging process visible on the body of the blade. This will reveal a pattern in the steel that looks like a wood grain effect, called the *jihada*. He will also show the subtleties of the *hamon* in vivid and contrasting detail, and breathe life into the blade. The steel itself becomes a beautiful work of art.

KISSAKI (point)

The *kissaki* is the point of the sword. If the sword is of normal construction with a ridgeline (*shinogi-zukuri*) then there will be a line joining the *shinogi* to the cutting edge. This line is called the *yokote* and separates the *kissaki* from the rest of the sword. The *kissaki* is a very good indicator of the quality of both the blade and the polishing as it is considered the most difficult part of the sword to work on. Indeed, a poor or unscrupulous polisher might be tempted to move the *yokote* (the vertical line that defines the start of the kissaki or point) in order to make the point smaller and less of a challenge.

Kissaki are usually des-cribed by size, as follows:

O-kissaki: Large or long *kissaki*.
Chu-kissaki: Medium length or sometimes as "extended" *chu-kissaki* if it is a little longer than usual.
Ko-kissaki: Small *kissaki*.

An important element of the *kissaki* is the shape of the *hamon* within it. This is called the *boshi*, which is a name of the old court caps worn in Japan. The *boshi* is the hat or cap of the sword. As individual schools and swordsmiths had particular styles of both *kissaki* and more importantly of *boshi*, these elements are of huge significance in correctly appraising a sword.

LEFT: This 13th century blade by Nagamitsu is dated 1297 and demonstrates the low *koshi-zori* associated with Bizen swords in particular. Nagamitsu was a leading swordsmith from the Osafune school, which was founded by his father Mitsutada.

MUNE (back)

The *mune* is the back edge of the blade and is mostly triangular or *iori-mune* – that is, roof shaped. However, there are a couple of other shapes, such as *maru-mune* (rounded back) and *kaku-mune* (square or flat back). The *mune* is also described as being either high or low.

LEFT: A 14th Century shortened *tachi* blade with the intact inscription, "Bishu [Bizen province] Osafune Kagemitsu".

ZORI (curvature)

Nearly all Japanese swords are curved and the *zori* (or *sori*) refers to the curvature of the blade. Curvature is mainly of three types but they are sometimes known by different names. These are:

Saki-zori: Curvature at the top part of the sword, near the *kissaki*.

Tori-zori: Evenly curved throughout the length of the blade and named after the curve of the gate of a Shinto shrine or *tori*. It is also known as *naka-sori* (middle *sori*) or *Kyoto-sori* as this was popular with swords made in Kyoto in the *koto* times.

Koshi-zori: Here the centre of curvature is low down the blade nearer the handle and is so named as the curvature is near the hip or *koshi*. As it is also a characteristic of blades from Bizen, it is sometimes known as *Bizen-zori*.

In addition, there are:

Uichi-zori: This is a reverse curvature that curves in the direction of the cutting edge and is usually only found on tanto or daggers.

Mu-zori: No *zori*, in other words, a straight blade.

The *zori* is also very important when appraising the age of manufacture of a blade.

LEFT AND RIGHT: A straight *tanto* signed with the two characters, "Kunihiro". This blade is by Horikawa Kunihiro from Kyoto who did much to establish the *shinto* methods of swordmaking at the end of the 16th Century and beginning of the 17th. The blade is mounted in a richly decorated *aikuchi-tanto koshirae* (left).

SUGATA (shape and form)

The *sugata* is the overall shape of the blade. This encompasses all of the features mentioned above, as well as the width of the blade (*mi-haba*) and any tapering towards the point. An appreciation and understanding of *sugata* is of the utmost importance when judging a sword, though it is sometimes somewhat subjective. For instance, it is said that a sword with a good *sugata* cannot possibly have been made by a poor swordsmith. However, when looking at the *sugata* of a blade, one has to make a judgement about whether it may have been altered by shortening or because of damage. In other words, the *sugata* you are inspecting may not be the original *sugata* of the sword. This is especially important in the West where amateur restoration or other mistreatment may have altered the sword greatly.

The *sugata* is an important factor in judging the age of a sword. For instance, if a sword has *o-kissaki* and is broad, then this is the *sugata* of the Namboku-cho period (1333-1392). However, this *sugata* was also widely adopted in the *shinshinto* period (1780-1868), so other considerations must be taken into account. Similarly, a very narrow blade, which tapers to a very small *ko-kissaki* and has strong *koshi-zori*, may point you towards the *ko-Bizen* school of the late Heian or early Kamakura period. However, similar *sugata* were sometimes produced in the Muromachi period and so, a degree of *saki-zori* might make you revise your judgement on this sword.

RIGHT: A blade by Bizen Osafune Yasumitsu and dated 1396. He is known as Oei Bizen Yasumitsu after the name of the period. The sword has a sober *katana koshirae*.

JIHADA (pattern of the "body" steel)

The *jihada* is the pattern of the *jitetsu* or *jigane* (steel) that is visible on a properly polished sword. It is found between the edge of the hamon, or quenched and hardened edge, and the *shinogi* or ridge line. The area between the *shinogi* and the back of the sword, the *shinogi-ji*, is usually burnished brightly and in the majority of swords, apart from very early ones, a straight grain effect may be seen. Depending on how the swordsmith has folded and hammered the steel in the forging process, the jihada may show a number of different wood-grain like patterns. These are generally either known as *mokume-hada* or *itame-hada*. The former is quite round like the grain of a log cut across the grain, while the latter is more elongated or stretched like a log sliced along the grain. A third type, known as *masame-hada*, is a much straighter grain and a characteristic of Yamato swords. A sword's *jihada* may show any number or combination of these three and *jihada* is variously described as *o* (large), *ko* (small) as well as prominent, strong, weak, loose, tight, or visible. A further type of *jihada*, known as *muji-hada* or "no-pattern", is commonly seen in blades of the *shinshinto* period (1780-1868). In reality these swords often have a very tight *jihada* that may be revealed by modern polishing techniques. Finally, there is a very wavy pattern known as *ayasugi-hada*. It was popularised by the Gassan swordsmiths of Dewa province and is produced by the modern Osaka Gassan school. It is sometimes found on certain old Naminohira school blades from Kyushu island as well.

Other features may be seen in the *jihada* such as various types of *utsuri* (the shadow or reflection of the *hamon*) or *ji-nie* where the crystal pattern has spilled over from the *hamon*, as well as subtle colours of the steel. A study of the *jihada* is very important when appraising a sword and may indicate age or province of manufacture.

RIGHT: An example of the famous *gogi-mei* (5-character signature) of the Tadayoshi school, which reads Hizen (no) Kuni Tadayoshi. The graceful blades of Tadayoshi have a unique *jihada* known as *konuka-hada*.

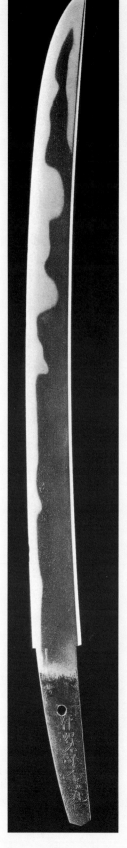

LEFT: A *hira-zukuri tanto* by the 17th century Kyoto swordsmith, Kinmichi. The inscription incorporates his title and reads Iga (no) Kami Kinmichi.

HAMON (hardened edge)

The *hamon* is the main thing that sets the Japanese sword apart from any other. Without the hardened edge, formed in the manner described above, the cutting ability of the Japanese sword would be like all others, rather than the awesome weapon it is.

Coating the sword with the clay or *tsuchi-dori* is a skilled process that will produce a number of "activities" or *hataraki* in the blade, associated with the production of the *nie* and *nioi* (the martensite crystals). The configuration of the *nie* may produce a number of patterns within the *hamon* as well as spilling over into the *jihada* when they are known as *ji-nie* or sometimes *chikei*. Such activities are greatly admired in the sword and add much to its artistic appeal and value. Some, such as *ashi*, may also add to the practical effectiveness of the blade by creating fracture zones to limit damage or absorb shock in combat.

It is quite possible to have a combination of both *nie* and *nioi*. If the *nie* predominate, the result is known as a *nie-deki hamon*. Early Bizen blades were *nioi* dominant in the *hamon*. It was not until later, when the Soshu school, which was *nie-deki*, influenced Bizen sword production, that *nie* became more common in Bizen swords and they became a hybrid known as *soden*.

There are an almost infinite variety of shapes to the *hamon*, ranging from a simple straight line (*suguha*) to hardened spots dotted all over the blade (*hitatsura*). Although most groups of swordsmiths practised *suguha* at one time or another, many schools favoured distinctive shaped hamon that became virtually their trademark.

An important part of the *hamon* is the part that goes into the point of the sword, known as the *boshi*, the hat or cap of the sword. This is the part of the sword that is reputed to show the swordsmith's level of skill most obviously and it might return (*kaeri*) along the back edge or *mune* of the sword.

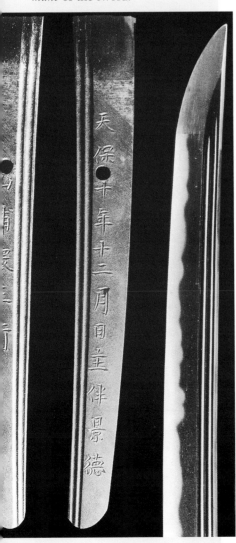

HORIMONO (carvings)

Horimono means carved things. Swords were carved for a number of different reasons. Most commonly they carry religious motifs to inspire and protect the wearer in times of war. They were hand carved using small hammers and chisels. Specialist *horimono* carvers were highly rated and some were even mentioned in the inscriptions on the *nakago*. Munenaga, for example, was the *horimono* carver to the first generation Tadayoshi of Hizen province in the early seventeenth century and an exceptionally talented student of Umetada Myoju. Today, specialist *horimono* artists still practise their skills. In most cases, however, the swordsmith or his apprentices were responsible for the carvings. In the later *shinshinto* and Gendai periods (late nineteenth century and early twentieth century) masters of the Gassan school of Osaka were highly rated for their skill, along with Kurihara Nobuhide from the Kiyomaro *mon* or group.

Earlier *horimono* tended to be simpler, but with the beginning of the Tokugawa peace, greater emphasis began to be placed on the artistic properties of Japanese swords and more decorative designs were introduced. These designs include realistically carved flowers, branches of plum blossom, bamboo etc., as well as dragon and simple sword designs. These limited subjects for *horimono* have been expanded on by certain post-war swordsmiths, not always with altogether successful results.

Hi or grooves were cut for both decorative and practical reasons. It might be possible to lighten the weight of the blade with a full length *hi* without significantly weakening it. It is also said that the *hi* would allow air to enter a wound and facilitate the blade's withdrawal. Modern day practitioners of *iaido* (the martial art of sword drawing) favour full length *hi* as they feel it necessary to hear a whistling noise as the blade cuts through the air – such is the mind of the modern-day *budoka* in the West.

LEFT: Although this is a *katana* blade by Bishu Osafune Geinbenjo Sukesada and dated 1577, it has been mounted in an *ito-maki tachi*, which has the Tokugawa family *aoi-mon* lacquered on the *saya*.

HORIMONO (carvings) *continued*

A *horimono* favoured by many swordsmen was the figure of Fudo, who is often depicted standing on a rock, with a *vraja*-hilted straight sword in his right hand and a rope in his left. As a guardian of Nirvana, his fierce visage scared away evil, while his rope was to bind the wicked and his sword to punish them. He is often shown surrounded by fire and has been likened to the patron saint of swordsmen. The rock on which he is standing is beautifully carved, showing the small lichens growing on it. The details of Fudo himself, his clothing, his hair, his body and his terrifying eyes, are rendered in the precision and depth of the cutting, showing the artist's skill in a miniature piece of sculpture. The debased Indian Sanskrit character known as *bonji* is cut above the image of Fudo and is the character for Fudo Mio. The following description of Fudo is from the display card accompanying on a wooden carving of the deity in the British Museum.

"Sometimes depicted alone, sometimes as the foremost of the 'Five Kings of Light' of the esoteric Shingon Buddhist sect and sometimes with his acolytes Kongara Doji and Shitaka Doji. Attributes of the deity are minutely described in a *sutra* of AD 709 (although in sword carvings he is usually depicted alone). His fierce aspect shows intolerance of wickedness, which he seeks out to chastise. The rope binds illusory enemies of enlightenment, while the sword cuts through the illusory world revealing Kongotai or the ultimately real world. His sword hilt is in the form of a three-barbed *vraja* symbolising Buddha, the Lotus and Konotai. Fudo's name 'Unmoving' indicates the unchanging nature of ultimate reality beneath the illusion of his warlike exterior. As he represents the ideal spiritual attitude of the swordsman, he is considered to be their patron deity."

LEFT: Another blade by Tadatsuna of Osaka with a dragon *horimono*. The inscription reads Awataguchi Ikkanshi Tadatsuna, Hori-do saku, affirming that Tadatsuna made the carving himself.

RIGHT: A deep and skilfully carved *horimono* of Fudo Kaen on a blade by Ikkansai Kasama Shigetsugu who was especially famous for this depiction. The inscription, as well as dating the sword and giving other useful information, states that the carving was by Shigetsugu's own hand. The sword was made in 1939 for presentation to Adolph Hitler.

Two parallel grooves may be carved at the bottom end of the blade are known as *gombashi–hi*. Unlike the *hi*, these serve no practical purpose but, like the Fudo carvings, have religious significance. They represent a set of ritual Japanese chopsticks (*hashi*) that are used to handle the incense in the Buddhist rights of exorcism. It is sometimes possible to appraise a sword from both the subject and style of the *horimono*.

ABOVE: An example of the famous *gofi-mei* (5-character signature) of the Tadayoshi school, which reads Hizen (no) Kuni Tadayoshi. The graceful blades of Tadayoshi have a unique *jihada* known as *konuka-hada*.

NAKAGO (tang)

A good Japanese sword will always have a well-finished *nakago* or tang. Ideally this would be *ubu* or in its original unaltered condition. That is to say it will not have been shortened from the butt end, possibly losing any signature or inscription (*suriage*), or extended at the top end to effectively shorten the working part of the blade (*machi-okuri*). All these things, including the addition of extra *mekugi-ana* (peg retaining holes) are encountered and may decrease the value of the sword to a greater or lesser degree. Such alterations are more acceptable on swords that have been in existence for many hundreds of years but, generally speaking, the later the blade the less desirable any changes to the *nakago* become. Certainly, a modern sword from the twentieth century, for instance, should be *ubu*, although if it is a copy of an old *suriage* (shortened) sword it might reproduce the *suriage* effect of the original.

LEFT: This is the signature of the first generation Tadayoshi after he received the title Musashi Daijo and changed his name to Tadahiro. The full inscription reads Hizen Kuni Ju Musashi Daijo Fujiwara Tadahiro.

Usually a sword's *nakago* will be rusty as it is not polished like the rest of the blade. It is important that this rust is left untouched and that no effort to remove it is made. The colour and patination of this rust will often indicate the age of the sword. The swordsmith will have filed both surfaces of the *nakago* and sometimes even the *mune* or back. The pattern of these file marks, known as *yasuri*, were passed from teacher to pupil. So they are important, as is the shape of the *jiri* or butt of the *nakago*.

Most Japanese swords have an inscription on the *nakago*, which will impart various useful pieces of information. The inexperienced collector will often go to the inscription first when given a sword to study. This is a mistake. An inscription on a nakago is relatively easy to fake and there are many convincing fakes around. It is more advisable, therefore, to appraise the blade itself first and decide what school or period it came from. If the inscription confirms the appraisal then you can feel more comfortable, but if it differs wildly you have every right to be suspicious of the inscription.

When they are not fakes, these inscriptions will provide information such as the maker's name, any titles he may have had, where he worked and, occasionally, who the sword was made for. This will usually be found on the front side of the *nakago* known as the *omote*. If the sword is made to wear thrust through the sash, with the cutting edge uppermost, such as in the *katana*, the *omote* will be the side facing outwards. On a slung sword or *tachi*, the *omote* will be the other side. There are, as always, exceptions to this general rule. While the main inscription is usually to be found on the *omote* side of the *nakago*, sometimes the date is on the reverse side or the *ura*. These inscriptions are usually carved by the swordsmith with a cold chisel, so it is possible to become familiar with his handwriting, a further help in deciding on the authenticity of a

signature or *mei*. In cases where a signature has been lost completely due to shortening (*o-suriage*), occasionally a gold inlaid attribution (*kinzogan-mei*) has been added. Or, on a previously unsigned blade, there may be a lacquered inscription or *shu-mei*.

The result of a cutting test is considered to be very desirable on a *nakago*. Usually these are also recorded in gold inlay and form three columns of inscription on the *ura*. The right-hand column is the date on which the test was carried out; the middle, the name and details of the tester; while the left-hand column is usually carries the result of the test: for example, "Cut two *do* [waist] cuts into the sand" – that is, right through. These grisly attestations usually appear on swords of the *shinto* period. In the *shinshinto* period it seems they were more commonly engraved by the swordsmith himself, rather than inlaid in gold.

The blade of a *samurai* sword needs its furniture. Although this was functional, it was often a *samurai*'s greatest indulgence. It was considered unmanly for a *samurai* to wear jewellery of any kind, but to lavish money on his sword was quite acceptable. All the furniture or mounts of a *samurai*'s sword, everything excluding the blade, are known collectively as the *koshirae*. The making the *koshirae* combined the efforts of a number of skilled artisans including wood workers, handle wrappers, and artists in metal work and lacquers. The swordsmith who had been commissioned to make a blade would be the team leader and he would give out the orders for work to all these people, including the polisher.

LEFT: A fine *wakizashi* by the renowned Edo *shinto* swordsmith, Kotetsu, with the inscription Nagazone Kotetsu Nyudo Okisato. On the reverse is the result of a cutting test by one of the Yamano family. The sword cut through two bodies.

THE MOUNTINGS OF JAPANESE SWORDS

"Treasure swords of Japan are obtained from the east by merchants of Etsu. Their scabbards are of fragrant wood,
covered with shark skin, gold, silver, copper and metals adorn them, hundreds of gold pieces is their cost.
When wearing such a sword, one can slay the barbarians."

Ou YangSung Dynasty (1007-1072)

While all other parts of the sword may be considered as secondary to the blade, on a well-mounted sword, the fittings compliment and enhance it, and allow the blade actually to be used. Very early mounts seem to have been imported, along with most other things, from the Asian mainland in the third and fourth centuries AD. Many of these Chinese- and Korean-style mounts were more ceremonial and decorative than practical. Indeed early swords had quite inferior blades that would not have stood the test of combat. Many appear to have had elaborate handles with rings on their pommels and were richly decorated in gold and silver and coloured enamels. A number are preserved to this day and are considered very important artefacts in the history of the Japanese sword.

The *koshirae*, the full set of mounts not including the blade, comprise the *kodogu* (metal mountings), *tsuka* and *tsukamaki* (hilt and hilt wrap), the *habaki* and the lacquering and construction of the *saya* (scabbard). These are all made by various collaborations between different artist and artisans with their individual specialties, while the *katana kaji* (swordsmith) and *togishi* (polisher) work on the blade itself.

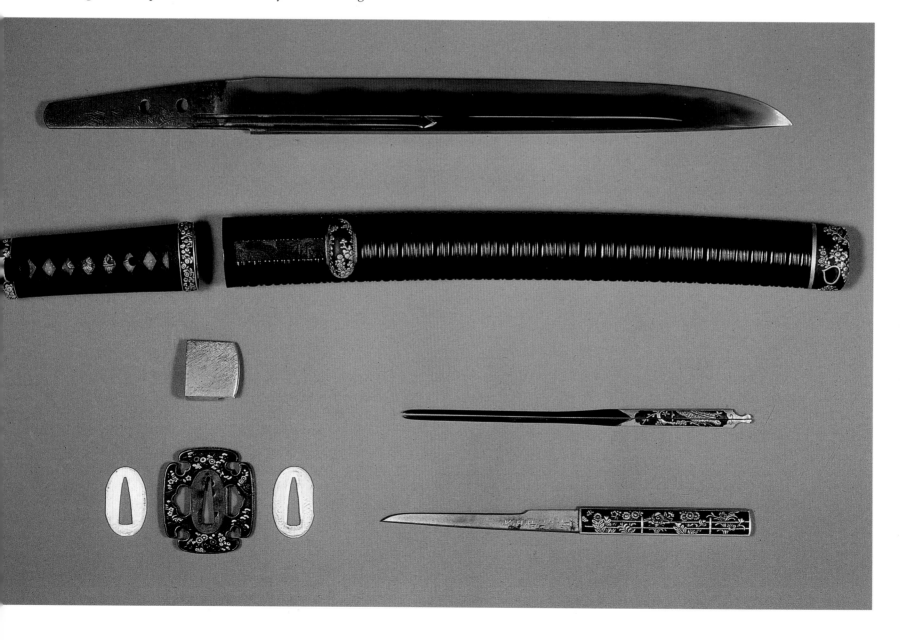

TSUBA (hand guard)

Of all the parts of the Japanese sword, the *tsuba* or hand guard is ranked second only in importance to the blade. It must protect the right hand of the user. Unlike a European hand guard, that of a Japanese sword does not encase or wrap around the hand. It is more usually of a disc shape and is designed as much to prevent the user's hand slipping onto the blade as blocking or warding off an attack.

Tsuba fall into two main categories. There are those made of plain iron, often with a cut-out or silhouette design, which are known as *sukashi-tsuba*. Or they are made in a variety of soft metals, when they are known as *kinko* work. The latter usually have a base plate made up of various Japanese alloys, such as *shakudo*, *shibuichi* or even plain iron, all of which are patinated to give them colour. Both types may have a variety of other metals such as gold, copper or silver, applied in a number of techniques such as flat or raised inlay. Numerous designs are found on *tsuba* and may take their subjects from religion, nature or legend, or depict *mon* (family crests). The skill in both design and execution in such a limited and difficult shaped space is incredibly rich and often unbelievably skilfully executed. There were

LEFT: A *wakizashi* short sword by Etchu (no) Kami Masatoshi who originally came from Mino province but migrated to Kyoto early in the 17th century. The stripped down sword shows the component parts including *tsuba*, *seppa*, *kozuka* and *kogai*. Exquisitely decorated in the Mino style, this would have been the short sword of a *daisho*.

RIGHT: The top *tsuba* is of an iron *sukashi tsuba* where the design is shown in silhouette and this one represents warblers in a budding plum tree. The bottom two *tsuba* are for a *daisho* and incorporate a number of soft metals on *shakudo nanako* plate in their realistic design from nature. With the exception of the top piece all are the work of the Ishiguro school in the late Edo period and all demonstrate the high level of artistry attained at this time.

THIS PAGE: A group of 18th and 19th century Choshu school iron plate *tsuba* with various designs. The top two are a pair of *sukashi tsuba* for a *daisho*, and the others are of a solid iron plate.

many schools and artists often signed their *tsuba*. However, as with blades, many forgeries exist.

It is said that the ancient warrior preferred the more austere iron *sukashi* type of *tsuba* which were designed for combat and reflected the *samurai* taste, while the more decorative reflected the taste of the merchant class. It is also thought that many of these early iron *tsuba* were made by swordsmiths or armourers, whose knowledge of metalwork was easily adapted to this sideline. But from the later Muromachi period, many specialised artists concentrated on *tsuba* production.

Arguably the best in the Edo period, though rather stylised and lacking a certain creativity, was the work produced for the *shogunate* by the Goto family. They worked mainly with gold decorated *shakudo-nanako* (a fine punch design on the *shakudo* plate resembling fish-roe or *nanako*). As well as making *tsuba*, they produced many *kozuka*, *kogai* and the *fuchi kashira* discussed below. Their imitators and members of other branches of the family could seldom reach their standard.

During the later Edo period, the making of fittings, especially decorative *tsuba*, reach a zenith in skill and artistry. By this time, many of the *samurai* were greatly in debt to the increasingly affluent merchant class. It was often this despised and socially inferior group who provided the finance and patronage that allowed many of the fine *tsuba* and fittings of the period to be made.

Tsuba and fittings makers were often organised into schools or family groups and passed on the trade secrets in a similar way to blade makers. Although special commissions for work might produce unique creations, schools often confined themselves to a limited number of designs and techniques. Such designs would be repeated and reproduced sometimes for several generations, each generation signing their work in the same manner. Such work is sometimes known as *machi-bori* or town carving – the Soten school is a well-known example.

ABOVE: A *sukashi tsuba* of the Tetsugendo school depicting the first encounter between the legendary Minamoto hero Yoshitsune and his faithful retainer Benki on the Goto bridge in Kyoto. Details are in gold silver and copper.

LEFT: A modern *tsuba* maker carefully applies a raised design onto the plate. Today *tsuba* are still made in the traditional manner that they have been for hundreds of years.

TSUKA (Handle)

The Japanese *samurai* sword mounting is a very functional thing. While being decorative and artistically constructed, everything about it owes its existence to practical considerations forged by the experience of war. The *dai-to* or long sword, for instance, must have a *tsuka* or handle that is able to accommodate a two-handed grip comfortably. This grip is usually helped by wrapping the handle in silk or thread. A great variety of wrapping styles are to be found and wrapping a *tsuka* became an important job in itself. These styles differed by the type of thread used, the style of wrap (flat or raised), the shape and size of the *bishi* (open diamond-shaped spaces) and the way they were tied-off. Some of these represented regional differences and had names such as *Musashi-maki* – wrap from the Musashi province. *Tsuka-maki* or hilt wrapping became a specialised job performed by an expert known as a *tsukamaki-shi*. He would provide the correct style and colour wrap to compliment the rest of the *koshirae*.

The wrap covers a *same* or ray-skin which is glued onto the wooden handle base. Also highly valued among the *samurai*, the *same* helps the wrap to be firm, reinforces the wooden base and provides a non-slip surface so that the silk or thread will not move around when the sword is in use. On a more expensive *tsuka*, the *same* would fully wrap the wooded base,

BELOW: A pair of *menuki* or hilt ornaments that are found under the wrapping, partly to aid the purchase of the thread and also to facilitate the grip on the handle. This silver pair has been made to celebrate the year of the snake.

ABOVE: A *tsukamaki-shi* or specialist hilt wrapper tying off the knot at the top of the *tsuka* or handle. As with other crafts of the Japanese sword, hilt wrapping is still practised today using only the traditional materials and methods.

overlapping with no gap. This was known as *maedare-kise*, but was by no means always used. For reasons of cost, two separate panels of *same* might be used, one on either side of the *tsuka*, in the style known as *tanzaku-kise*. Considered most important in judging the quality of the *same* are the large nodules, which were usually placed near the *kashira* (pommel) end of the *tsuka*, on the *omote* (front) side of the sword where they could be seen most easily. The pattern of these nodules was of great importance and there are instances where they are faked or enhanced by later addition. Full skins of particularly good quality *same* were dressed up in a presentation style and given as valuable and desirable presents.

The often beautiful small metal hilt ornaments, known as *menuki*, also provide purchase for the wrap as well as assisting the grip. Also on the *tsuka* are the *fuchi* and *kashira* which finish either end of the *tsuka* – the *fuchi* nearest the hand-guard, the *kashira* forming the pommel. The *kashira* provides a convenient place to tie off the loose ends of the *ito-maki* (handle wrapping). The *fuchi-kashira* pair are made in the full range of metals and

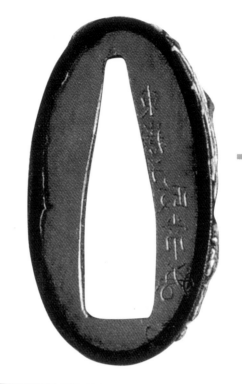

THIS PAGE: Two pairs of *fuchi-kashira*, the metal fittings at the top and bottom of a *tsuka*. One pair (bottom) depicts a bamboo grove under a crescent moon made of the alloy called *sentoku*. The other, in *shakudo nanako*, has insects and flowers. Both these designs taken from nature are highlighted in precious metals and date from the 18th century.

alloys employed in Japanese sword furniture and depict similar subjects, such as a family *mon* or crest. Also found is a formal hilt of the Tokugawa period with a normal *fuchi* but a plain black horn *kashira* which the wrap passes over.

The *tsuka* will also have a hole to accommodate the *mekugi*, a wooden peg that passes through the *tsuka* and through a hole in the *nakago* called the *mekugi-ana*. This peg is usually of smoke hardened bamboo. It fits tightly and holds the whole *koshirae* together. Occasionally metal screw-type *menuki* are found, often with ornamental heads.

There were many subtle variations in style and shape of *tsuka*. These variations were all given different names and were often regional styles, such as *Higo-tsuka* or *Izumo-tsuka*. Over fifty different *tsuka* styles are recorded.

SAYA (scabbard)

In the early days, most *saya* or scabbards were decorated in plain black lacquer, which provided a certain amount of protection from moisture. *Uchigata*na were mainly the property of the lower ranking foot-soldier.

However, by the Muromachi period, those of rank were beginning to display more decorative and much brighter coloured *saya*, employing techniques such as having gold flakes sprinkled over wet lacquer that was polished down when dry. Those of the Momoyama period (late sixteenth century), in tune with the general tendency of the time, became richly flamboyant and show incredible creativity.

By the time that the regulations of the Tokugawa were in force, black was again the preferred colour, particularly on formal occasions. However, as the Edo period progressed, a greater variety of lacquered finishes came to be seen, although probably the most common would include a family crest or *mon* of the owner. Another interesting effect was to have same wrapped around the *saya* and polished down to an attractive smooth pearlite type of

BELOW: The *sayashi*'s job is to make the scabbard for either a newly made or a newly polished sword. The finished work may be lacquered for a new *koshirae* or left plain for *shira-saya*, a storage mount. Only the finest seasoned Japanese *hinoki* wood is used.

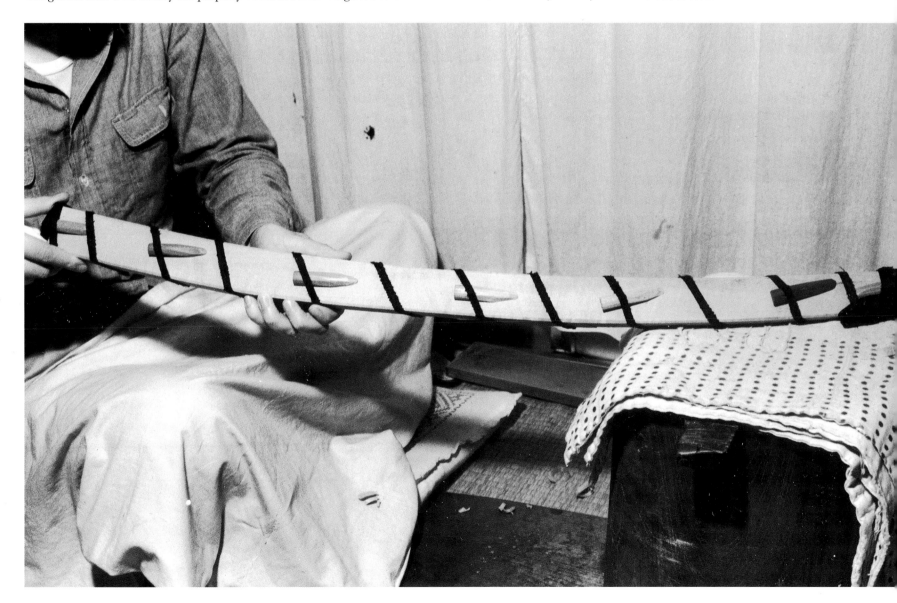

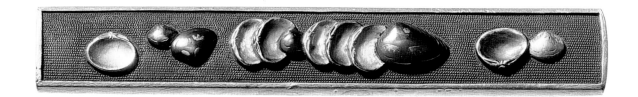

The panels on this spread are known as *kozuka* and are the handles of the small auxiliary knife known as *ko-gatana*. The exception is the matched pair of a *kozuka* and a *kogai* below. All are made of a variety of soft metals, mostly with a *shakudo* base on which gold, silver and copper are applied. The subjects are taken from nature, myth, legend and family *mon* or crests. Both the *ko-gatana* and *kogai* are usually fitted into slots on the *saya* of short swords such as *wakizashi* or *tanto*, but may be occasionally found on *katana*.

finish. The art of lacquering became a sophisticated and highly skilled art in other areas as well as decorating *saya*. Well over fifty different types of *saya* are recorded.

The mouth of the *saya* is known as the *koi-guchi* or carp's mouth, a named taken from its elliptical shape. This is sometimes reinforced with horn or a metal fitting as it is particularly vulnerable to wear if the sword is in constant use.

A few inches down the outside of the *saya*, on the *omote* side (the outer or front side when worn in the traditional manner of a *katana*), there is a loop known as the *kurikata*. This is usually made of wood or horn – though sometimes of metal – is to help retain the sword in the *obi* or sash of the wearer. Through the centre of the loop there may be two small fittings, usually in brass, known as *shitodome*. These have small teeth and help to retain the *sageo* or cord that further assists the retention of the *saya* in the *obi*. Often in a slot in the side of the *saya*, there is a small auxiliary knife, known as a *ko-gatana*. Its handle, known as a *kodzuka*, is sometimes a small work of art in its own right. The *kozuka* would be made by a skilled artist, such as the one who made the *fiuchi-kashira*, the *menuki* and the *tsuba*. Indeed he may have made all the metal fittings for the sword in a matching design. Sometimes the *ko-gatana* was replaced by a skewer shape tool known as a *kogai*. They are mostly found on *wakizashi* (short swords) and *tanto* (daggers), though both may be found together on better quality long swords.

A number of strange or unusual, not to say weird, types of *saya* are recorded though seldom encountered. The *ireko-saya* had a very practical inner lining which could be removed for cleaning, while the *kotsubuire-saya* had a small draw built into the inside to carry coins. Also for storing coins was the *shirigane-saya* at the butt end which, according to one theory, acted as a balancing weight for the shorter blade. The *itame-saya* was made of very thin wood so that the sword could be used without even drawing it, while the *mise-saya* or "show-off" *saya* was made to give the impression that it contained a far longer blade than was actually the case. Possibly the most amusing was owned by a well-known politician of the Meiji period who wore a sword of such great length, compared to his modest stature, that he found it necessary to put a small wheel on the end of the *saya* to stop it dragging along the ground.

HABAKI (collar)

The Japanese sword, unlike those of other nations, is not held tightly in its scabbard. Usually it is only the *mune* or back edge of the blade that is in contact with the inside of the scabbard. However, it is necessary to stop the sword rattling and falling from the *saya*, so a collar was given to the blade which fitted onto the blade in the machi area – the *mune-machi* and the *ha-machi* are where the blade proper meets the *nakago*. This collar is called the *habaki* and this area of the blade is known as the *habaki-moto*. Originally, in some very old *tachi*, the *habaki* was actually part of the blade and, a little later, swordsmiths were making their own *habaki*. It appears to have been common practice during the Muromachi period, that swords

mounted as *uchigatana*, which had *tsuba*, were fitted with single piece *habaki*, while those swords with no sword guards were fitted with a two piece *habaki*. Later, during the Edo period, it was customary for *koto* (pre-Momoyama period) swords to be fitted with the double variety and later swords to be fitted with the single versions. This custom is no longer observed and seems to have died out since the end of World War II.

Today, those skilled in the art of making *habaki* are often employed by polishers to provide new *habaki* for their clients. Commonly they are made of copper, which usually provides a base over which either gold or silver foil may be wrapped. Others are made of various alloys or even solid gold or silver and are sometimes skilfully carved with a variety of designs including the family crest or *mon*. There are over forty different names or styles of *habaki*, which again vary in design, such as *niju habaki* (two-part *habaki*), or material, such as *kinkise habaki* (gold *habaki*), or by location, such as Mito or Osaka *habaki*.

SAGEO (cord)

While not strictly considered as part of the *koshirae*, the *sageo* or cord maybe three to four feet long (90-120cm). It is passed through the *kurikata* or retaining knob found on the *saya*. It is there to help the retention of the *saya* in the *obi* or sash and may be of a variety of colours or designs.

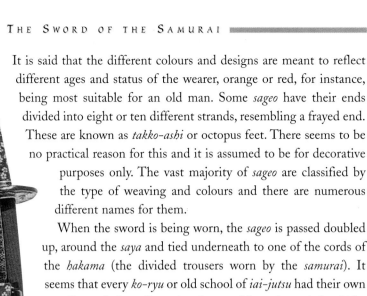

LEFT AND RIGHT: The three holes in the *nakago* of this sword indicate that it has been altered more than once in its lifetime to fit different sets of mounts. It is signed Bishu Osafune Sukemitsu on the *omote* or front side and dated February 1464 on the *ura* or reverse. The blade shows the low centre of curvature (*koshi-zori*) that is a characteristic of Bizen province blades as well as a certain amount of curvature near the point. Known as *saki-zori*, this feature is found on blades from the Muromachi period. The *katana koshirae*, which dates from the 19th century, has an ornate wrap and matching *sageo*.

It is said that the different colours and designs are meant to reflect different ages and status of the wearer, orange or red, for instance, being most suitable for an old man. Some *sageo* have their ends divided into eight or ten different strands, resembling a frayed end. These are known as *takko-ashi* or octopus feet. There seems to be no practical reason for this and it is assumed to be for decorative purposes only. The vast majority of *sageo* are classified by the type of weaving and colours and there are numerous different names for them.

When the sword is being worn, the *sageo* is passed doubled up, around the *saya* and tied underneath to one of the cords of the *hakama* (the divided trousers worn by the *samurai*). It seems that every *ko-ryu* or old school of *iai-jutsu* had their own peculiar variation of exactly where and how the end should be tied. When the sword is at rest on the *katana-kake* (sword rack), knots are tied in the *sageo* to keep them tidy, but they were tied so that they could be undone with a single pull in the case of an emergency. Such knots go by the name of *cho-musubi* (butterfly knot), a complicated but aesthetically pleasing arrangement, or the more simple *daimyo-musubi* (Lord's knot), or even *ronin-musubi*. In the case of a *daisho* (matched pair of swords), the two *sageo* should also match.

All the above are common to *katana*, *wakizashi* and regular *tanto*, varying only by the size and style.

KOSHIRAE (mounts)

There are various types of *koshirae*, most of which are dictated by the size of the blade.

DAI-TO (long swords)

The *dai-to* may come with a number of different types of *koshirae*, regardless of what type of blade it may be (*tachi* or *katana*). Of these, probably the most familiar is the *uchigatana* or *katana koshirae*. This, if you like, is the definitive "samurai" sword". The word "uchigatana" is a contraction of *uichi*, to strike and *katana*, a sword, meaning a sword suitable for striking an enemy. The *uchigatana* style of mounting, began to replace the *tachi* around the end of the fourteenth century, prompted by the change in battle tactics from mounted combat to combat on foot and the resulting lighter armours such as *domaru* and *haramaki*. Before this time, even as far back as the Heian period, the *uchigatana* had only been used by those of lower rank, but the advantage of a shorter sword worn cutting edge up became apparent to those of more exalted status at this time.

Usually, the *saya* will have no metal mounts, but a huge variety of lacquered designs are used to decorate it, although originally plain black was preferred. The lacquer had the added benefit of

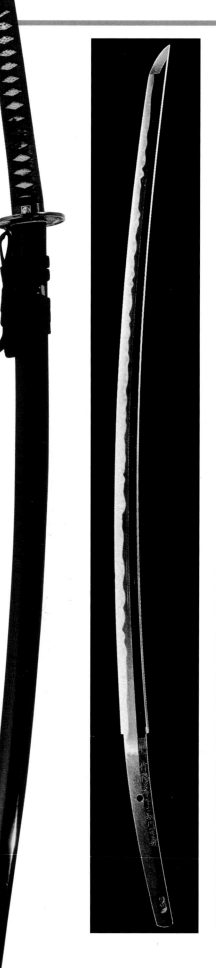

being resistant to water or damp. So, as in many Japanese art forms, it has a practical as well as decorative function. Certainly by the Momoyama period at the end of sixteenth century, boldly designed and flamboyant lacquer work was seen, reflecting the mood of the time. A reasonable number of these important Momoyama-period *koshirae* have been preserved. These include those on the swords owned by Toyotomi Hideyoshi as well as those of the Ii *daimyo* from Hikone. They are illustrated in many catalogues and books on the subject, and are frequently exhibited in Japan.

The *saya* of the *uchigatana koshirae* will also have the *kurikata* or retaining "hook" on the *omote* side, which is made of either soft metal, wood or horn, and is worn tucked through the *obi* with the cutting edge uppermost in a manner familiar to all practitioners of *iaido*. On some *saya*, there is a hook known as a *kaerizuno* whose function is to catch the *obi* and prevent the *saya* from coming completely out of it when the sword is drawn. The presence of *kaerizuno* is often an indication of a superior *koshirae*. At the closed end of the *saya* there is a lacquered cap known as

LEFT AND BELOW: The inscription on this sword reads "Sakuyoshi Bakkashi Hosokawa Masayoshi" and the *ura* states that it was made in the spring of 1837. The restrained *katana koshirae* compliments this fine blade by Masayoshi very well.

RIGHT AND BELOW: Signed Oite Kishu Nanki Shigekuni Tsukuru Kore, this sword was made by the second generation sword-smith of that name. Shigekuni was skilled in both the Yamato style and, as with this sword, the Soshu style of sword-making.

a *kojiri*. Usually all three of these – the *kurikata*, *kaerizuno* and *kojiri* – are made of horn, though sometimes metal. This also applies to the open mouth of the *saya*, the *koi-guchi* or carp's mouth.

The *koshirae* is complete with a *tsuba* and *tsuka*, which will have *fuchi-kashira* and *menuki* variously, and sympathetically decorated. On more formal mountings, all the metal mounts may simply depict the owner's *mon* or crest. In this case the *saya* is usually plain, black lacquer. All these various mounts show great art in miniature, and as such, are avidly collected on their own account.

Tachi Koshirae

Unlike the *katana*, the *tachi* was a slung sword, worn with the cutting edge down and was originally an ancient style designed for combat while mounted on horseback. The *tachi*'s *saya* has metal mounts – various rings, a chape and hanging devices, whose the design or decoration is often repeated on the *tsuba* and *tsuka*. Most commonly it bears the *mon*, the heraldic or family crests. Better quality *koshirae* will have metal mounts in *shakudo-nanako* and other soft metals. One *tachi* style has the top third of the *saya* wrapped in the same manner as the *tsuka*. This *koshirae* is known as *ito-maki tachi koshirae* or thread-wrapped slung-sword mounting. The *tsuba* on most *tachi* were known as *aoi-gata* or *mokko-gata*, a lobe shaped peculiar to this mounting, rather than the more usual round or oval shape found on *uchigatana*. The lacquer on the *saya* is often richly gold flecked in the *nashiji* – pear skin-like – style. On *tachi koshirae*, the *kashira* at the butt end of the *tsuka* is differently shaped from that of the *uichi-gatana koshirae* and is known as *kabuto-gane* (metal helmet).

Most extant examples of this style of mount would have been used with formal dress during the Edo period, but a number of variations were worn during hunting or other leisure pursuits. One of the more unusual is called *ho-ho-no-tachi*. The *ho-ho* was a mythological bird, the equivalent of the phoenix in Western culture. The *ho-ho-tachi* will have a metal bird's head instead of the *kabuto-gane* on the end of the *tsuka* and this gives it the Westernised name of "bird's head" *tachi*. All other mounts on the *saya* are likely to be of a standard *tachi* design but the *tsuka* will often be covered with *same* but left unwrapped. Such designs are said to have been worn for falconry.

Rarely found are normal *ito-maki-tachi* which have a fur covering on the bottom half of the *saya*. Very occasionally these are made of tiger skin, but more usually of bear fur. I have seen an example of the latter where the bear fur may be easily removed from the *saya*, returning it to its normal *itomaki-tachi* state. These are known as *shiri-saya*, not to be confused with *shira-saya*, and were made in imitation of very early battle *tachi*. They were considered to be the correct dress when hunting or dog shooting (a particularly unpleasant equestrian sport) during the Edo period.

Further variations include the *efu-no-tachi*, which has a peculiar cylindrical *tsuba*, again with no wrapping on the *tsuka*, just plain *same*. This is a formal mount, said to have been used at court and dates from Heian times, but was much copied later.

LEFT and BELOW: This sword is by Naminohira Yukiyasu from Satsuma province in the south of Kyushu. Swordsmiths of this name were active in Satsuma for some 900 years and their swords usually have a conservative and ancient appearance. This sword is mounted in an *ito-maki tachi koshirae*, the *saya* of which is covered with a *shiri-saya* simulating a tiger's tail. Although such "tiger tail *tachi*" appear to have been worn in battles by persons of rank, this was most probably worn when hunting during the Edo period.

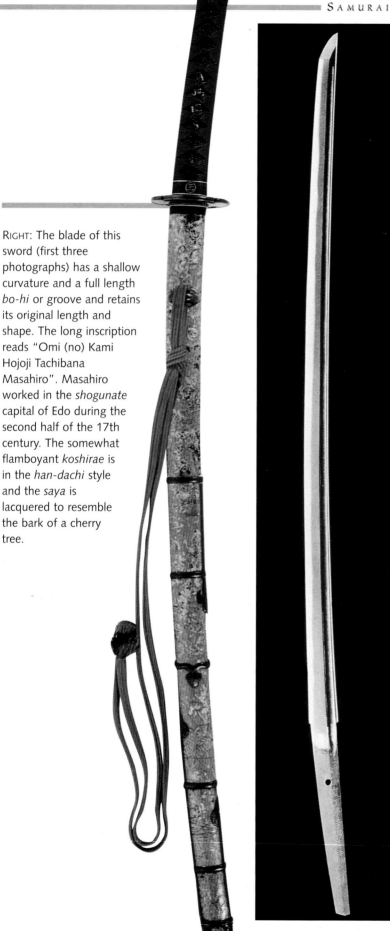

RIGHT: The blade of this sword (first three photographs) has a shallow curvature and a full length *bo-hi* or groove and retains its original length and shape. The long inscription reads "Omi (no) Kami Hojoji Tachibana Masahiro". Masahiro worked in the *shogunate* capital of Edo during the second half of the 17th century. The somewhat flamboyant *koshirae* is in the *han-dachi* style and the *saya* is lacquered to resemble the bark of a cherry tree.

During the Meiji period, when swords were often mounted for export, a good number of *katana* were remounted as *tachi*. A silver-mounted example in my own collection came to me with the wrapping in tatters. I decided to have it professionally rewrapped. When it had been stripped in preparation, it was apparent that originally a *kurikata* had been attached to the *saya* and that it had actually been a *katana*. Fortunately, the *mon* on the *saya* were of a rounded design and did not appear upside down after the alteration. There are also twentieth century examples around, usually with brass mountings and of lower quality. Many of these were made to celebrate the coronation of the Taisho and Showa Emperors. On many examples, the

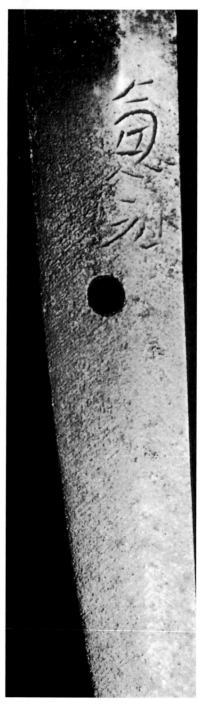

saya and metal fittings are decorated with *mon* but the blades seldom show great quality.

Han-dachi Koshirae

One style of *koshirae*, which is a mixture of both the *uchigatana* and *tachi koshirae*, is known as *han-dachi* (half-*tachi*). It owes slightly more to the *katana koshirae* than to a *tachi* and was very popular during the Bakamatsu or the end of the Edo period. At this time many longer-than-average examples seem to have been made. They became popular with royalist sympathisers, hence they were known as *kinno-to* or emperor-supporting swords.

Han-dachi katana were usually worn in the fashion of *katana* and not *tachi*, but would retain a number of the *tachi*'s metal *saya* mounts and would also have a *kurikata*. As with a *tachi*, the *han-dachi* usually also have a *kabuto-gane* at the end of the *tsuka*, rather than the *kashira* of the *uichi-gatana koshirae*. The majority of *han-dachi katana* seem to have a *mokko-gata* or lobe-shaped *tsuba*.

Chisai-Katana (short or small swords)

On a small *katana*, the *koshirae* differs only from that on the regular *katana* by virtue of its size. Although some made in the early sixteenth century were for one-handed combat (*kattate-mono*), many were also later made for the affluent merchant class who were subject to restrictions on the size of weapons they were allowed to wear. Such swords are often very richly mounted and the *saya* are ornately lacquered reflecting the ostentation and wealthy tastes of their owners. This contrasted to the more subdued and restrained taste that was the ideal of the *samurai* class. However, it was often to the wealthy merchant class that the artisans looked for patronage and without whom many of the later artists would probably have been unable to produce such exquisite work.

The *chisai-katana* is similar in size to the very early *uchigatana* worn by the lower ranks before it was generally adopted in the late fourteenth century.

Shin-gunto and kai-gunto (Imperial Army and Navy swords)

During the Showa period (1926-89), the *shin-gunto* (new army) and *kai-gunto* (navy) mountings were produced for the Imperial Army and Navy. These mounts are inspired by the old *tachi koshirae*. Their design was certainly in imitation of the old *tachi* and they are probably the most commonly encountered *koshirae* outside Japan. There were many subtle differences in the customising of the *shin-gunto*, whose numbers are far in excess of their naval counterparts, the *kai-gunto*.

LEFT: This *katana* blade has the simple two-character inscription, "Kanemoto". Several generations of Kanemoto worked in Mino province in the 16th century and developed a distinctive *hamon* known as "*sanbon tsugi*", or three cedar trees. The highly decorative *han-dachi koshirae* accompanying this blade may be regarded as being in somewhat questionable taste.

The *shin-gunto* is usually a field brown colour overall with a metal *saya* on which there are brass mounts similar to those of a *tachi*. Towards the top of the *saya*, a single suspension ring is found. A solid cast brass *tsuba* separates the *saya* from the *tsuka*, which has a brown thread wrap. Occasionally the *tsuba* is not solid but pierced right through. Swords with *tsuba* such as these often seem to have superior blades and are always worth a second look. The metal mounts are again brass, often patinated to a rich brownish colour and the *menuki* depict three cherry blossoms. A button is inset into the *fuchi* which releases a brass lever that secures the blade into the *koi-guchi* or mouth of the *saya*.

The naval version is similar, but is either black or dark blue overall, including the *same* which, unlike the white army version, is black. The metal mounts are very similar to the army's, but tend to be gilded rather than brass. The *saya* also has two suspension rings, unlike the single one of the army. Unlike the army's, the navy's *tsuba* is usually ovoid in shape and patinated to a dark blue or black colour. All metal mounts on both Imperial Army and Navy swords are decorated throughout with a cherry blossom design, the favourite emotive blossom of the *samurai*.

On both army and navy swords, an interesting customisation is the addition of a small silver family *mon* on the *kabuto-gane* of the *tsuka*. These are usually thought to accompany a sword that has a better than average quality blade, the thinking being that higher class, ex-*samurai*, families were the only ones whose family possessed a *mon*. In reality, most families had adopted one or more *mon* during the Meiji era, and they probably have little real meaning. It would be a mammoth and probably fruitless task to attempt to trace the previous owner of a sword by reference to the *mon*. When surrendering swords with this feature, the officer would sometimes deface the *mon* in order to lessen the disgrace to his family name.

Both types of sword will often be found with a leather combat or foul weather cover over the entire *saya* and sometimes also the *tsuka*.

SHO-TO (short swords and daggers)

The *wakizashi* or "companion sword" was designed as the *sho-to* (short sword) that accompanied the *dai-to* in the matched pair of swords, known collectively as the *daisho*. The two blades of a *daisho* might occasionally be by the same maker, but the *koshirae* would always be an obvious, although not necessarily an exact, matched pair. Often *daisho* have been split up and it is a collector's dream to reunite the two swords of a *daisho*.

Slots to accommodate the small *ko-gatana* (auxiliary knife) or *kogai* (a kind of skewer) are often found near the top of the *wakizashi*'s *saya* and, rarely, these may also be found on *katana-koshirae*. The handle of the *ko-gatana* is known as a *kozuka* and is usually made of soft metals similar to the other mounts. The rectangular

LEFT AND BELOW: A *wakizashi* blade signed by Tadakuni of Hizen province with the title Harima Daijo and the ancient family name of Fujiwara included in the inscription. This broad blade has a full length *bo-hi* or groove and the *suguha* or straight *hamon* favoured by many Hizen swordsmiths. The excellent *koshirae* has a *tomoe* (comma) *mon* on the *fuchi* and the hilt binding goes over the horn *kashira* in the formal manner. It would have formed part of a *daisho*.

panel of the *kozuka* is skilfully decorated in a similar manner. The blades of these auxiliary knives were crafted by swordsmiths and often bear their signatures, although they are seldom of the quality of a sword blade and the signatures are often apocryphal. However, nowadays, modern swordsmiths make good *ko-gatana* blades and sell them grandly signed as souvenirs for tourists. As they lack the *mekugi-ana* (hole), they are not subject to the same quantity restrictions placed on swords. The function of the *kogai* is not known for certain. Fashioned in a similar manner to the *kodzuka*, but with an integral blade made of all one metal, they are avidly collected. There are various theories regarding their use. Some say that they were used to arrange the hair of the *samurai*. Or that they were used to help pick up the head of a decapitated foe. Or that they were even an ear-cleaning implement. Whatever the truth, together with a matching *kozuka*, they make a beautifully crafted accessory to a sword and are highly valued by collectors.

A variation of the *kogai* is the *umabari* or "horse-needle". These are usually only made of iron by artists from Higo province and frequently have brass inlay. It is variously said that they were used to prick the side of a horse to release trapped air, to remove stones from horses' hooves or to encourage the horse to go faster. Another variation of the *kogai* is split into two parts which could easily be adapted to make *hashi* (chopsticks)

The *wakizashi-koshirae* is only different from the *katana* or *han-dachi koshirae* by virtue of size and the *kojiri* (butt end) of the *saya*, which tends to be rounded rather than squared off in most cases.

Custom-made blades for *wakizashi* began to be made around the Oei period in the early fifteenth century, coinciding with a move towards more fighting on foot and the wearing of the *daisho*. Occasionally, older blades may be found in these *koshirae*, but the old blade would have to be shortened to accommodate this *koshirae*.

During the early Meiji period, many swords appear to have been thrown together quickly and cheaply, supposedly to arm the insurgents from Satsuma province. These swords, which seldom have anything other than a most inferior blade, are easily recognisable. Most are *wakizashi* sized. They have a cheap flat *ito-maki* (hilt wrap), often plain or sparsely decorated iron mounts (*tsuba* and *fuchi-kashira*) and a plain iron disk for the *menuki*. In the West, these are popularly known as "Satsuma Rebellion mounts" and are not greatly sought after by collectors.

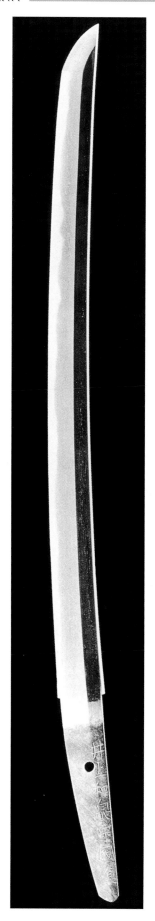

LEFT: A very richly mounted *wakizashi* in the *han-dachi* style. All metal mounts are of a floral design on a *shakudo-nanako* base in the Mino-Goto manner. The *saya* is exquisitely lacquered showing cherry blossoms on the green ground, and the *tsuka* is wrapped in doe-skin. It contains a blade by Kanemoto.

RIGHT AND ABOVE: Made by the famous Osaka swordsmith, this sword is signed Inoue Izumi (no) Kami Kunisada. As he is the 2nd generation, he is better known as Shinkai and was a leading light in the so-called Osaka *shinto* school. This *wakizashi* is dated 1670.

Tanto Koshirae

The *tanto* or dagger might be worn as part of a *daisho* instead of the *wakizashi*, in which case the mounts would often be match those of the *dai-to*. They were also commonly worn in conjunction with a *tachi*. There are three basic types of *tanto koshirae*, which might all contain similar types of blades:

1. *Tanto*: with a normally formed (but smaller) *tsuba*, all the normal *tsuka* mounts found on a *katana* or *wakizashi* and a lacquered *saya*. They might also accommodate the *ko-gatana* in the same manner as a *wakizashi*.

2. *Hamidashi tanto*: similar to the above but often slimmer overall and with a *tsuba* that has most of one side cut away usually to accommodate the top of the *kodzuka* handle of the *ko-gatana*.

3. *Aikuchi Tanto*: literally close-fitting mouth, with no *tsuba* at all, the *fuchi* is flush with the *koi-guchi*. Very often the *tsuka* will have no *ito-maki* (thread wrapping) and the *menuki* will be fixed directly onto the *same* which covers the *tsuka*. This style was originally designed for wearing with armour.

Another type, often of late manufacture, is known as *kwaiken*. Usually with no metal mounts, except perhaps a *menuki*, this is almost a miniature *tanto*. It was said to be a woman's weapon that could be hidden in the sleeve of the kimono.

Tanto appear throughout the history of the Japanese sword and were made by most schools of sword-making. Many *tanto* are very beautifully and intricately mounted. Most of these mounts tend to be nineteenth century. It should also be noted that, before the Meiji period, silver mountings are virtually unknown. So a silver-mounted *tachi* or *tanto koshirae* is unlikely to be earlier than mid-nineteenth century.

SHIRA-SAYA (plain wood storage scabbard)

Finally, all lengths and styles of sword blades might be found in *shira-saya*. This is a storage rather than a practical mount and is in plain, undecorated wood. A rich *daimyo* or *samurai* might have several different sets of *koshirae* for one blade and would keep the blade in a *shira-saya* when it was not being used. The *koshirae* would be kept together with a wooden blade, known as *tsunagi*. The *shira-saya* is undecorated, though sometimes an appraiser may brush an attribution onto the *saya*, especially for an unsigned or shortened blade. Known as a *saya-gaki*, this might tell of presentation details. *Saya-gaki* are at their most reliable when the name of the writer is included and such attributions, especially by the Honami family or other well-known sword appraisers, are greatly prized by collectors. If a *saya-gaki* is anonymous, then attribution is less reliable. Some *shira-saya* have the *koi-guchi* (mouth of the scabbard) reinforced with black horn. This may also surround the *mekugi-ana*. Called *tsune-guchi*, these are purely decorative embellishments and have little or no practical use.

Nowadays, when a sword is sent off for polishing, it will be returned in *shira-saya* and, if it has a *koshirae*, a *tsunagi* would be made for it. Sadly, in this situation, it is not possible to return the blade to the *koshirae* which may have traces of dirt or grit that would cause damage to the polish. A good *shira-saya* also has the advantage of being almost airtight, limiting the blade's exposure to dampness and lowering the risk of it rusting.

FAR LEFT: Tsunaie from Osafune in Bizenmade this *hira-zukuri tanto* in 1522 from Osafune in Bizen province. It has a silver mounted *aikuchi tanto koshirae*. Sword fittings made of silver like this example are seldom found until the very end of the Tokugawa period and the beginning of the Meiji period (1860s).

LEFT: After polishing, the blade is kept in the plain wooden storage mount called *shira-saya* which is airtight and dust free, since it may harm the polish to return it to its original *saya*. Any *koshirae* is then kept together with a wooden replica of the original blade known as a *tsunagi*. This *koshirae* is a Hizen province style of *han-dachi koshirae*.

RIGHT: This type of sword rack is made exclusively for a *tachi koshirae*. Here an *ito-maki tachi* is placed in the correct manner on the rack with the *tsuka* or handle at the bottom. The rack itself is heavily lacquered and depicts hawks swooping over crashing waves.

SWORD HANDLING ETIQUETTE

"As a whole, one had better refrain from paying a visit uninvited unless necessity dictates. When invited conversely, one cannot be a real guest unless his demeanour can convince the host of his being a pleasing and thoughtful guest."

Yamamoto Tsunetomo – Hakakure

To wear a Japanese long sword, together with the short companion sword (*wakizashi*) in feudal Japan was indeed a great honour. It meant that the wearer was of the *samurai* class with all the privileges that accompanied that rank, but many responsibilities and formalities accompanied these rights. The *samurai* were a proud and haughty bunch whose honour was often prickly and easily upset. Any perceived insult to his sword was exactly the same as an insult to the owner and would need to be rectified, often by drawing the sword with the bloody consequences this might bring. A situation known to practitioners of *iaido* to this day is called *saya-atte*, or scabbards hitting. If two *saya* collided, instant retribution would follow, as the sword had been struck and this was tantamount to striking the owner. As soon as the *saya* touched, the sword would be drawn and an attacking cut would be made (*nukitsuki*) all in the one action. *Saya-atte* might even happen deliberately, so that a ne'er-do-well would have the opportunity of testing both his sword's cutting potential and his own technical ability, all in the one swift incident. To avoid accidental *saya-atte*, it was considered best to walk to the left of a path or road and allow any walker approaching to pass on one's right side, away from the *saya*. It is even thought that this is why the Japanese drive on the left-hand side of the road. (The British, it is said, drive on the left-hand side of the road for a similar reason. A falconer would always carry his bird on his gloved left hand which would also hold a horse's reins, leaving the right sword hand free. It was

considered essential to keep to the left and have others pass on the right, so one could defend oneself, if attacked.)

Even civilised social contact could easily give the wrong impression, so great care was taken to neither offer or invite provocation. This was done by following a rigid code of etiquette in any given circumstances. It was usual when visiting a person of higher rank, for instance, to leave one's long sword at the entrance to the house. It would be taken, very deferentially, by a servant or a page who handled it with a silk cloth, then placed it on a sword rack ready for collection on departure. The visitor would be allowed to keep his short sword, which he would be careful to keep in a position where he could easily draw it if surprised or attacked. No *samurai* would ever be totally unarmed. Even with the sole comfort of the short sword, care was taken to keep the left hand away from the *tsuba*, as pushing the *tsuba* forward with the left thumb, thus loosening the blade in the *saya*, was the first move made when drawing the sword.

The display of non-aggressive intent was even more important if the long sword accompanied one to a meeting or social engagement. Here it would be removed from the *obi* or belt as one made oneself comfortable, sitting on the tatami mats. The sword would ideally be removed with the left hand, passed over to the right hand and placed on the mat on the right-hand side of the owner. Here it was relatively difficult to pick up and draw quickly. It was seen as highly suspicious if the sword was placed on the left, especially

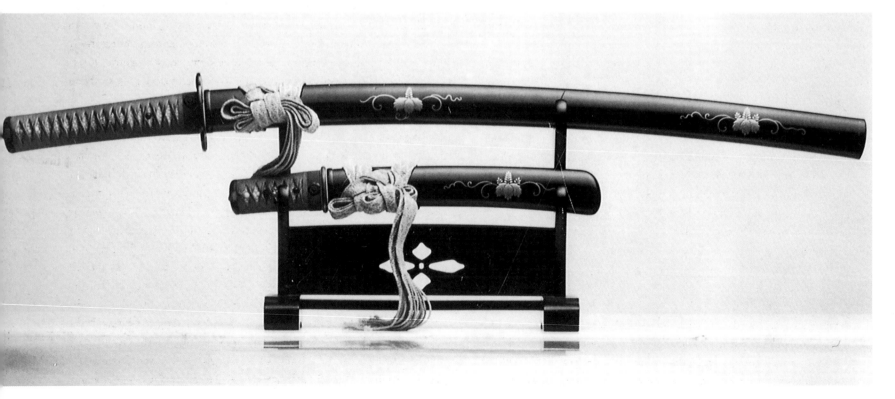

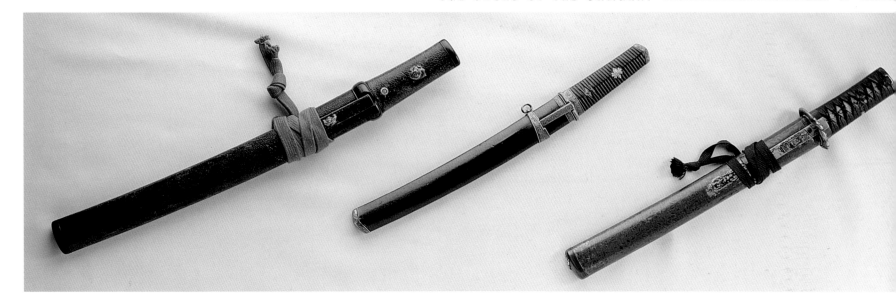

LEFT: A *daisho* correctly placed on a *katana-kake* (sword rack), with a *tanto* as its short sword. The *mon* is the Oda family heraldic crest.

ABOVE: Three types of *tanto koshirae*, including (left to right) an *aikuchi tanto*, a *hamidashi tanto* and a standard *tanto* with a *tsuba*.

with the cutting edge of the blade away from the owner. From this position it was very easy to grasp the *saya* with the left hand while reaching across and drawing the blade with the right. The significance of where the sword was placed meant that the owner was either relaxed, expecting or offering no trouble if it was on the right, or wary and ready to fight, if on the left. Whichever the case, the mood of the meeting would be quite obvious to all.

Today, in a modern *kendo dojo*, the members always kneel in *seiza* (on both knees) when formally starting and finishing the session, with their *shinai* (bamboo swords) to their left, in state of preparedness and *zanshin* (awareness). Incidentally, even today in a modern *kendo* or *iai dojo*, the practitioners and teachers start and finish a session with a formal bow with everyone kneeling in a prescribed order. All should know their position in this line, which is in ascending order of rank or status, the lowest being at the end nearest the door. In the case of an attack on the *dojo*, the lowest grades would provide themselves as delaying cannon-fodder and sacrificial lambs, while the higher ranks had more time to prepare to defend themselves. This no doubt provided a great incentive to advance in the art and progress down the line towards relative safety.

There are also correct ways of placing a sword on a *katana-kake* or sword rack. If the sword is a traditional *katana*, *wakizashi* or *daisho*, it should be placed on the rack with the cutting edges uppermost, the *katana* at the top and the *wakizashi* on the bottom in the manner they are worn. A further refinement might be that the *kurikata* (retaining knob on the *saya*) should be visible – in other words the *omote* side of the sword is showing and the *tsuka* (handle) is to the left hand side. Once again, it is surprisingly difficult to pick up a sword from that position and draw it immediately without changing hands and slowing down the action. To my mind, the swords also

happen to be better presented in this way. To display the swords with the *ura* (reverse side) showing was considered acceptable but, as they could be drawn from this position in an instant, it was seen as a far more aggressive position and, for this reason, favoured by many warriors. Indeed, it would be possible to tell the state of any house or castle's martial preparedness, simply by seeing how the swords were displayed on their racks.

A *tachi* or slung sword ideally has a differently designed rack than that made for *katana*. A *tachi* rack or stand has a shaped base and a vertical stem with a slot to accept the *saya*. *Tachi* should be placed on these racks with the end of the handle, the *kabuto-gane*, resting on a small indentation in the base. It will then stand vertically with the butt end of the *saya* free in the air. Should it be necessary to place a *tachi* on a conventional *katana-kake*, then it should be placed with the cutting edge down, in the opposite manner to a *katana*. Once again, this is the way the sword would be worn. A beautifully made and lacquered sword rack will enhance the display of a sword "at rest" but it is incredible how unnatural a sword looks when placed incorrectly on the rack or stand.

There would have been occasions when a fully mounted sword was passed between two persons, possibly for inspection, study or appreciation. This would usually be accomplished while in *seiza*, the formal kneeling position on the tatami – *seiza*, with legs folded under the buttocks and toes flat, is considered to be a position from which an attack is difficult to mount swiftly. After a short bow to the sword, the giver would remove it from the rack, clean it and pass it over, usually horizontally, with both hands fully outstretched. The cutting edge would be towards the giver and the *tsuka* to his left. The right hand would be near to the end of the *saya* and the left would be palm uppermost near the *tsuba* with the thumb on the *mimi* or rim of the *tsuba*. This ensured that the blade did not inadvertently slip from its *saya*. The recipient would grip inside of the giver's hand on the saya and take over the position by the *tsuba*. He would immediately turn the cutting edge towards himself, give a slight bow of respect and proceed to examine the piece. Traditionally, this might be accompanied by a bow from the giver and,

to be easily removed from the *tsuka*. If two or three attempts at this fail – by which time this self-flagellation would be causing considerable pain – the blade is unlikely to be freed in this manner. I have occasionally found myself in this position. Not wishing to be responsible for causing any damage, either to my left hand or the sword, I have asked the owner to remove it for me. He is familiar with the sword and, if he also has difficulty, it is best to leave it intact.

LEFT: The formal and correct way of studying and appreciating the *sugata* or form and shape of a blade held at arm's length.

ABOVE: When viewing the *hamon* or *jihada*, the sword must be supported by a *fukusa* or other soft cloth and brought up to eye level.

if the rank of the receiver was exalted or the sword was known to be especially important, the bow would place the sword at head level. Out of good manners and respect for another's property, especially if exceptional lacquer work was evident on the *saya*, a silk cloth called a *fukusa* would be used when handling the sword. This may be supplied by the host, but it was advisable to carry one's own and be fully prepared.

The normal method for removing the *tsuka*, from either a mounted sword or one in *shira-saya*, is to first remove the *mekugi* or peg with a *mekugi-nuki*. Then hold the *tsuka* near its base in the left hand with the blade at a slight angle, say 20 to 30 degrees from the vertical, with the inclination across your front side and the cutting edge uppermost. With a tight left hand grip, strike the top of your left hand smartly with your clenched right fist, on the little finger side rather than with the knuckles. The shock of the strike transmits through your left hand, through the *tsuka* and usually loosens the hold of the *tsuka* on the *nakago*, allowing the blade

A sword might have to be passed from one person to another minus its *saya* but retaining its *tsuka*. In this case, the giver would hold the end of the *tsuka* firmly at the end nearest the *kashira* with his left hand, again keeping the cutting edge facing himself. The aggressive intent in doing it otherwise is evident. This time the receiver will accept the sword by grasping above the giver's hand with his left hand and nodding to acknowledge that he has a firm grip, possibly acknowledging this verbally too. It will be noted that in this procedure both parties always have their right hands free. Once the sword, complete with mounts, is safely in the viewer's hands he may study it. First, he should look to see whether the *mekugi* (peg) is inserted in the *tsuka*, rather than discover by accident that it is not when the blade falls out.

A close examination of the fittings and the lacquer work should proceed the drawing of the blade. A sword with fine fittings should be examined while wearing white cotton gloves if possible, or with a *fukusa*, if not. The sweat from hands may cause discoloration or even rust which should

obviously be avoided. To draw the blade, the *saya* should be gripped in the left hand held slightly lower than the *tsuka*, but with the cutting edge uppermost and drawn in one smooth action. The *saya* should be placed safely aside, beside you on the tatami or back on the rack or table. It is good form to cover the end of the *saya* with a cloth, or the flap of the sword bag if one is present, while you are examining the blade, to prevent any dirt or grit entering the *saya* and causing damage to the blade later.

Most properly, you should place a silk handkerchief in your mouth to prevent spittle fouling the blade. Speech should be avoided when a blade is naked for the same reason. A blade should only be withdrawn completely from the *saya*. It is considered the height of bad manners to examine a blade a few inches at a time while being slowly withdrawn from the *saya*. Care should be taken that the blade is not waved around or pointed at anyone. The handle should be removed to inspect any inscriptions only with the expressed permission of the owner. The blade may be examined in detail, but should not be handled other than with a *fukusa* or some other suitable soft fabric. If the *tsuka* is removed, it is permissible to handle the *nakago*, while supporting the rest of the blade with a *fukusa*. It is usual to leave the

habaki in place while examining an otherwise bare blade.

To pass a fully stripped blade, the *nakago* must be gripped in the same manner as the *tsuka* on a mounted blade. The sword will be passed vertically to the receiver in exactly the same manner as described when the sword retains its *tsuka*. However, in this circumstance, it is advisable that the free right hand be placed under the *nakago-jiri* (butt end of the *nakago*) for extra support. When replacing the sword into the *saya*, the back of the *kissaki* is rested on the inner part of the *koi-guchi* and the blade is then replaced in the exact reverse of the method described for drawing it. This applies in all circumstances.

The over-riding consideration is that the person handling the blade is at the mercy of the blade should he mishandle it. This was, and remains, the etiquette involved in handling a mounted sword. It emphasises great respect for the sword, personal safety and a high degree of *zanshin* or awareness. Although today we may not fear an attack, the other factors are still relevant. The proper etiquette should always be observed to show respect for the *samurai* whose swords we are privileged to examine and enjoy today.

Handling unmounted swords presents similar problems, along with one or two others. When swords are laid out for *kantei* (appraisal) sessions, for instance, they usually rest on a table with the few inches

LEFT: This *wakizashi* is signed Gensaimonjo Nobukuni and is dated August 1414. Several talented swordsmiths were named Nobukuni and this is the 4th generation of the line who worked around 1394-1427. Many fine *horimono* or carvings are found on blades with a Nobukuni signature.

RIGHT: This sword was made by the second generation of Hizen swordsmiths named Masahiro. The signature reads "Hizen Kuni Kawachi (no) Kami Fujiwara Masahiro". The powerful Nabeshima clan retained the Masahiro line for eight generations. This sword was made in the mid-17th century.

nearest the *kissaki* supported by a small silk pillow or *makura*. When lifting this naked blade, care should be taken that the *kissaki* does not dip and touch the table itself. The sword needs to be almost scooped up so that the *kissaki* immediately rises. It goes without saying that the blade should not be pivoted on the *kissaki*. When clear of the table the methods and rules for examination are as described above. When replacing the sword back on the *makura*, similar care should be taken.

These days a light source is usually available when studying a blade. This enables the *hamon* and *jihada* to be seen clearly, in detail. However, this often involves a certain amount of twisting and turning in order to obtain the best angle between light and blade. Great care must be taken in this situation and a good grip must be kept on the *nakago*, while the other hand supports the blade with a *fukusa*.

Often viewing will entail several people studying several blades between them, at the same table, either standing or in a kneeling position. It is then of the utmost importance that all blades are kept facing to the front and not waved around. A clash of swords would be an unforgivable breach of etiquette and probably result in the perpetrator catching the next plane home. It is difficult to imagine how one would ever be invited back after such an incident. In all other respects, group viewing should follow the same rules as previously described.

On various visits to study swords in Japan, both accompanied and alone, I was aware that our sword handling etiquette and ability was closely scrutinised by our Japanese hosts and *sensei*. Often in this situation, museum curators or NBTHK officials will watch closely and have been known to comment on the "manners" of the guests. The etiquette does not go unnoticed and is a direct reflection on oneself and one's teacher.

CARE, RESTORATION AND PRESERVATION

"Until fifty or sixty years ago, the samurai would, every morning, take a tub bath, shave the front part of his head, smoke his hair with incense, trim his nails and scour them with pumice and further polish them with wood sorrels, being thoroughly careful not to neglect his personal appearance. Furthermore, he would dust his weapons and keep them polished and free from rust."

Yamamoto Tsunetomo – Hagakure

The Japanese sword has two deadly and unremitting enemies that are a constant threat to its very existence. They may work together, but are just as dangerous if they attack the sword individually. Their names are ignorance and rust. Of these, the worst is ignorance. The effects of rust are often reversible, at a price. Ignorance will always be more difficult to combat as it has allies in self-importance, arrogance, well-intentioned misdirection, embarrassment and loss of face. Education is necessary, though it is not always welcome.

Ignorance may even be seen in those who should know better, such as high grade martial arts *sensei*. In the past, I have found it necessary to remonstrate with high grade Japanese *kendo* or *iai* teachers, who have mishandled or shown a reprehensible attitude towards a genuine Japanese sword. Even such exalted individuals must be left in no doubt when they are in error. The alternative is to perpetuate their ignorance and possibly jeopardise a sword's existence at some stage in the future. The fact that you may have a hard time in the *dojo* later should be considered a small price to pay.

Preservation as an aspect of Japanese sword collecting should not be underestimated. If one appreciates and admires an object then it is natural to take care of it. Even so-called *shinto* or "new swords" may date back nearly four hundred years and are only around today because they have been preserved by many generations of previous owners. Indeed, ancient swords from the Heian and Kamakura periods are often important historical objects as well as great works of art and have been lovingly cared for, often at great personal cost, for a thousand years or more. It seems highly unreasonable, not to say immoral, that their final resting place should be in the hands of an ignorant foreigner who wants to cut his shrubbery with his "*samurai* sword". Similarly, old swords should not in my opinion, be used for *iaido* or any other martial art where they risk irreparable damage.

Museums, surprisingly, are another great source of Japanese sword abuse and trying to tell curators, who often look on their charges as their personal property, how to conserve Japanese sword blades is a task that requires the artfulness of a politician and patience of Job. Swords would often be better preserved by the genuine collector who knows how to look after them. In this way, future generations will still be able to marvel at their beauty and revere them as important historical artefacts.

It is difficult for the uninitiated to be conversant with the often demanding necessities of Japanese sword care and conservation. Even in Japan, 99.99 per cent of the population will never have handled a sword. Their only contact with one may have been on a school visit to a museum as a child. It is a sure bet that if you are reading this book, you will have far more contact and appreciation of Japanese swords than most Japanese and are, therefore, in a better position to help preserve them. No opportunity should be lost. This may mean "liberating" the sword from an owner, before it is further vandalised. On many occasions I have "rescued" swords that I had no desire to own, simply to ensure their future safety.

Once a sword has been rescued and is in the hands of one who appreciates it, decisions then need to be made about its future conservation. Obviously, if it is already in a fine state of preservation, nothing other than regular maintenance is required. Sadly, this is rarely the case and we will assume that it is covered in rust and that little is discernible on its surface.

Firstly a close study of a blade must be undertaken to see whether restoration is possible. Obvious problems, such as edge chips, broken points, deep rust pitting and bends in the blade, need to be carefully assessed. Other less obvious problems, such as has the *shinogi* or ridge line, being rounded off and having lost its shape, or are any of the other lines badly distorted, should also be assessed at this time. The presence of any of these, depending on the degree of damage, may mean that the sword is a write-off or only partially restorable. If in doubt, this may be a good time to seek the advice of a more experienced collector or, indeed, a professional polisher. Whatever the case, it is most inadvisable to attempt to do anything yourself, unless you are professionally qualified. Amateur restoration will, in all probability, be worse than none at all.

This is a good point to define what I mean by "professionally qualified" polisher or restorer. There are a number of artisans working outside of Japan who may have had some Japanese instruction, but many are self taught. The best of these may approach the standard of some of the less accomplished Japanese-trained polishers and some of their work is even good enough to be submitted to *shinsa* or Japanese judging panels. Their work is adequate in so far as the best of them will do no damage to a blade that cannot be reversed or improved on at a later date. These people may provide a useful service, in that their work stops further rusting or corrosion and a sword that otherwise might suffer terminal damage may be saved. However, those that are competent to do this are few and far between and I would not allow them to polish a very good blade. An adequate cleaning job should enable one to see what is on a blade that one could not see before. However if such a polisher does not understand, in minute detail, the characteristics that an individual sword possesses, he may adopt the wrong polishing techniques for that blade, to its detriment. So he should be skilled at *kantei* or sword appraisal. This can easily be tested. One can easily draw one's own conclusions if he will not partake in *kantei*.

If he is not skilled at the initial foundation work of the polishing, for instance, this may be difficult to reverse and all subsequent stages of polishing will be incorrect. Ignorance may be found even among skilled artisans and genuine lovers of Japanese swords. Of all those claiming to be *togishi* or polishers in the West, no more than three or four should be trusted. The rest should be avoided. Many are vandals who may do irreparable damage to a Japanese sword. Their motivation is purely financial, their knowledge of Japanese swords is negligible and, often, their arrogance is unbelievable. Because of the profit involved, many work as fast as possible. This leads to the greatest act of vandalism – cleaning a sword with acid. This hideous shortcut has untold and long-lasting effects on a sword. Because the sword has a laminated structure, the acid will actually get inside the blade. It may be eating away at the innards of a blade for years like a cancer, causing the metal to gradually flake away. If such a sword is encountered it must be taken directly to a proper *togishi*, who will hopefully know how to neutralise the malignant action and be able to polish the blade correctly. This practice is not confined to the West. Some of those polishers from Japan, advertising their services to Westerners, may to some degree, use acid to enhance the *hamon*, for instance, and save themselves the difficult and time-consuming finishing work. Beware the cheap polisher who can get a sword back to you within two or three months.

ABOVE: Arguably the most important aspect of sword preservation is the polishing of a blade. Here a master *togishi* does the foundation work of the polish. All qualified polishers undergo a rigorous apprenticeship; work is carried out using traditional tools and methods.

In an ideal world, one should know the polisher, talk to him about the sword and what you expect from the polish. Even among the top class of polisher in Japan, some are better at polishing the harder steel of *shinto* and *shinshinto* blades, while others excel at the softer *koto*. Different swords may need to be polished by different artisans and you should seek them out and try to establish a relationship with them. If they have won prizes in NBTHK polishing competitions, you will have a good idea of their prowess. Wherever possible it is advisable to see examples of their work or take the recommendation of another collector. The best work may be described as "art polishes" and the subtleties they are able to show in both *hamon* and *jihada* are usually far removed from the Western attempts. And for the best work you will naturally have to pay more and wait longer.

A sword may have to be sent or taken to Japan for polishing, so you should also be aware of the procedures. All Japanese swords that are taken into Japan require a permit. The only exceptions are modern *iai-to*. These are, in fact, not real swords anyway. They do not have a forged blade and are

ABOVE: It is essential that the *togishi* has a deep and fundamental understanding of swords. He must be expert at *kantei* (appraisal) and understand the original shape and structure of the sword. Without this understanding it is impossible to correctly restore and polish the sword and to expose the original work and features that the swordsmith created.

simply reproductions made for the martial arts. If however, they are the so-called *shinken* (modern hand-made swords, also made for martial arts) they will require proper registration and certification. A *shinsa* paper from the NBTHK, NTHK or some other organisation, does not constitute an import permit and should not be confused with one.

The procedures may be rather time consuming and irksome, but it is essential that they are always carried out to the letter. Otherwise you risk not only the confiscation of the sword or swords, but criminal prosecution. It is a criminal offence to have an unregistered sword in Japan, as serious as having an un-licensed firearm in the UK.

If you do take a sword to Japan, you must declare it at customs on entering the country. It is worthwhile planning a delay of two or three hours as the customs officials will probably have to send for a police officer who has some knowledge of swords. He will then examine the sword and issue a temporary permit to you, which will allow you to take the sword out of the airport and go about your business. You may find this rather a frustrating business, but it is unwise to argue. Making a fuss about the bureaucracy will only delay you further. This temporary permit is only valid for a maximum of three weeks. If you allow it to expire, then you will be in contravention of the law and risk all that it entails.

No permit will be issued for a *Showa-to* that carries any kind of *kokuin* (stamp). Such swords are considered merely as weapons with no artistic merit. They are illegal in Japan and will be immediately confiscated and destroyed. Even if you believe the sword is *gendaito* and traditionally made, if it has a stamp of any sort, you will be running a grave risk trying to import it. You will be relying on your skill in the Japanese language to convince the police that this is not a *Showa-to* but a hand-forged sword. Regardless of the rights and wrongs of the argument, you may still lose your sword. You will then be faced with trying to recover it. I would strongly advise against attempting to import this type of sword.

Please note that with a personal import in this manner, you are only allowed to bring a maximum of three swords per person into Japan, but this may include modern swords (without *kokuin* or stamps, of course).

A full licence needs to be obtained from the local Board of Education (Kyoku-inkai) which is the agency acting for the Bunka-cho or Cultural Affairs Department, before the temporary permit expires. In Tokyo, this is done at the Tokyo Metropolitan Office in Shinjuku where a *toroku-shinsa* is held on the second Tuesday of the every month. This *shinsa* is for local blades as well as the foreign imports. At the *shinsa* the official permanent licence, called a *toroku-sho*, is issued. It costs 6,200 yen and shows the dimensions of the blade together with any inscription. Unlike other *shinsa* it makes no attempt to value or appraise the sword in terms of authenticity or quality. Once you have this, usually in the form of a plastic coated card, it must be kept with the sword at all times. Many owners have it sown to the bag in which the sword is kept to avoid losing it.

By far the easiest way to import swords is to use an agent or polisher. If your sword is going to a polisher, he will often take care of all the necessary paperwork, as will an agent. In this case it is important that, when sending the sword, you clearly mark the destination and contents of your parcel on your customs declaration. I always write "Japanese sword for restoration purposes only". I also try to have it arrive in Japan around the second Tuesday of the month or reasonably close to the third Tuesday of the month when the *toroku-shinsa* is held at the Tokyo International Post Office Customs. When the package arrives in Japan, the customs will inform the recipient who then arranges to pick it up and take it for full registration on the appropriate day. Of course, the agent or polisher will add a handling charge for this service as there is a lot of running around to be done. But usually the charge will be the same for several swords as for a single one. There is no restriction on how many swords you send by this method, unlike the limit of three per person that you can carry with you. Besides, the handling charge is small compared to the hassle of doing it yourself – or the potential problems should you fall foul of the law.

I do not recommend sending modern swords. If they are not a hundred years or older, they are not recognised by the authorities as antique Japanese swords. Swords younger than a hundred years old invite very complicated procedures, similar to those needed for the import of commercial machinery. Particularly modern swords of the Taisho, Showa and Heisei periods should be avoided as some *toroku-shinsa* judges may reject them and issue no *toroku-sho*. This depends entirely on the judge's generosity. It is easy to understand why I have not attempted to take the Fuhrer's sword that I own to Japan for a *shinsa* and restrict it instead to *shinsa* conducted outside the country where such laws do not apply.

It is advisable to check on current regulations before taking swords to Japan as the rules may change and ignorance of the law is no excuse. Apart from the possibility of criminal proceedings and the confiscation of your sword, you may cause problems for others in the future. I also understand that Japanese prisons are not the most pleasant of places and are best viewed from the outside and at a distance.

Once the blade has been given a proper polish in Japan, it will be returned with an NBTHK certificate of authenticity. Although this will have been costly, you will have saved the sword from further abuse. It is now in pristine condition and all the details of the sword are apparent. It will have been mounted in a new *shira-saya* (plain wood storage mount), probably had a new *habaki* made – usually it is the polisher's responsibility to commission any necessary work from other artisans, such as a *habaki* maker or *sayashi*. It will probably be dripping in *choji* (clove) oil. If it had a *koshirae* (set of mounts) these will now be held together by a wooded replica of the blade, called a *tsunagi*.

Although now, with this particular sword, we have vanquished the first enemy, ignorance, rust is poised to mount an attack. Water is used throughout the polishing process and a small amount may be still trapped in the folds of the steel of the blade. Over the first few months after polishing, this may "sweat" out onto the surface of the sword and can result in rust spots. If left untreated this will obviously disfigure the polish and may even mean that the sword will need to be returned to the polisher. As the polishing process removes metal from the blade, it can only be

undertaken a certain number of times before exposing the *shingane* or core steel. This is undesirable. So the newly polished blade must be constantly checked and cleaned, every couple of days for the first month and once a week for the following three or four months. This involves applying *uichiko* powder to remove the *choji* oil, cleaning and re-oiling the blade.

To do this, the sword, it is removed from the *fukuro* (bag). Usually the *saya* is replaced in the bag and the mouth of the *saya* covered by the overlapping piece that would normally accommodate the *tsuka* or handle. This ensures that no dust or dirt can enter the *saya* while the sword is out and damage the blade when it is replaced. The sword is then stripped of all mounts which are likely to be only the *shira-saya* and *habaki*. It is important that the *habaki* is removed. *Uichiko* powder is then applied liberally over the entire blade, including the *mune* or back edge, but not the *nakago*. Holding the blade by the *nakago*, *nugui-game* (Japanese fibrous paper) is then used to dust the surface very lightly. (If this *nugui-game* is new, it will be necessary to crumple it up to soften it.) As good *uichiko* is ideally a powder made from the polisher's finishing stones and, therefore, slightly abrasive, this dusting action will clear away any coarse pieces that might be on the blade's surface and prevent an unsightly scratch. Still gripping the blade by the *nakago*, use the *nugui-game* to wipe the *uichiko* from the blade, firmly but gently. Initially, the first few inches are wiped down the blade, towards the *nakago*. This avoids picking up any rust or dirt from the *nakago* and wiping it onto the clean surface of the blade. The same thing applies to any *horimono* or carvings on the sword. There may be dirt in the *horimono*, so the wiping action is towards the *nakago* rather than the *kissaki*. After this the rest of the blade should also be wiped in a single motion towards the *kissaki*. All wipes should be in one stroke, avoiding short rubbing actions, which may cause circular scratches to appear on the blade. Obviously the paper should be held around the *mune* or back edge of the blade rather than along the *ha-saki* or cutting edge, when cleaning. Preserving one's fingers intact is also a desirable thing.

This procedure should have removed all the *choji* oil from the blade, which may then be polished with a soft dry cloth. This is exactly the same process that would be used simply to be able to study and appreciate the details of a sword, which is not possible when it is soaked in *choji* oil. If the sword is to be re-oiled, this should be applied with a soft cloth, ensuring that it is evenly spread on all surfaces of the sword. In Japan it is necessary to have swords constantly oiled as the climate is rather humid. It is not always necessary to do this in the West, depending on one's local climate and how one's swords are stored. In my own case, I usually only oil them during the summer as the English climate is not particularly humid and the swords are kept in a constant temperature. Some collectors enjoy this cleaning process as the aroma of the clove oil is quite pleasing. Only pure *choji* oil bought from a sword dealer should be used. Ordinary clove oil available in a chemist's shop is not pure or refined enough for applying to sword blades and, when it dries, it will stain the blade and prove difficult to remove. Another small point regarding *choji* oil is that, although it is sweet smelling, it is actually quite toxic. It is certainly best not to get it on your hands if you have any kind of scratch or open wound. While unlikely to kill you, it may cause an unpleasant irritation.

A side effect of constant oiling is that the oil eventually soaks into the *shira-saya* and stains the wood right through from the inside to the outside, changing the colour of the *shira-saya* in a not altogether unpleasant manner. If swords are kept oiled they should not be stored in a vertical position, propped up against a wall, for example. Such a storage position will mean that the oil on the blade will all run towards the lowest point and accumulate in the bottom of the *saya*, with detrimental effects to the wood and possibly causing a dirt trap. Store the swords either on a *katana-kake* or lying on a flat surface, in a drawer, for instance.

It is an absolute and fundamental rule that a Japanese sword blade, especially one with a new or well-polished surface, should never be touched by the naked hand. The salty and acidic properties of sweat will cause an almost instant rust patch on a blade. Although the resulting fingerprint might help identify the perpetrator, this is less than desirable. If swords have been lent for display purposes or out of your possession for any reason, it is always advisable to thoroughly *uichiko* and clean them on their return. The same process should be undertaken on a regular basis in order to maintain the condition of the blade.

This deals with cleaning the polished surface of the blade, but not the *nakago*. The *nakago* is never polished but left to rust and patinate with age, a process which may even be assisted by handling. Even on a blade that has no signature or inscription of any kind, much valuable information may be found on the *nakago* that may help identify its age and maker. This includes the overall shape of the *nakago*, the number of *mekugi-ana* or holes, the *yasuri-me* or file marks and the colour or patination of the rust of the *nakago*. Obviously inscriptions are of great value giving names, dates and places. But under no circumstances should the *nakago* be cleaned since much of this information will be lost if this is done. The patination may be lost completely and, depending on the abrasiveness of the cleaning, the inscriptions may be damaged irretrievably.

The *koshirae* or mounting of the sword may also deteriorate if left in humid or damp conditions. This should obviously be avoided. Lacquer and soft metal fittings may be lightly dusted whenever the blade is cleaned. In extreme cases, mild soapy water may be used with a soft brush to clean off surface dirt. This must be done with the utmost care and you must be careful not to overclean fittings, especially soft-metal pieces. I have seen what was beautifully patinated black *shakudo*, polished to a bright copper colour, by the ignorant. Over-enthusiastic polishing may also obscure delicately carved details irreversibly. No cleaning fluids should ever approach such mounts and the advice given in B.W. Robinson's *Arts of the Japanese Sword* should be studiously ignored. The old patination processes of the original makers were secrets and few now know how to replace lost patination correctly. If such over-cleaned pieces do need repatination, have this done professionally. This still may not bring back the original patination colour, which is probably lost forever, but may result in a satisfactory replacement. All the cleaning that is normally required is for any

dust to be removed with a soft cloth, but there should be no rubbing or polishing at all.

Sasano Masayuki, in his book on *Sukashi Tsuba*, suggested that cleaning iron *tsuba* with a sharpened piece of horn, bone or wood and a soft cloth was a reasonably safe method of removing surface rust. Using warm soapy water and a soft natural bristle brush will also be effective for removing grease or other surface dirt from iron fittings, but such treatment is certainly inadvisable for all materials other than iron, which is naturally quite tough and can take this treatment. This may then allow the piece to naturally repatinate over time, although this may take several years. One strange method that I have heard, but never seen or done myself, is to freeze the object so that it is coated with ice. Gently removing the ice loosens stubborn rust spots that may then be removed with a horn spatula. Certainly metal tools, wire brushes, steel wool, acid or abrasive cleaners should never come near your fittings nor should attempts to repatinate in hot ashes or fire be even remotely considered. Soft white cloth gloves should be worn at all times when handling *koshirae* or metal fittings to prevent moisture from one's hands adversely effecting the piece. A silk cloth or *fukusa* is a quite acceptable substitute.

Finally, it is advisable always to keep your sword in a tied cloth bag when not being viewed. These bags come in a variety of cloths and designs and it is customary to use different bags for different types of mounting. For instance, when a sword is returned from a polish, it is usual that, if it is in a *shira-saya*, it will be in a silk bag. The usual custom is that this bag is in a plain purple colour and the *himo*, or ties, are of the same material and attached. Such bags may or may not be lined and I have encountered, white, green and blue *shira-saya* bags of varying quality and thickness. Also for *shira-saya*, cotton striped bags with black *himo* are used. These bags, as well as preserving the *shira-saya* from any knocks or dents, when secured correctly, will prevent the sword from moving in the *saya*. More ornate brocade bags are used for fully mounted swords or *koshirae*. These will have a set of tasselled *fusa-himo* or ties, which are attached via a loop on the side near the opening. They are wider than the *shira-saya* bags in order to accommodate the *tsuba*. Again they are of differing quality, ranging from, heavily padded with a thick lining to the lighter and thinner varieties. The former are generally used for more valuable or delicate *koshirae*. Similar bags, but wider, are used for *tachi koshirae* to accommodate the greater curvature and more ornate *sageo* which often accompanies this type of mount.

When placing a sword into a bag, ensure that is all the way in and that there is no slack at the top or bottom of the bag. Then bring the flap of the bag over the *kashira* of a mounted sword or the butt end of the *tsuka* on a *shira-saya* and bring it down tightly before tying securely with the *himo*. This will ensure that there is no opportunity for the sword to move around in the *saya* and causing any kind of damage. A variety of attractive style decorative knots may be used which add to the display. It is quite acceptable in these days of relative peace, to keep the sword in its bag on a *katana-kake*. I think it is always worth while buying the best quality bags for swords. It

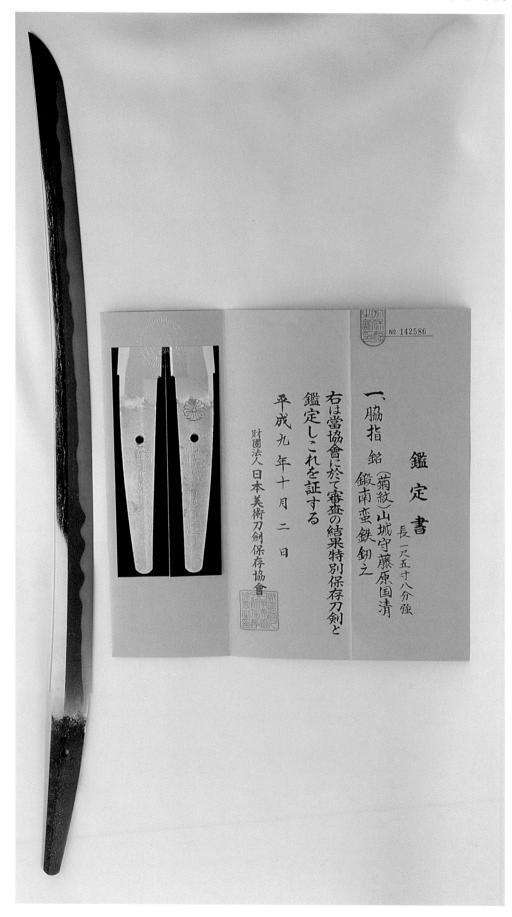

右は當協會に於て審査の結果特別保存刀劍と鑑定しこれを證する

一 脇指
　　銘（菊紋）山城守藤原國清
　　　　鍛南蠻鉄釯之

鑑 定 書

長一尺五寸八分強

平成九年十月二日

財團法人日本美術刀劍保存協會

No 142586

LEFT: Known as *origami* or folded papers, certificates of both quality and authenticity for both blades and fittings are issued by several organisations in Japan. They are proof that a panel of experts in a *shinsa* has judged a sword and this is their official written appraisal. Various different papers are issued to state the degree of quality of a given piece. The above is issued by the government organisation called the Nihon Bijutsu Token Hozon Kyokai (The Society for the Preservation of Japanese Art Swords, NBTHK). The NBTHK only hold their *shinsa* in Japan and this is an example of their *Tokubetsu Hozon* certificate. The sword is a 17th century *wakizashi* blade by Yamashiro (no) Kami Kunikiyo.

seems churlish to spend a lot of money on a polish or a sword and then place the sword in a cheap bag, when even the best bags cost so little compared to the price of the sword.

If a sword blade is in Japan for polishing and has been through the tiresome bureaucratic channels of importing it into the country, it may as well be submitted to a Japanese *shinsa* or judgement team for their opinion on both authenticity and quality. There are two main *shinsa* in Japan and they both deliver opinions and issue certificates on fittings as well as blades. The first and most authoritative is that conducted on a regular basis by the Nihon Bijutsu Token Hozon Kyokai (NBTHK) at the Japanese Sword Museum in Yoyogi. The second is the Nihon Token Hozon Kai (NTHK) run until recently by the late Mr. Yoshikawa, who many years ago fell out with the NBTHK and started his own organisation. This latter conducts many *shinsa* outside of Japan and is far more friendly to the Western collectors, especially those in the USA, where a number of local sword clubs are directly affiliated to the NTHK. One of the reasons that the NTHK is so visible outside of Japan may be that it is now conducting far fewer *shinsa* inside Japan where its "papers" are considered of little value.

Both societies issue certificates which attest to both the authenticity of a sword or fitting and to their quality. Great credence is placed in these certificates,

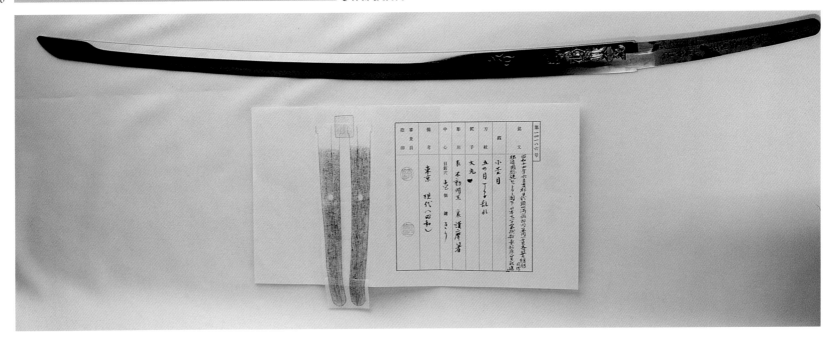

which are called *origami* or folded papers. Nowadays they also act as a kind of log-book for the sword. It would be difficult to sell a sword in Japan without some kind of certificate of authenticity, so most of the Japanese dealers who buy swords in the West immediately submit them to NBTHK *shinsa* on their return to Japan. Although the societies issuing certificates have different names, their basic judging criteria is similar. The following is the NTHK's most common criteria for failing a sword or fitting in *shinsa*:

- Any sword or fitting, whose maker is still alive, will not be considered.
- Quality. As the *origami* is partly a reflection of quality as well as authenticity, a sword or fitting will fail if it does not reach a high enough standard.
- *Gimei* or wrong signature. The NTHK's paperwork points out that there are forgeries, made for commercial reasons in all parts of the art world. If possible, the team will try to indicate who they think actually made the piece.
- Condition. If a sword is not in a state where it may be adequately appraised then it will fail. If the condition is reversible – for example, it is polishable – after the necessary work it may be resubmitted with a chance of passing. A failure because of condition is not always a sign that the sword is no good, only that it is not possible to appraise it in the current condition. Hopefully, this will be pointed out to the owner who should probably have realised this anyway before submitting a sword to *shinsa*.
- Similarly if the sword or fitting has actually been damaged or is flawed, though this is more serious. A higher tolerance level is allowed in very old blades, especially if they are of historical interest. The younger the blade the less allowance is made. Conditions that will fail a sword, include *ha-giri* (a vertical crack in the *ha-saki* or cutting edge), no *boshi*, *saiha* (retempered) and other major *kizu* or flaws.

- In *kodogu*, there are three main reasons for a rejection. These are if the piece has suffered by being burnt in a fire (which is also a big problem for a blade), if it is a cheap reproduction such as a cast-iron *tsuba* or, like a sword, it is *gimei*.

The NTHK's *shinsa* literature gives good commercial advice onwhat to do in the event of failure: "Even when receiving a 'pink sheet' [a notice of failed *shinsa*] the important thing is to maintain an even perspective. To receive an *origami* is very good, but not to receive one is not the end of the world. Also do not become so discouraged by a pink sheet as to cause you to sell the sword foolishly. It is an unfortunate fact that some unscrupulous dealers wait for the unwary holders of pink sheets to relieve them of their swords cheaply. It is not uncommon to later see these same 'junk' pieces with a new polish and good *origami*. We strongly urge everyone with a pink sheet to think twice before selling off the sword cheaply. Like people, swords should be cherished for what they are and not despised for what they are not."

The most common passes are for what might be termed "ordinary" swords. The NBTHK's lowest pass *origami* is known as *hozon token* and the next one up as *tokubetsu hozon token*. A good result in the latter might encourage the owner to submit for a even higher level, reserved for outstanding swords, known as *juyo token*. NBTHK *shinsa* only take place in Japan. The NTHK equivalent of *hozon token* is *shinteisho* (awarded 60-69 points in their system) followed by *ninteisho* (70-84 points). To reach the equivalent of *juyo token*, NTHK *shinsa* must take place in Japan where either a *yushu* or *sai-yushu origami* is issued. All these certificates will show the *nakago* of the sword (either a photograph or *oshigata*), a photograph of the *kodogu* or *koshirae*, an explanation and date of the *shinsa*, all in beautiful calligraphy. However, only a few years ago, a great scandal over forged *juyo* token certificates shook the NBTHK. Who knows how many fake ones may still be in circulation?

There are many people in the West who are, at least in part, earning a

LEFT: A similar certificate to that shown earlier, except that the Nihon Token Hozon Kai (NTHK) issued this at a *shinsa* held in New York in 1997. This level of certificate issued by this group is called *Ninteisho* and the sword is a *gendaito*.

BELOW AND RIGHT: This sword is by the father of the Masahiro shown on Page 93. It is signed Hizen Kuni Kawachi Daijo Fujiwara Masahiro and dates from the early 17th century.

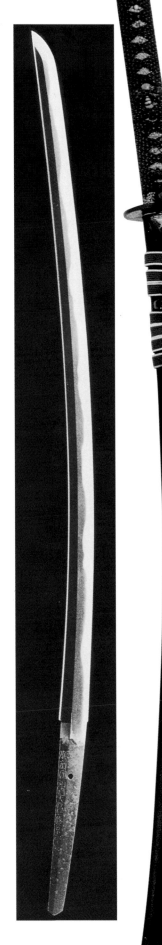

living by offering restoration work on Japanese sword fittings. The best of these are highly skilled artisans, some of whom have learnt under recognised teachers in Japan. These people include *tsukamaki-shi* (hilt wrappers), *saya-ashi* (scabbard makers), *habaki* makers, lacquerers, *tsuba* makers and even makers of *fuchi-kashira* and *menuki*, as well as the polishers already mentioned. The skill of these individuals varies from poor to accomplished, but using them at all brings the question: Where does restoration become replacement and at what point will it mean that the sword is no longer the same piece, or even in some cases, is no longer a Japanese sword?

It is important always to remember that we are dealing with antiques sometimes of historical significance. If a sword has a new *tsuka* and all new *kodogu*, together with a brand new brightly lacquered *saya*, all made in the West and all that is left is the original blade, can this really be called a Japanese sword any more? Or is it better described as a "Japanese-style" sword, or a sword that contains a Japanese blade? If the blade is made in the West, especially by amateurs with none of the formal Japanese training or apprenticeship, then it seems to me that this is certainly not a Japanese sword. The point is to what degree and in what manner is restoration acceptable? It is not possible to define this absolutely, but I would suggest that, when the essential character of the sword is changed, this is a step too far. Most obviously, gaudy coloured *tsukamaki* or *saya* lacquered bright "day-glow" colours lack the essential refined taste usually associated with a good Japanese sword mounting and say more about the taste of the "restorer", while the repair of a split *saya* or replacement of a damaged *koi-guchi* seem acceptable to me. The Japanese themselves are often guilty of simply replacing parts, rather than their sympathetic restoration, usually for reasons of time, cost and convenience. This also applies to armour where I have seen brand new *kuwagata* (horn-like crests) – bright and shiny when a little ageing might have looked far more appropriate – put on to old *kabuto* in order to make them more readily sellable. Maybe the benchmark should be that, if only traditional Japanese materials and methods are used by properly trained artisans, then the chances are that the end result will be acceptable.

I think that the mind-set generated by unsympathetic "restoration" is only a small step away from the irresponsible and reprehensible habit of taking fittings from swords and selling them separately, on the basis that the individual parts have more monetary value than the whole. Many important *koshirae* have been vandalised over the years in this manner and, of course, this is the antithesis of preservation. In many quarters, the concept of *ubu*, unaltered or original, seems not to be understood or, if understood, not appreciated. I was lucky enough to acquire a beautiful *han-dachi koshirae* from an Italian collection that came up for sale. The *kodogu* or metal fittings were all of good *shakudo-nanako* with *waki-goto* gold floral designs applied in relief and the *saya* was beautifully lacquered with a cherry blossom design. Both the *tsuba* and the *kogatana*, however, had been replaced. The *tsuba* replacement was a round iron piece, obviously too big for the sword, signed Fujishimi Kaneiie, while the *kogatana* was of *kaga* inlay style. The original *tsuba* was almost certainly also in *shakudo-nanako*, not iron. It

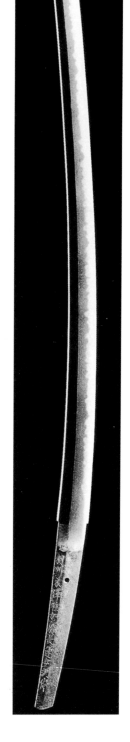

BELOW and RIGHT: This magnificently shaped *tachi* blade appears powerful and strong. It is tempered in the Bizen style of *choji hamon* by the *shinshinto* swordsmith Tsunatoshi who trained a number of skilled students who also followed the Bizen tradition. The signature reads "Ushu Yonezawa Ju Chounsai Kato Tsunatoshi" and is dated February 1836.

would have been *mokko-gata* in shape, not round, and made by one of the Goto branch families, not Kaneiie, probably with a similar design to the rest of the *kodogu*. Similarly, the *kozuka* of the *ko-gatana* would have been of *shakudo-nanako* rather than the flat polished *shakudo* of the *kaga* school. The previous owner, a well-known collector of sword fittings, should have known better. He could have, at least, made sympathetic replacements rather than the obvious misfits that he did. So far, I have been successful in at least finding a suitable *tsuba* for the sword. Both his replacement pieces were actually of quite good quality themselves, but hopelessly out of character with all the other fittings, so a possibly important *koshirae* is no longer *ubu* and has not been preserved intact.

SPOTTING A GOOD BLADE

There is a logical procedure for examining a Japanese sword blade and this is used in the practice of *kantei nyusatsu*. In *kantei* sessions, a blade is presented to a participant with any inscription there might be on the *nakago* covered. The maker's name, or at least the period of manufacture and school, must then be guessed at. If the procedures are followed, this apparently daunting task may be accomplished with less difficulty than might be expected. The procedure for *kantei* covers the points to look for to tell a good blade from bad.

First the *sugata* or shape of the blade should be examined. The shape should appear strong, the curvature natural and the *kissaki* should be in proportion to the width and length of the blade. There should be no "wasting" in the *monouichi* area which might indicate reshaping and the *fukura* must be natural for the same reason. All lines – such as the *shinogi*, *yokote* and *ko-shinogi* – should be correct and crisp, especially on a newly polished blade. It is important that the *shinogi* or ridgeline should not be burred, flattened or rounded. Remember that it is impossible to replace metal that has been removed. The *mune* or back edge's shape should be noted. This may be rounded (*maru-mune*), three-sided (*mitsu-mune*) or, most commonly, roof-shaped (*iori-mune*). In this latter case, the height of the *mune* should also be noted.

Any *hi* or other carvings should be studied to see if they are original or *ato-bori* (carved later) and of good quality. For instance, if a sword has been shortened or the *machi* moved, but the *hi* still stops above the *habaki* (and looks quite natural when the sword is mounted) then it must be a later addition.

When examining a blade's *sugata*, the blade is best held upright at arm's length. The *sugata* may impart a great deal of information about the age of the blade and sometimes about where it was made. However, if the blade has a good shape and sits comfortably in the hand, there is a fair chance that it has some quality. It is impossible for a good sword to have a bad shape unless it has been altered, damaged or repaired in some way. This frequently happens, so it is important to try and imagine the *ubu* (unaltered) shape of the blade before any shortening (*suriage*) has taken place.

The next area to study is the *hamon*. This is often referred to as the tempered edge, but is where the sword has been quenched to provide a high carbon steel area which will hold a sharpened edge. It contrasts with the body of the sword. The *hamon* may be in any number of patterns, but appears as a milky white colour on a properly polished blade. The upper edge of the *hamon* will be formed from tiny martensite crystals called *nie*. Sometimes these are too small to see with the naked eye and are then known as *nioi*. It is *nie* and *nioi* that border the *hamon* and form the pattern of the *hamon* and they should be examined very closely, ideally by holding the blade at eye level pointed towards a spotlight. The *nioi-guchi* (edge of the *hamon*) should form an unbroken and constant line from the *machi* area (bottom of the blade) along its entire length and into the *kissaki*. A break in the *hamon*, called *nioi-giri*, is a serious flaw and a blade with one should be avoided. It is also important that the *boshi* (the area of the *hamon* within the *kissaki*) is present and does not disappear off the edge. This is also a serious flaw in the blade and is only acceptable on great swords of historical and cultural significance. No compromise should ordinarily be accepted here. Various activities within the *hamon* should be noted. These may be small leggy lines coming down from the *nioiguchi* (*ashi*) or various flowing lines such as *kinsuji* (lightening) or *sunagashi* (drifting sands). These and other activities or *hataraki* greatly enhance the *hamon* and demonstrate the swordsmith's skill at *yaki-ire*, the quenching process.

If *sugata* and *hamon* pass muster, the sword should be okay. However, we need to assure ourselves that it is hand forged and not a cleverly mass-produced piece such as the *Showa-to* mass-produced during World War II. This is ascertained by examining both the *jigane* and *jihada*. The *jigane* is the actual steel from which the sword is made and might show subtle changes in colour and texture. The *jihada* is the surface pattern of the *jigane* caused by the forging process and emphasised by the polishing. This is mostly visible between the edge of the *hamon* and the *shinogi* or ridgeline. The *jihada*, appearing like a wood grain, is described by its type and size – for example, *ko-mokume* or small burl – and there are many criteria for judging the quality of the *jihada*. It should appear homogenous, natural and uncontrived, and may be enhanced by *nie* appearing on the surface, when they are termed as *ji-nie*. These *nie* may form patterns similar to the *sunagaeshi* in the *hamon* and, when appearing on the *ji*, are called *chikei*. Also visible on better quality swords, mainly but not exclusively *koto* period swords from Bizen province, is a feature known as *utsuri* or shadow of the *hamon*. This comes in a variety of shapes which may help identify the period of manufacture; however, this must not be confused with *tsukare* or tiredness in a blade which sometimes resembles a kind of *utsuri*.

The *kissaki* or point section of the sword should be examined when studying the *sugata* but may benefit from further examination as it is a very important part of the sword. It is in the *kissaki* that both the skill of the swordsmith and the polisher are most immediately apparent. Make sure that the *fukura* or the rounded and sharp part of the point is correct and appears natural rather than reshaped. It is unlikely that it will be straight (a common mistake amateur restorers make) and the *boshi* or tempered part of the *kissaki* will naturally follow this line, especially in *shinto* blades which tend to have *suguha* in this part of the *boshi*. The *boshi* must not disappear off the edge and any *kaeri* or "turn back" onto the *mune* should again be natural. Make sure

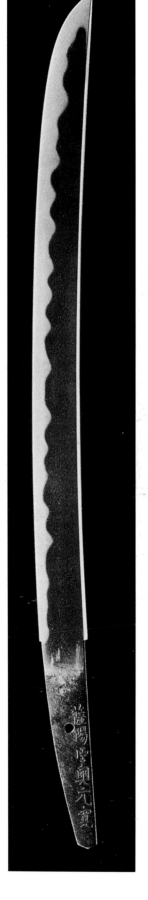

BELOW AND RIGHT: Although this is a late *tanto* blade, it demonstrates the old style of swords made by the conservative swordsmiths of Satsuma province in both shape and *hamon*. Dated 1828, it is by Motohiro who was taught by his highly talented father Motohira. It is quite unusual to see *wakizashi* in *hira-zukuri* (flat with no ridge line).

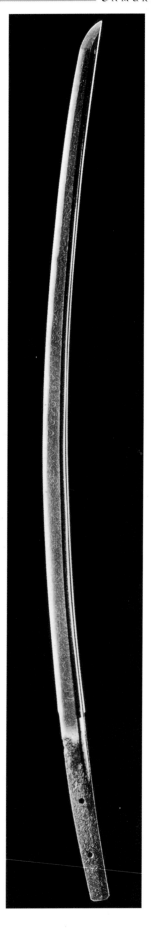

BELOW AND RIGHT: This old *tachi* is faintly signed with the two characters for Gassan. This group or family of swordsmiths is distinguished by their unique *jihada* known as *ayasugi-hada*. They seem to have died out at the end of the *koto* period but were revived in the *shinshinto* period in Osaka and still thrive today.

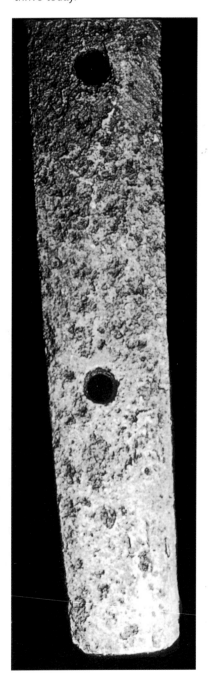

that there is a real temper line here and not a false one put on by an unscrupulous polisher. If it does not reflect the light like the rest of the *hamon*, then it has no *nie* or *nioi* and it is best to disregard the sword.

While undertaking this detailed examination of a blade, any flaws or faults will become apparent. Some of these may be more acceptable than others, depending on the age of the blade. A twelfth-century blade is entitled to have a few problems that would not be tolerated in a modern sword. However, all faults and flaws obviously detract from both the beauty and value of a sword. Look for holes or bubbles in the sword, which may indicate air, or impurities, have been included in the forging process and may be lurking just under the surface of the blade. Also check the *ha-saki* (cutting edge) very carefully for hairline vertical cracks running from the *ha-saki* into the *hamon*. Called *ha-giri*, these are often very difficult to detect, but they are very serious flaws since, if the sword were used to cut, at the point of *ha-giri*, it would bend or break. *Ha-giri* are not acceptable under any circumstance. Also check for *niogiri* or breaks in the *nioguchi*.

When the *shingane* or core steel begins to show through the *kawagane* or skin steel, the sword is becoming *tsukare* or tired. The cause of this is excessive polishing often on swords where the *kawagane* is thin in the first place. Early tiredness may appear as small darkish patches on the polished surface but full tiredness is recognisable as patches of *jigane* that have no pattern at all on them. Such *tsukare* is often found on *kazu-uichi-mono* (mass produced blades) of the Sengoku Jidai. Although a small amount of *tsukare* may not detract too much from a sword, it is obvious that a sword with *tsukare* cannot be polished further, as this will only compound the problem, and the sword is effectively at the end of its life.

Finally, the inspection of the *nakago* or tang takes place. The *nakago* on a good sword will always be carefully finished. The patination should be a good colour and the rust should not be cleaned off under any circumstances. If there are any inscriptions these will be of interest. A good *mei* will be skilfully and confidently written, not untidy, jumbled or hesitant. It almost does not matter whether you can read the inscription – most modern Japanese cannot read the old *kanji* in sword inscriptions. The important thing is that it looks confidently executed. However, beware of famous names on *nakago*. The odds are that it is a forgery and it would be better if the blade were not signed at all. If you have the necessary reference books, a detailed comparison with accredited genuine signatures might be undertaken. However, as a good number of forgeries may be several hundred years old this is by no means a guarantee of authenticity.

Of course, there are many subjective judgements to be made when judging a Japanese sword blade. But many times I have heard things like "there is something about it" or even "it speaks to me". This, of course, begs the questions: what is there about it and what is it saying to you? If one is to own a Japanese sword there is a certain amount of responsibility attached to it and, while we are all entitled to our opinions and gut feelings, it is far more satisfactory to have a reasonably informed opinion.

All flaws and faults in a blade obviously detract from it and some of the worst are mentioned above. Occasionally, the entire *hamon* may have been reinstated if the original is lost. The most common reason for the loss of a *hamon* is that the blade has been in a fire, as heat, including that generated by buffing, will have this detrimental effect. In fact, many *yakinaoshi* or reinstated *hamon* were made in the feudal era by skilled swordsmiths. The *shogun* Tokugawa Ieyasu's favourite swordsmith retempered many important old swords after they were damaged in a serious fire at Osaka castle. However, a sword with a retempered edge is not a desirable thing, as extra stresses and strains are put on the sword in the process which generally weaken it. Further, the appearance is usually not so fine as the original. Swords with this feature are usually reasonably easy to spot. The second quenching or *yaki-ire* required to reinstate a lost *hamon* will often give the sword an unnaturally deep curvature. Usually this is most apparent at the bottom end of the blade, nearest to the handle. Also the *hamon* will often have lost its clarity and may appear somewhat fuzzy and indistinct while the *jihada* or forging pattern might appear unnaturally coarse. The patination on the *nakago* will also not be natural and may appear rather "flaky". Finally a feature known as *mizukage* (literally water shadow) may be seen as a misty line rising from the beginning of the *hamon* and up into the *ji* at an angle of about 45 degrees. However, for some reason, this feature sometimes also appears on the original work of other swordsmiths, such as Shodai Tadayoshi and Kunihiro, where it is not a feature of retempering but a characteristic of their work. *Mizukage*, therefore, should not be taken as a sign of retempering on its own, better as confirmation when accompanied by other signs. Needless to say, blades with *yakinaoshi* should be avoided.

Finally I would make a couple of points which may prevent you making a costly mistake. The most commonly encountered swords in the West are *Showa-to*. These blades were made in the Showa period (1926-89) and the vast majority were mass-produced for the Imperial Army and Navy during the Pacific War period (1941-45).

These swords are not considered as true *Nihon-to* as they were not made by using the traditional methods. They are seen as symbolising Japan's recent militaristic past, so they are still illegal in Japan. *Showa-to* are reasonably easy to recognise from the small stamps on the *nakago* (usually *Seki* or *Showa*) and often they are signed with untidy and loosely carved characters. There is evidence to show that those with a star stamp (*hoshi kokouin*) may be superior *gendaito* or modern swords made traditionally and sold to the army as *gunto*. The *yasuri-mei* on the *nakago* will often be also very loose and untidy. Often an unsharpened inch or so of blade (known as *ubu-ha*) is found just above the *habaki*, but this may also be found on traditionally made swords of the period. As they have not been through a proper forging process, the body of the sword will not show any of the usual wood-like grain and will rather have a featureless and mirror-like finish. These heavy and clumsy swords are usually found in *shin-gunto* (army) mounts. Mostly they appeal to militaria collectors and I do not think they are suitable for *iai* practice or the serious study of Japanese art swords. Sometimes fine old family blades that were traditionally made may be found in the *shin-gunto* mounting but sadly, these are in a minority.

LEFT AND BELOW: The carvings on the blade of this *tanto* are debased sanskrit characters called *bonji*. They have religious significance from which the owner hoped to gain protection. The blade was made by Sukemitsu of Bizen Osafune, a name used by several swordsmiths and it is dated 1446. The later *koshirae* is very plain and sober in appearance.

CHAPTER 5
POLEARMS
(Yari, Naginata and Nagamaki)

"The naginata is inferior to the yari on the battlefield. With the yari you can take the initiative; the naginata is defensive. In the hands of one of two men of equal ability, the yari gives a little extra strength. Yari and naginata both have their uses but neither is very beneficial in confined spaces. They cannot be used for taking a prisoner. They are essentially weapons for the field."

Miyamoto Musashi —Go Rin No Sho

BELOW: A heavily armoured Lord with his retainer who is wearing a much lighter armour and is holding a large *naginata*.

In the Heian period (794-1184), we have seen that the metalworking capabilities of the Japanese swordsmith far exceeded that of their mainland counterparts. They were producing blades that, even today, are considered as "National Treasures" and "Important Cultural and Art" objects in Japan. As well as developing sword-making, these same smiths were producing *yari* (spears) and *naginata* (glaives or halberds).

These weapons were made by using the same technology as that which was employed in sword production. They were most probably developed from agricultural implements such as the scythe. Both were mounted on poles of varying lengths which enabled the user to keep his opponent at a distance.

Unlike a Western spear, the Japanese *yari* was designed to cut as well as stab. The side edges, as well as the point, were quenched and hardened to produce a *hamon* as on a sword. The forging process of early *yari* usually produced a straight-grained pattern on the body of the blade, known as *masame-hada*. As this is a characteristic of swords made in the Yamato tradition of sword-making, it is thought that many may have been made in the Yamato area of Japan. While this may have some validity, it may also have been simply that *yari* were traditionally forged in this manner, where the steel was only folded in one direction rather than the more complex methods that produced other patterns in the steel.

In the Heian period, most of the *yari* produced were *su-yari* (straight bladed), then in the middle-to-late Heian period the production of *naginata* became popular. Like the *yari*, this weapon was mounted on a pole but the blade was more substantial and curved with a single cutting edge that swelled out towards the point. The power of the great Buddhist monasteries was at its height at this time and the *sohei* or warrior-monks were invariably armed with *naginata* as well as swords. The fact that many of these monasteries were based in the Nara region in Yamato province adds to the speculation that Yamato-den developed the forging tradition used to make these weapons. Along with the *sohei*, the emerging *bushi* or *samurai* class favoured the *naginata*, which seems to have eclipsed the *yari* at this time.

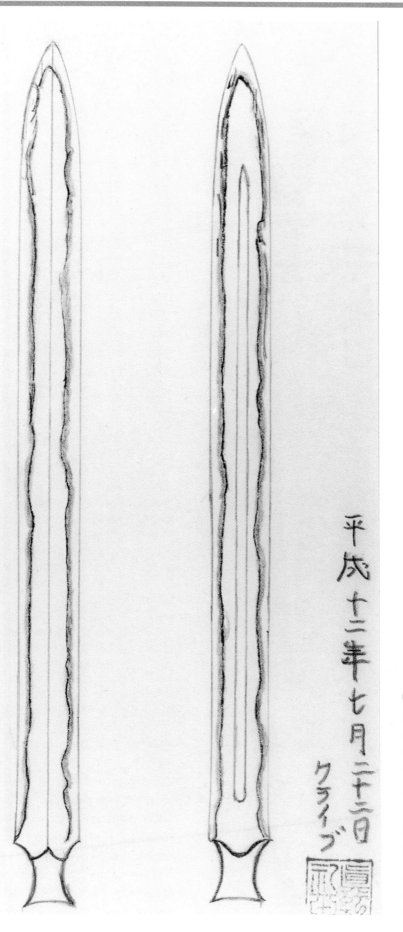

LEFT: An *oshigata* or drawing of a *suyari* or straight spear blade. It is of a triangular section and on the front side a *hi* or groove is found. The *hamon* may be clearly seen on both sides. It is signed Takeda Ju Sukechika, an unrecorded smith of the Takeda school from Bungo province in Kyushu. The school made highly functional swords and *yari* and it is believed that this example dates from the mid-16th century.

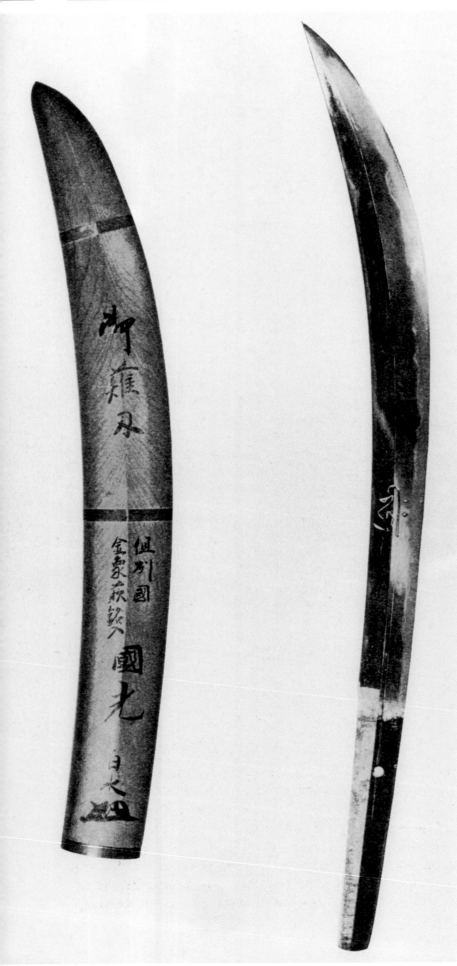

LEFT: A magnificent early *naginata* blade by the 13th century swordsmith Hojoji Tanshu Kunimitsu. As it has been shortened for use as a sword blade, thereby losing its signature, a gold inlay attribution has been added. A *bonji* is carved on both sides of the blade and the beautifully brushed *sayagaki* (attribution on the *saya*) is by a member of the Honami family of appraisers.

RIGHT: This print shows a number of *ashiguru* or foot soldiers running into battle armed with *yari*. The leading figure carries a *kama-yari* or sickle style spear. Also note the *hadome* or parrying cross bar which is used to trap a shaft or deflect an attacking blade.

At the end of the Heian period, the Gempei Wars between the Taira and Minamoto clans finally established the rule of the *samurai* at Kamakura. During these wars both sides employed *sohei* in their ranks and the *naginata* was widely used. Several battles took place at the Uji River, a strategically important point south of Kyoto. On one occasion, according to the Heike Monogatari (Story of the Heike (Taira) Clan), a bridge across the Uji was being defended by the Minamoto troops in the spring of 1180. It was here that the warrior monk Gochim-no-Tajima earned himself heroic immortality.

"Gochim-no-Tajima, throwing away the sheath of his long *naginata*, strode forth alone onto the bridge, whereupon the Heike shot at him fast and furious," the Heike Monogatari relates. "Tajima, not at all perturbed, ducking to avoid the higher ones and leaping over those that flew low, cut through those that flew straight with his whirling halberd, so that even the enemy looked on with admiration. Thus it was that he was dubbed Tajima the arrow-cutter."

Possibly the most famous of these warrior monks was Saito-Musashi-bo Benki, the faithful companion and retainer of the legendary Minamoto general Yoshitsune, who was the younger brother of the first *shogun* Yoritomo. Benki was reputed to be a giant of a man and is always depicted in Japanese art carrying his huge *naginata* with which he defended his master to the death. His *naginata* is popularly thought to have been made by a swordsmith named Munenobu. It was said to have had a blade that was 4 feet 8 inches (142cm) in length and a shaft of 7 feet 6 inches (228cm).

Following the establishment of the Kamakura *shogunate*, the Mongol

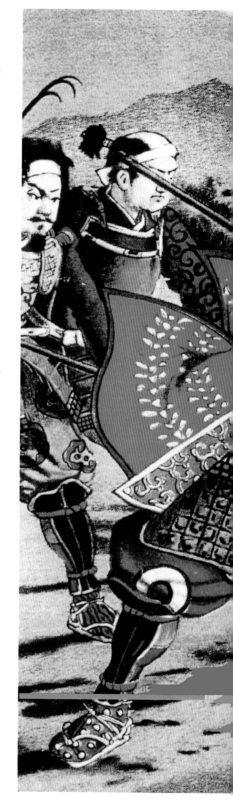

invasions of Japan in 1274 and 1281 raised sword-making to one of its golden ages and the quality of *naginata* and *yari* rose accordingly. *Naginata* are seen in many of the screens depicting the invasions. Quality further improved during the imperial "rebellion" by the Emperor Go-Daigo that began the Namboku-cho period.

The Muromachi period (1332-1573) was a period of almost constant warfare and the demand for all types of weapons was great. It was during this period that *yari* came to be extensively used on the battlefield while *naginata* also remained popular. Spears came in other designs apart from the *su-yari*, such as *hoko* (hook shaped) and *magari-yari* (cross shaped), often called *jumonji yari* after the Japanese character for "ten" which is a cross. The *magari-yari* had no less than six different cutting edges. This provides many problems for polishers today.

At the same time *nagamaki*, which are similar to *naginata* but tend to be less curved and far more like a sword blade in shape, were also used on the battlefield. As the Muromachi period progressed, more reliance was placed on massed formations of foot soldiers carrying *yari* as well as *yari*-bearing cavalry.

Naginata of the Muromachi period are not as large and impressive as those of the preceding Namboku-cho period, although they have a strong

saki-zori (curvature at the point) and their long points give the impression of sharpness. This configuration made them easier to use on the battlefield.

The end of this period saw the rise of Oda Nobunaga, one of the great unifiers of the country. While he is largely famed for his use of *teppo* (firearms) he was also convinced of the value of spears on the field of battle. It is recorded that he argued with his chief instructor of *so-jutsu* (the martial art of spear fighting) about the relative value of the short *yari* and the long *yari*. Nobunaga's commoner general and later ruler of most of Japan, Toyotomi Hideyoshi, was a fan of the long *yari* and put his argument to the test. The superior strategy and tactics of Toyotomi triumphed over a less-organised band armed with short *yari*.

Oda himself was said to have used a *yari* that was an incredible 18 feet (5.5m) in length when most were between 10 and 12 feet (3 and 3.7m). Their most effective use was against cavalry and some were fitted with iron cross sections on their poles called *hadome*. Often secured with a peg (*mekugi*) through a hole to prevent movement, this could be used to parry a sword blow or entangle the enemy's feet and trip him. At the bottom of the pole there was a heavy iron butt known as a *hirumaki*. This was a very important part of the pole as it not only helped prevent damage should the pole hit the ground, it also provided a counterbalance to the blade and could even be used offensively as part of the weapon itself. Both *yari* and *naginata* have similar but differently shaped *hirumaki*. These sometimes have simple inlay designs that are occasionally signed with the maker's name.

A *nagamaki* in the author's collection has a relatively short pole but, unusually, also has a section near the top of shaft that is wrapped over *same* in the style of a sword handle. Additionally there is a *tsuba* (sword guard) which is not of the quality one would expect on a sword. This is a reasonably common feature in *nagamaki*. The *hirumaki* has some silver inlay and the unsigned blade is 1 foot 10 inches (56cm) in length with a *nakago* (tang) of 1 foot 9 inches (53cm) – another expensive polishing nightmare. *Nagamaki* are considered to be difficult weapons to use on foot but are ideal when mounted on horseback. The technique was to stand in the stirrups and, leaning forward over the horse's head and shoulders, describe a large figure of eight, cutting to both sides of the mount. This was also a technique used with *yari*. At full gallop, it must have been amazingly effective at dispersing an enemy on foot, though the equestrian skills required must also have been formidable.

A number of *yari* from this time became quite famous, such as the large *su-yari* (straight *yari* with a triangular section) nicknamed "Nippongo". This spectacular *yari* is 2 feet 7 inches (79cm) in length with a deeply carved dragon in a groove entwined around a straight sword on the flat side. Nippongo is believed to have been made by one of the Kanabo group of swordsmiths. The *tombogiri* (dragonfly cutter) *yari*, like "Nippongo" is recognised as among the three best *yari* in Japan.

Spears were thought of very highly at this time and the *samurai* were eager to show their expertise with both *naginata* and *yari* on the battlefield. When Toyotomi Hideyoshi, Nobunaga's general and successor, defeated Sakuma Morimasa at the battle of Shizugadake in 1583, Toyotomi's seven most valiant *samurai* all used *yari*. Their heroic deeds were recorded and they subsequently became known as the "Seven Famous Spearmen of Shizugadake". One of the seven was the renowned Kato Kiyomasa (1562-1611) from Higo province who on this occasion used a long *yari* that was 2 feet (60cm) in length and made by the swordsmith Sukesada, from Osafune in Bizen province.

Kato Kiyomasa further enhanced his reputation with the *yari* when he

RIGHT: Kato Kiyomasa again, planning an attack on a Korean stronghold. Clearly shown is his unique *jumonji yari* with the uneven side blades.

went on Toyotomi's Korean invasion of 1592. There he used a *yari* which was similar to the *magari-yari* in shape (cross shaped) except that one of the side blades was much longer than the other. Known as a *katakama-yari*, this *yari* is often depicted being used by Kiyomasa to kill a Korean tiger. This *yari*, with its mother-of-pearl-encrusted shaft, is preserved today in the Tokyo National Museum in Ueno. This style of *yari* was used extensively in the late sixteenth century as it was considered effective for both cutting and stabbing.

The Momoyama period (1573-1600) ended with the battle of Sekigahara where the victorious Tokugawa Ieyasu placed great reliance on spearmen, although *naginata* were considered as old fashioned and clumsy by then. After the Tokugawa family began their *shogunate* dynasty, the practical use of the weapon decreased and its artistic and decorative properties were emphasised. Unlike swords, which it was mandatory for the *samurai* to wear, *yari* and *naginata* were optional extras. They continued to be made and became important accessories especially in the *daimyo* processions as they regularly travelled from their fiefdoms to Edo under the law of *sankin kotai* (alternate attendance).

In these processions the *daimyo* found it necessary to show the world at large that they were men of substance and that they commanded well-armed retainers. This was demonstrated by those in the procession, which could number several thousands (it has been estimated that Maeda *daimyo* of Kanazawa in Kaga province may have had up to four thousand in attendance), carrying long *yari* and *naginata*. Their poles and *saya* (scabbards) would be richly decorated and finely lacquered showing the lord's *mon* or family crest or they would be kept under silk coverings similarly adorned. Poles might be decorated with mother-of-pearl and *saya* were often particularly ornate. If not lacquered with *mon*, they were covered with bear fur, horsehair or some other extravagance. The *magari yari*'s distinctive cross shape or a ceremonial *naginata*, suitably embellished with the clan's *mon*, would be seen at the head of the procession borne by the *yarimochi* (spear bearer), a much sought-after position of honour.

The *naginata* tended to become lighter and less substantial as practical needs declined, while *magari yari* were often thicker and less manageable. Both old *yari* and *naginata* were sometimes remounted as *tanto* or *wakizashi* (daggers or short swords), usually losing their long *nakago* (with any signatures) in the process.

A very light version of the *naginata*, with a proportionately smaller pole, also emerged. It is thought that women of the *samurai* class, who needed arms to defend their homes and their honour, adopted this and were taught how to use it from childhood. Existing wood-block prints depict women using these weapons. Even today, women are the main practitioners of the martial art of *naginata-do*.

LEFT: Two ornately lacquered *naginata saya*, one embellished with a *shakudo-nanako* gilt edged *kojiri* and both showing *mon*. These would have been carried in *daimyo* processions to Edo.

BELOW: A variation on the *jumonji yari* by Hojoji Masamitsu with extra shoulders on the cross blades; 19th century.

BELOW: An *oshigata* of a 17th century *jumonji yari* made in Kyoto and showing all the various surfaces and edges. It is signed Yamashiro Ju Kunishige.

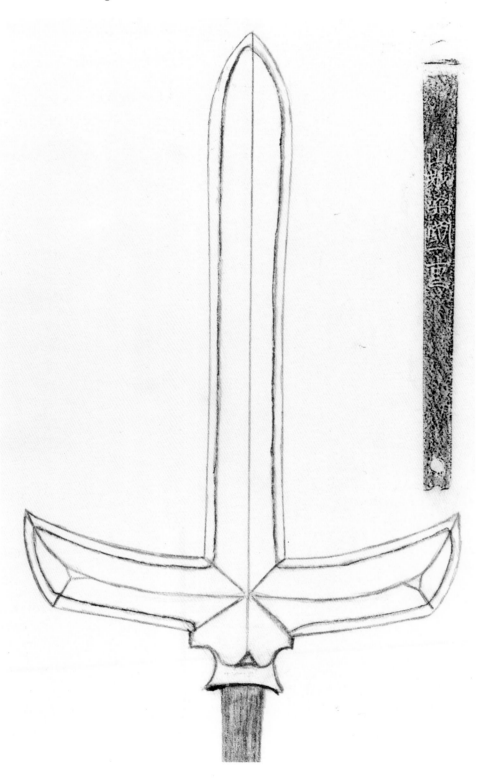

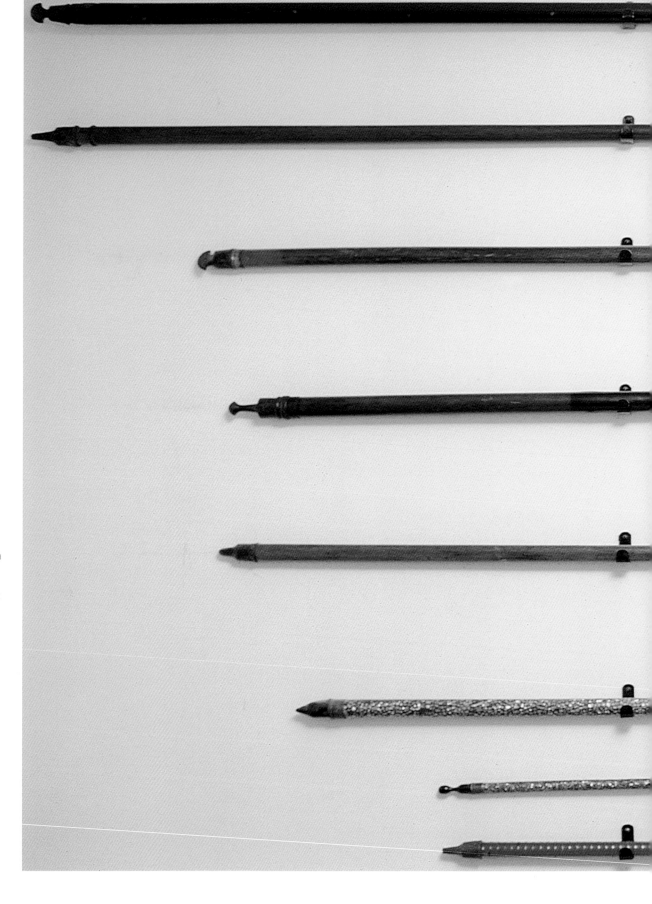

RIGHT: A display of polearms in a Western collection. The small one at the bottom is a *makura* (pillow) *yari* which would have been kept by the bed for protection at night, while the next one up is possibly a small *naga* or throwing *yari*. The third is a *jumonji yari* with a mother of pearl decorated pole and the fourth has a bear fur covered *saya*. The long bladed *nagamaki*, complete with a sword style *tsuba* and sword style hilt wrapping, is the fifth, followed by a conventional *naginata*. Seventh from the bottom is a *su-yari,* while the top piece is another *naginata*. Note the different shape of the *hirumaki* or butt end of the pole between *naginata* and *yari*.

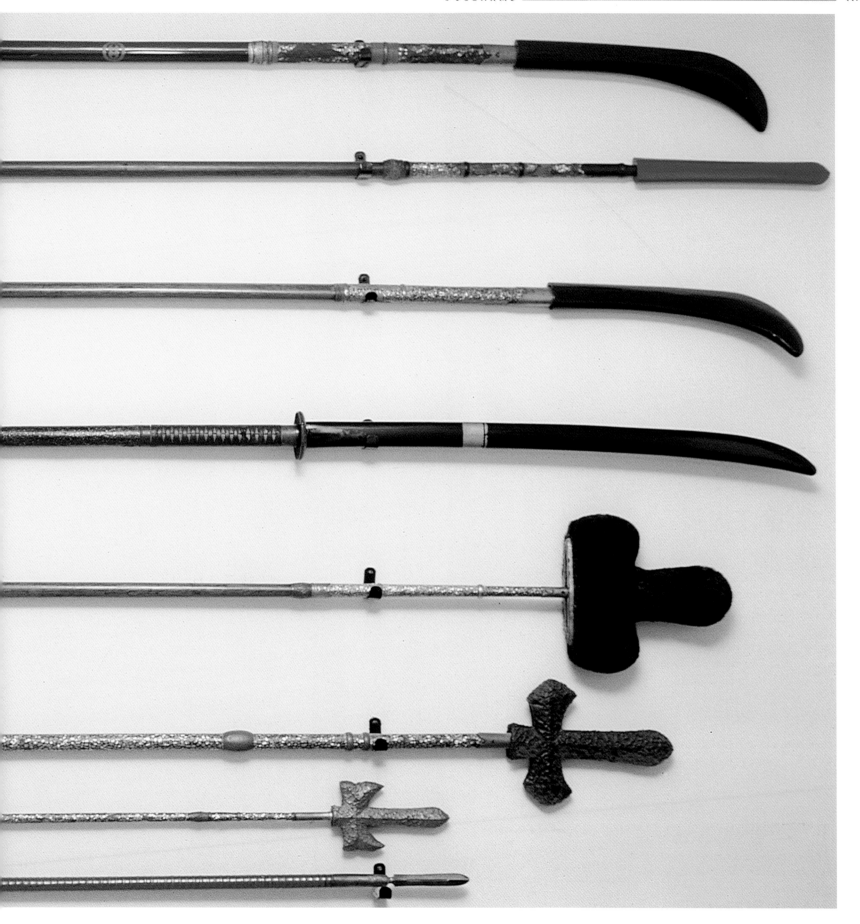

ABOVE : A richly lacquered *naginata* mount and blade featuring several *mon*, which include the *manji-mon* or swastika crest, an old Buddhist symbol.

ABOVE: A mid-19th century posed photograph of three *samurai* with a variety of weapons including a *naginata*, a *su-yari* and a bow. The middle figure also has a bear fur covered *saya* on his sword.

RIGHT: An 18th century *sode-gara-mi* or sleeve entangler used mainly by the Tokugawa police to ensnare the loose sleeves of a felon. The shaft is fitted with iron spikes and barbed hooks. Although never of any great quality, they were undoubtedly effective at the job for which they were intended.

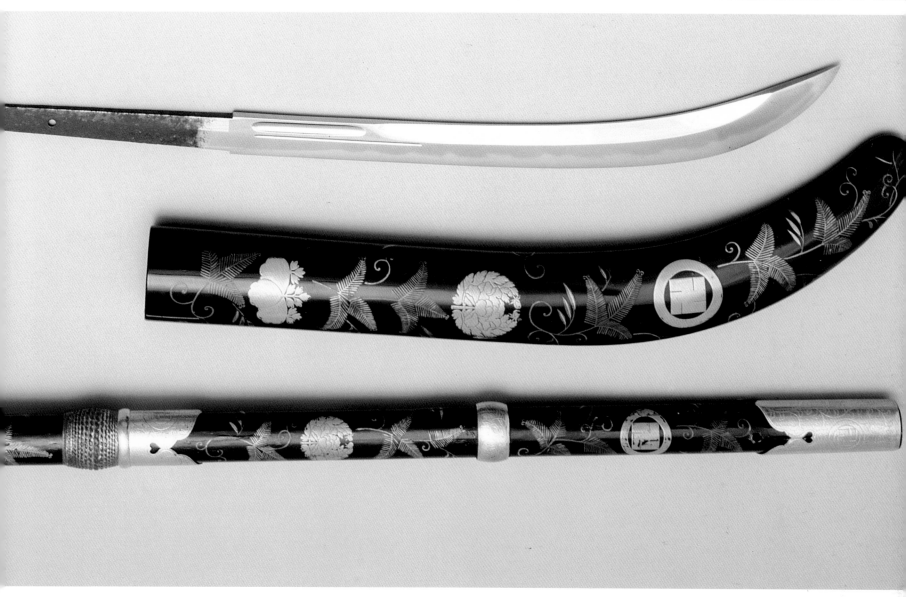

Although new trends in blade construction developed, good swordsmiths still made substantial *naginata* in the older style occasionally and, to a far lesser extent, *yari*. These may have been made only as special commissions, but quality pieces do appear throughout the Tokugawa period. There do not appear to have been makers who only specialised in this work and it definitely took second place to their main business of making swords. Further there was no regional centre and the author has seen examples from Hizen, Kyoto, Seki, Osaka and Edo. Most of the *yari* made at this time were primarily for ceremonial use.

Under the heading of "polearms" there are a number of more unusual weapons besides the more conventional *yari*, *naginata* and *nagamaki*. These include:

- *Makura yari*: The pillow (*makura*) yari is similar to conventional *yari*, but with a much smaller and simpler pole. This would be kept beside the bed in case of a night-time emergency and was suitable for use in a confined space. An example in the author's collection has a ribbed red lacquered pole with a proportionately sized *hirumaki*. The blade is of the socketed variety – that is, the blade does not have a *nakago*, but the pole fits into the bottom of the blade which wraps around the top of the pole. The blade maker has signed his name on the outside of the socket.
- *Ono*: This is basically a large war axe mounted on a 6 foot pole (1.8m), which was favoured by the *sohei* or warrior priests.
- *Otuschi*: A war-mallet of similar proportions to the *ono*.
- *Sode-Garami*: The name means literally "sleeve entangler". This was a multi-barbed polearm designed to arrest or detain criminals by tangling in the loose clothing. These with other similar pieces were often kept in racks at the Tokaido checkpoints through which all travellers were compelled to pass. They are mainly Tokugawa police restraint weapons rather than true *samurai* arms.

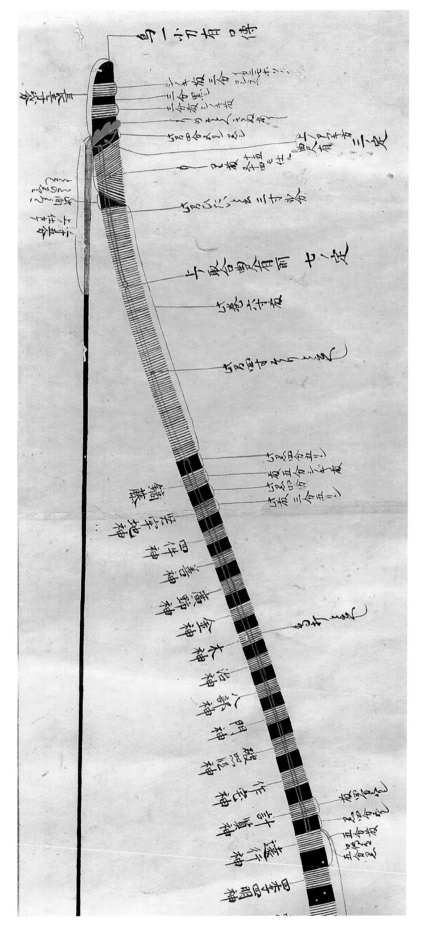

CHAPTER 6
ARCHERY
(Yumi and Ya)

"The bow is tactically strong at the commencement of battle, especially battles on a moor, as it is possible to shoot quickly from among the spearmen. However, it is unsatisfactory in sieges, or when the enemy is more than forty yards away. For this reason there are nowadays few traditional schools of archery. There is little use nowadays for this kind of skill."
Miyamoto Musashi – Go Rin No Sho

A variety of different bows were seen in Japan including large and small cross bows (*o-yumi* and *teppo-yumi*), repeating cross bows (*dokyu*), short battle bows (*hankyu*) and similar short bows for hunting and sports (*yokyu*). The Buki Niyaku, a martial treatise, lists five types: the *maru-ki*, a rounded wood bow, the *shige-no-yumi*, wrapped in rattan, the similar but smaller *bankyu*, the *hankyu* and the *hoko-yumi* or Tartar-style bows. However, the classic Japanese long bow is immediately recognisable for three distinct features. Its curve is most graceful and pleasing, while its length, usually between 7 feet 4 inches and 8 feet (2.2 and 2.4m), seems extraordinary. One owned by Yuasa Matashichiro, preserved at Itsukishima, is 8ft 9in (2.7m). Thirdly, it is gripped off-centre at about one third of its length from the bottom, which would appear to make it very difficult if not impossible to shoot.

The bow (*yumi*) has been associated with Japan from its earliest days and its origins are shrouded in myth and legend. Hachiman, the God of War, as well as many other deities are often depicted with a bow. Although it may have been used in rituals and tribal conflicts in the early centuries of the Christian era, it was undoubtedly primarily used for hunting. Ceremonial archery was adopted from China. Its practice was seen as the mark of a well-educated gentleman. The bow was the main weapon of the warrior in the Nara and early Heian periods, even taking precedence over the sword. During the Nara period highly ritualised competitions in mounted archery, which required a high level of equestrian skills, took place regularly. And hunts of all kinds – with deer, wild boar and other game as the quarry – tested archery skills. In this relatively peaceful time, it was said "a warrior who took deer or wild boar attained honour just as if they killed an enemy general". Minamoto Yoritomo, who was soon to become the first *shogun*, was delighted when his son shot a deer on the slopes of Mount Fuji and his pleasure was recorded in a letter written to his wife.

It is easy to see how the emerging *samurai* class of the late Heian period

LEFT: A section from a 17th century hand scroll describing a particular bow. Each individual section has been named after a total of thirty-six gods and twenty-eight constellations.

RIGHT: Two different types of quiver, one lacquered black with two *manji-mon* and the other of tanned leather with black leather imitating metal mounts. The *aoi-mon* on the latter is associated with the Tokugawa family.

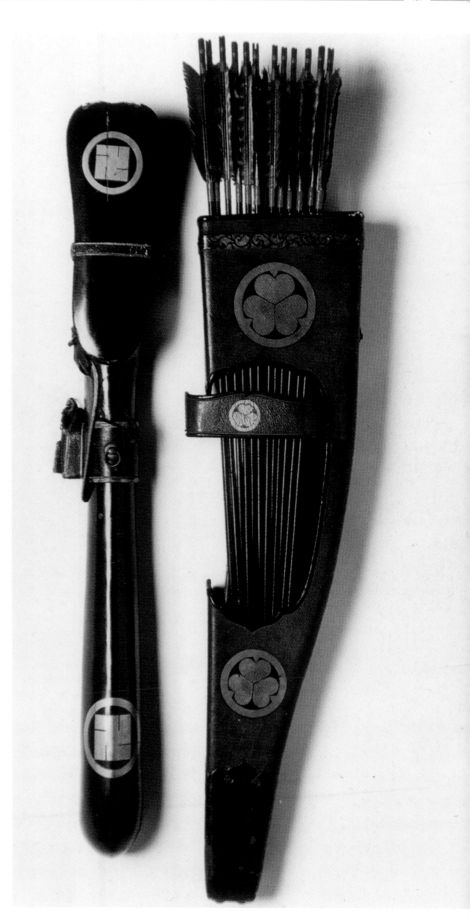

found it relatively easy to adopt these skills and adapt them to warfare. As the *samurai* developed into a force to be reckoned with, various martial *ryu* (schools) formed to teach *kyujutsu* (the art of archery) and the major clans came to depend on the expertise of these archery schools. With the clash of the Minamoto and Taira clans at the end of the Heian period (1180-1185). archery techniques and skills developed dramatically.

In legend, many stories are told of warriors' prowess with the bow. That of Minamoto Tametomo is famous. Tametomo was the uncle of Yoritomo, the first Minamoto shogun, and was a giant of a man. So big was he that it took five men to bend his enormous bow for stringing and his arrows measured "twelve hands and two fingers". The number of men required to string a bow was a standard measure of its power.

Tametomo was a prodigious archer and in the Hogen War (1156-58), a preliminary skirmish before the Gempei Wars, he killed two men with one arrow, but was captured by the Taira clan forces. So that he would never be able to draw a bow again, the Taira maimed him by removing the sinew from his arm, then they exiled him to the island of Oshima in Izu province. Such was his personality that he ruled the island as though it were his own personal fiefdom, refusing to pay any taxes and secretly training his arm to draw the bow again. Anticipating a degree of trouble, the governor of Izu sent twenty small ships to collect the taxes owing. On seeing them approach, Tametomo decided to fire a warning arrow across the bow of the leading ship. The arrow, however, struck the lead ship below the waterline. The ship sank while the rest of the fleet fled.

The Gempei Wars between the Taira and Minamoto clans provided many legends and heroes and there was no greater hero than the renowned archer Nasu no Yoichi. The Taira had been beaten at Yashima on the Inland Sea and were forced to retreat by ship. Most of their boats were lost and they were sailing away from the defeat when the last ship turned back and issued a final symbolic challenge to the victorious Minamoto. Seventy yards from the shore they hoisted a fan to the top of the mast and the Minamoto were invited to shoot at it, if they were good enough. Yoichi took up the challenge and road his mount into the sea and prayed for the breeze to drop as he took aim. The wind stilled as he loosed the arrow, which struck the target and shattered it. A roar of approval rang out from both sides. Failure would have meant an incredible loss of face both for Yoichi personally as well as the Minamoto army, so the stakes were very high indeed. The sword worn by Yoichi on this day remained in the possession of the Nasu family who handed it from generation to generation at least until Showa tenth year

(1935) when it was designated as an Important Cultural Property by the Japanese government.

After establishing the *bakufu* at Kamakura, Yoritomo used archery games and competitions to train his *samurai* and maintain their martial fitness. One of these competitions, known as Kusajishi, was derived from deer hunting. In it, two teams of five would compete by shooting the effigy of a deer from a set distance. A referee would call out whether or not a shot was any good. Strangely, the shooter was then able to argue the point if he disagreed. This is still practised today and I have seen it take place at the Yasukuni Shrine in Kudan, Tokyo where, instead of a deerskin-covered target, a plastic inflatable deer was shot at with blunt arrows. All the archers were magnificently attired in period costume, including a *tanto* at the waist. But, unlike in the Kamakura period, one of the shooters was a woman.

Similarly, Yoritomo encouraged mounted archery in a form known as *yabusame* and he instructed Ogasawara Nagakiyo, the founder of the Ogasawara ryu, to teach this to his *samurai*. In *yabusame* the mount charges at full tilt while the archer, standing in the stirrups, shoots at three relatively small wooden targets. He gives a loud *kiai* (shout) with his shot, then "reloads" from his quiver. Performed annually at Kamakura, *yabusame* is a magnificent, colourful and exciting spectacle. *Yabusame* has been performed at the Tower of London in London by a visiting team from Japan.

LEFT: Made by Miyao Eisuke of Yokohama during the Meiji era (1868-1912), this parcel gilt bronze group depicts an arrow maker and his apprentice. The smith is forging a pierced arrowhead on his anvil while the arrowheads in a group at his side have been put into hot clay. The apprentice waits attentively for instructions with his hammer poised. In the background is a rack of fully fletched and finished arrows.

RIGHT: The bow shown in full and in detail on the right, richly lacquered in gold and inlaid shells, dates from the 16th century and was registered as an Important Art Object by the Japanese government in 1940. The other bow is signed Fukuyama Kanuemon. Two *ebira* or light quivers are seen in front of the arrow rack, one with the *mon* of the Oda family.

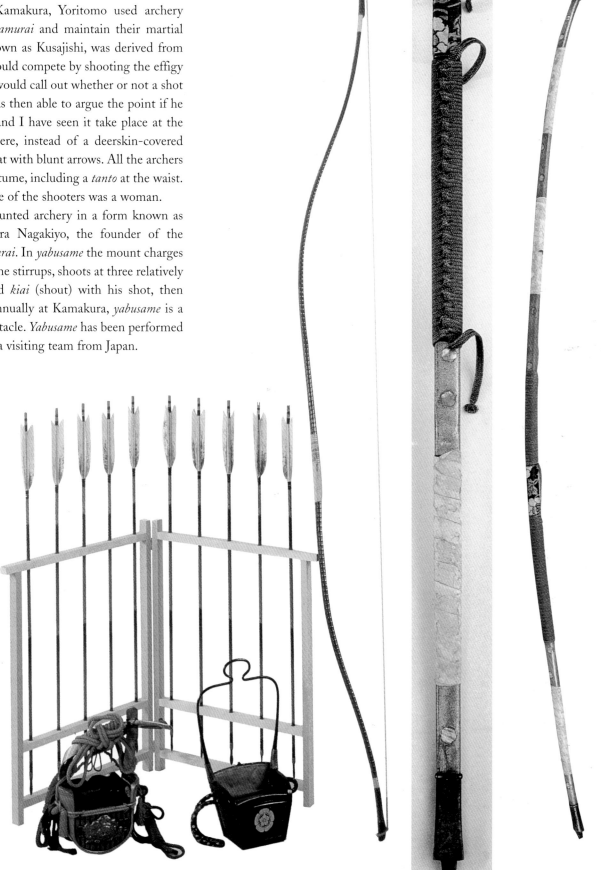

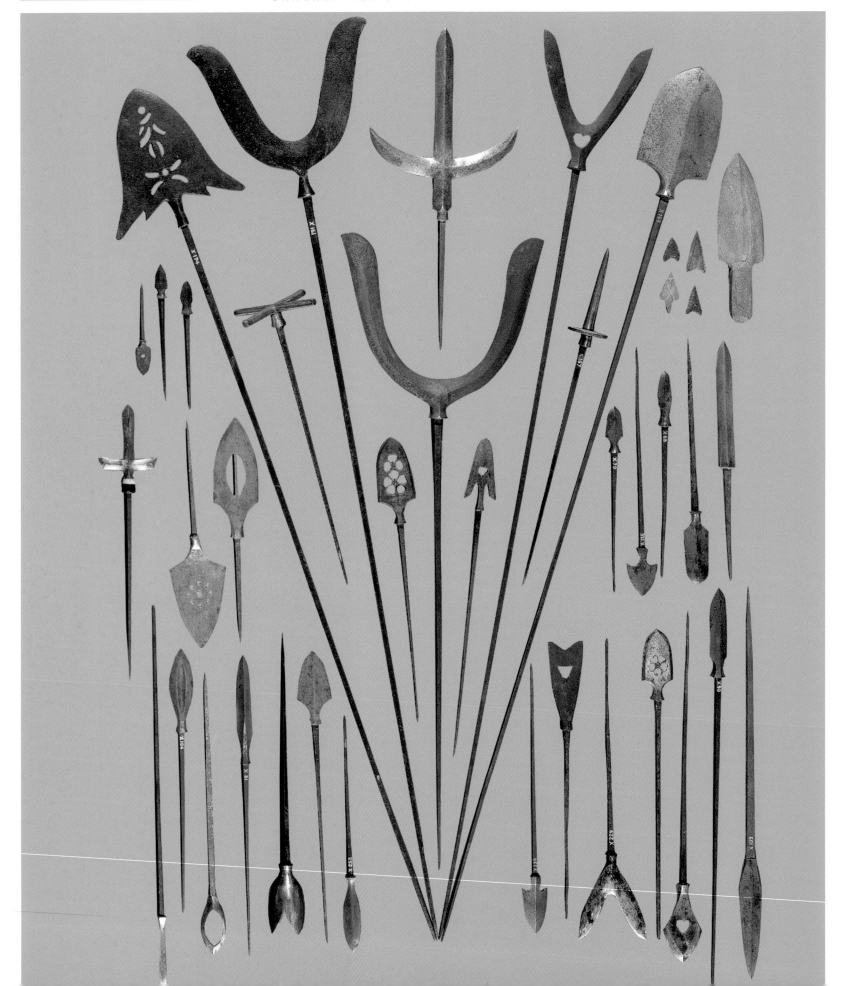

Bows or *yumi* were made of a laminated structure. A deciduous wood was given a backing of bamboo on the side of the outward curve at first. Later, in the Heian period, this was also applied to the inner curve. However, the glue that held it together was not very reliable and the bow was bound with rattan to strengthen it. Additional pieces of wood were inserted in each end to strengthen the nocks for stringing. The handle, set low, was again of rattan binding with leather to give grip. Most *yumi* were lacquered black, as with sword *saya*, both to strengthen it and as a protection from moisture. The *tsuru* or string was made of plant fibre, usually hemp, and coated with wax.

The arrow (*ya*) shafts were made from bamboo, ideally cut in November or December. After shaving off the nodes and outer skin, the nock that accommodated the bow string (*tsuru*) was made immediately above a node for strength, then finished by binding it with lacquered fibre to prevent splitting at this vulnerable point. The fletcher or arrow maker, called a *ya-haki*, would sometimes sign his name on the nock. A barrelled shaft was made for long-distance shooting, while tapered shafts provided greater accuracy at shorter ranges. Finally the shaft was fletched in a variety of feathers, mainly hawk, eagle, crane or pheasant's tail. There are usually three flights, though sometimes four.

The *yajiri* (arrowheads) came in hundreds of different shapes and designs. Many of them looking like miniature *yari* (spears). They were attached to the shaft by means of a long thin *nakago*, again similar to most *yari*. The simple designs were used for hunting or war, while the more elaborate were reserved for ceremonial functions. Sometimes specialist smiths forged them, but a number of top class swordsmiths also produced intricate *yajiri* to demonstrate their talents – they often signed them. Arrowheads are more commonly referred to by the more modern name of *yanone* and some of the most commonly encountered types are:
- *Hira-ne*: Flat shape with sharp edges, often heavily decorated especially with *mon* (family crests).
- *Karimata*: Shaped like a two-pronged fork, they come various sizes from quite small to very large. Reputedly used to cut armour lacing, ships' rigging or to cripple horses, this arrow required a four-feather shaft to counteract its tendency to spin. They could be adapted with a wood or bulbous horn cover to make a whistling arrow that was used to signal the commencement of an action.
- *Muto-ya*: Used for target practice and the more humane dog hunts.
- *Kabura-ya*: Signalling arrows, also called *hiniki-ya*.
- *Yanagi-ba*: Willow-leaf shaped.
- *Togari-ya*: Pointed arrows.

LEFT: A collection of *yajiri* or arrowheads of many shapes and sizes, including five of stone which may be neolithic. It will be seen that several of these are similar to miniature *yari* in design, while others are elegantly pierced with cherry blossom motifs or *bonji*. Some of the larger ones seem impractical and may have been made as votive offerings.

- *Watakushi-ya*: Flesh tearers or barbed arrows.

The reason the *yumi* developed with the off-centre grip is that this is thought to facilitate its use on horseback. Other cultures solved this problem by using a smaller bow. But for Japan the length was set. A long bow decreased the tension and stress of the draw – this is important with the poor glue they used. The bow then had to be shot with the low grip to make it manageable on horseback. In order to nock the arrow, the bow was raised above the head, then pushed away as it was lowered to face height ready to release the arrow.

The *samurai* archer would carry a quiver (*ebira*) at his right hip. The box-like base had a grid for the arrowheads to fit into and a framework rising at the back to retain the shafts. Drawing an arrow from the *ebira* meant grasping the shaft just above head of the arrow and lifting it clear of the grid, while maintaining a grip on the *yumi* with the left hand. Performing this manoeuvre while mounted on a charging horse is hard to imagine but is the same action employed by the yabusame men of today. Drawing the bow above the head in this manner was the method originally taught by the Ogasawara Nagakiyo of the Ogasawara ryu.

During the Sengoku Jidai, Japan's period of almost uninterrupted warfare in the fifteenth and sixteenth centuries, massed archers were often used at the start of the battle. The archers were kept in constant practice and both technique and shooting improved significantly. Heki Danjo came from Yamato (present-day Nara prefecture) or Iga (present-day Mie prefecture) and was the most influential archer of the time. Born in 1443, he lived to the age of fifty-nine and claims to have experienced a spiritual revelation in archery, which he called *hi, ken, chu* (fly, pierce, centre). He conducted many experiments on different ways of holding the bow and shooting, and discovered a new devastatingly accurate method, which revolutionised archery. The Sengoku Jidai *samurai* swiftly adopted the techniques of Heki Danjo and followers teaching his new methods started many new schools.

However, from 1543, the introduction of firearms changed everything. *Kyujutsu* was suddenly obsolete as a weapon of war and the arts of the bow were in danger of being lost forever. To save *kyujutsu*, early in his reign as the first of the Tokugawa *shoguns*, Ieyasu inaugurated the famous competition at Sanjusangendo in Kyoto.

Sanjusangendo is a narrow corridor some 131 yards (120m) long, with a low roof with hanging beams and one side open to the air. A target is set at one end and the archer is 131 yards away at the other. The object is to hit the target as many times as possible within a 24-hour period, from dusk to dusk. Apart from the stamina required, this is particularly difficult because of the low roof. Many scarred beams bear witness to this. In the 250 years up to the end of the Tokugawa period, 823 archers took up the challenge of Sanjusangendo and only thirty left any score of note.

One of them, Hoshino Kanzaemon, was determined to be the greatest archer in Japan. In the Sanjusangendo competition, he scored an amazing 8,000 hits out of the 10,542 arrows shot. Seventeen years later, a strong *samurai* named Wasa Daihachiro beat this record with a little help from an onlooker. After several hours of constant shooting, Wasa rested, then found

that he was unable to attain his previous accuracy. An old *samurai* who had been watching Wasa's efforts approached him and rebuked him for resting. The old man then took out a knife and made several small incisions in Wasa Daihachiro's left hand causing it to bleed. Wasa's hand had been so swollen from his exertions that he had been unable to hold the bow properly. The cuts relieved the pressure and he was able to reach, and even surpass, his previous standard of shooting. In the 24 hours, Wasa Daihachiro shot a record of 13,053 arrows and scored 8,113 hits, beating the record set by Hoshino. Doing the arithmetic on this it means that he shot about nine arrows a minute or one every six or seven seconds, a truly incredible feat. It was not until later that Wasa Daihachiro found out that the old man who had helped him beat the record set by Hoshino seventeen years earlier was none other than Hoshino Kanzaemon himself.

Through the Kanbun and Genroku periods, as the Tokugawa peace rolled on and the threat of war diminished, the martial arts began to lose their function. At the same time the general populace began to learn them.

This applied equally to arts such as *iaijutsu* and *kenjutsu*, the sword arts, as it did to *kyujutsu*. The emphasis moved away from the strictly practical necessities of overcoming an enemy to the spiritual benefits to be gained from constant training. The practising martial skills were moving from *bujutsu*, martial arts, to *budo* or martial ways. In this latter term, the character "*do*", meaning road or path, is the "way" to enlightenment, *satori*.

Kyudo survived the trials and tribulations of the Meiji and Taisho periods and became more popular in the militaristic Showa period. Like the other martial arts, it was prohibited by occupation forces after World War II. It could be practised again only after these laws were repealed and, in 1949, the Zen Nihon Kyudo Remmei was formed. Today *kyudo* has some 500,000 practitioners throughout the world, and the correct etiquette, mental approach and physical form of shooting, rather than the purely combative necessity of hitting the target, are emphasised. Indeed, hitting the target is of secondary importance. Nevertheless the future of *kyudo* seems assured.

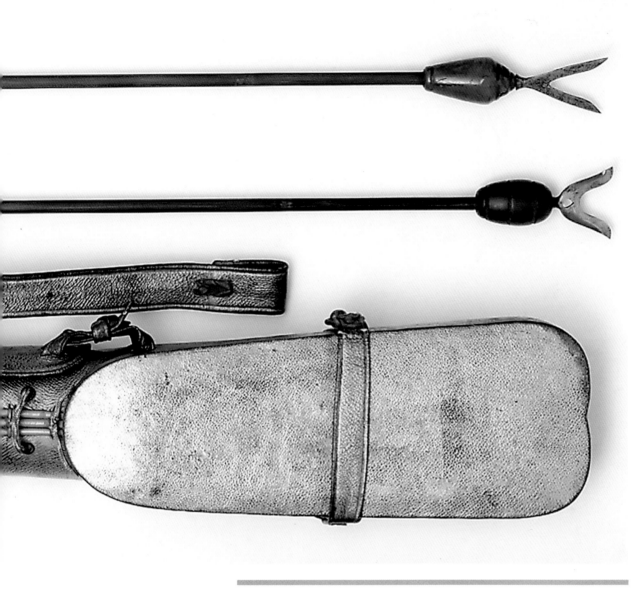

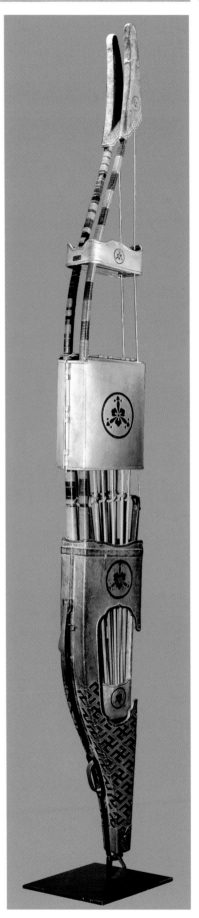

ABOVE: This type of quiver is known as an *utsubo*. This has a leather frame decorated in gold lacquer and is partially covered with white fur. The *kyu-mon* on a nine-circle crest may be seen in the mid-section. The two arrows are both whistling arrows and have been fitted with *karinata* or two pronged heads.

RIGHT: This fine *yumidai* (archery set) dates from the late 18th or early 19th centuries. Both bows are strung and lacquered black although one has sections of red lacquered bamboo. The double quiver is of metal and gilded leather with the *mon* of the Fuji family. It contains two sets of arrows and overall the *yumidai* stands 8ft 6in (260cm) high.

CHAPTER 7
GUNS OF THE SAMURAI
(Tanegashima)

*From inside fortifications, the gun has no equal among weapons.
It is the supreme weapon on the field before the ranks clash, but
once swords are crossed the gun becomes useless."*
Miyamoto Musashi – *Go Rin No Sho*

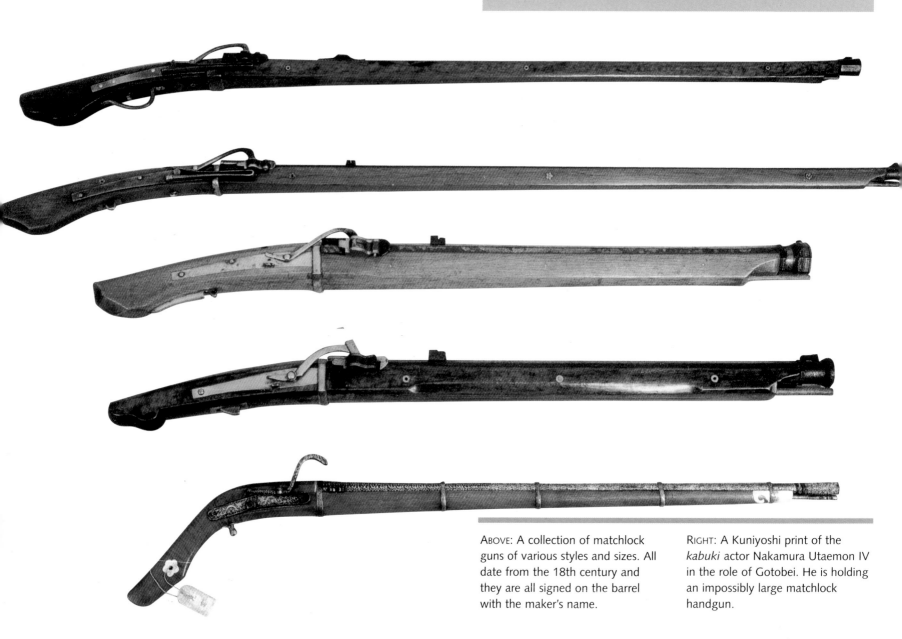

ABOVE: A collection of matchlock guns of various styles and sizes. All date from the 18th century and they are all signed on the barrel with the maker's name.

RIGHT: A Kuniyoshi print of the *kabuki* actor Nakamura Utaemon IV in the role of Gotobei. He is holding an impossibly large matchlock handgun.

In the year 1543, Japan experienced a technological breakthrough when Westerners arrived, bringing with them firearms. On the island of Tanegashima, just off the southern coast of Kyushu, three Portuguese adventurers became stranded after being blown off course by a typhoon in a stricken Chinese junk. These were the first recorded Westerners to set foot on Japanese territory. Two of them had firearms and ammunition, unseen in Japan before this date. When Lord Tokitaka, the *daimyo* of this island fiefdom, saw one of the Portuguese shoot a duck in flight, his amazement can be imagined and he immediately arranged

shooting lessons. Before long he had acquired both guns for an enormous sum of money and gave them to his local swordsmith to reproduce.

The story goes that the swordsmith was unable to reproduce the thread of the breach plug, or possibly the spring in the lock mechanism, and had to wait for several months before another Portuguese ship arrived at Tanegashima. He then persuaded his attractive seventeen-year-old daughter to befriend the ship's armourer – so, with Japan's first recorded piece of international industrial espionage, the problem was solved. Within a year, Lord Tokitaka had made at least ten guns and it was not very long

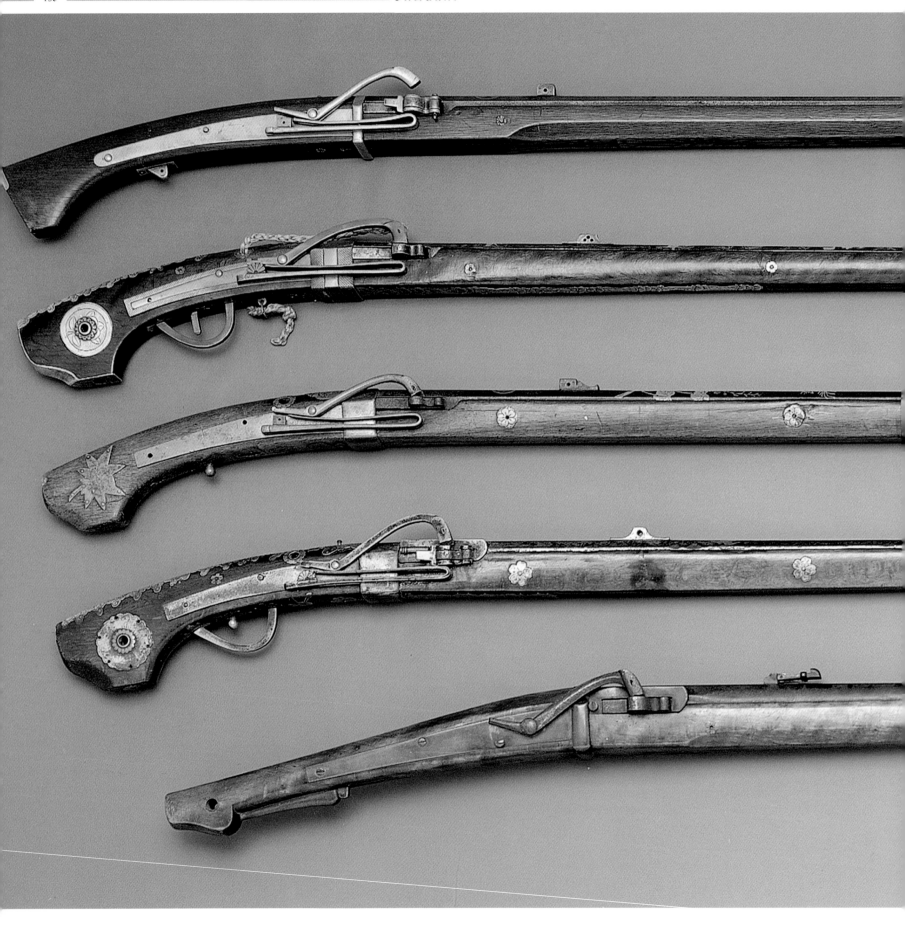

LEFT: A collection of five *teppo* all dating from the late 18th or early 19th centuries. The long top piece is signed on the reverse of the barrel "Kunitomo Kyubei – Ho" and is engraved with two dragons and a *bonji*. Of similar length, the second has an octagonal barrel that is flared at the end with a triangular fore sight and channeled rear sight. The hole in the stock is for the matchlock cord. The third unusually has an adjustable rear sight and lightly engraved barrel, while the fourth also has an octagonal barrel that is flared at the end. The shorter weapon, at bottom, which also has a flared barrel, is probably a carbine.

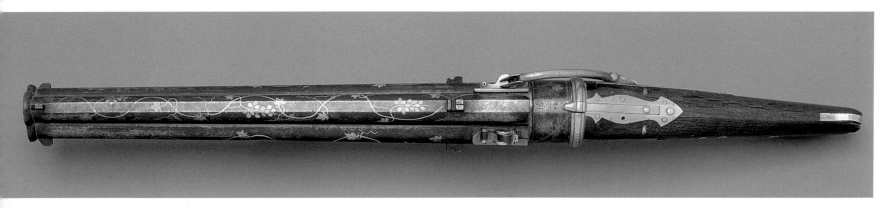

before they were in production throughout the country. Usually they were made by swordsmiths who had the necessary skills in working with metal. Meanwhile, Lord Tokitaka trained and drilled "all his vassals from far and near, and out of every hundred shots they fired many of them could hit the target a hundred times," according to *Teppo-ki* or *The History of Guns*.

The new weapons were known as *Tanegashima* at first. Later the name *teppo* took over. The arrival of guns into Japan was timely as Japan was in the middle of the Sengoku Jidai or period of the country at war. It was quickly to become a decisive factor in a number of important battles, but it was never to attain the status and respect reserved for the sword and, to a lesser extent, other edged weapons. Those who were trained to use the *teppo* were generally lower ranking *ashiguru* or foot soldiers, often recruited from farmers, whose social standing was below that of the *samurai*. It was quickly realised that such social inferiors, with only a few weeks training, could easily dispatch one of much higher rank, who would have spent years studying sword techniques. Further, the noble *samurai* may not have even been able to draw his sword from its scabbard before being hit from long range by a lead bullet.

The death of the twenty-seven year old Lord Mori Nagayoshi in 1584, illustrates this well. Mori, dressed in a white *jimbaori* or surcoat over colourful-laced armour, insisted on riding out in front of his troops, waving his sword in an attempt to inspire them. Such a tempting and conspicuous target must have been hard to resist and an unnamed and unknown matchlock man took careful aim at his head and shot him dead. This was far removed from the honourable ways of fighting, with social equals locked single combat, so the sword remained the preferred weapon of the gentleman.

One of the first to appreciate the potential of firearms was Oda Nobunaga, the first of the great unifiers of the country. He was a superb tactician and especially favoured the use of massed forces of spear men. However, it was he who first used *teppo* on a large scale at the battle of Nagashino in 1575. This battle was fought against Takeda Katsuyori, the son of Takeda Shingen, who had himself died of a bullet wound. Nobunaga's army numbered 30,000 men, of which 10,000 were armed with matchlocks as well as swords. The 3,000 most highly trained were placed behind a wooden palisade in three lines to await the charge of the famously feared Takeda cavalry. When the charge came, the front row knelt and fired, then retreated to the rear to reload while the second row fired. Once the second row had fired, it retired. Then the third row did the same, producing a continuous volley. This completely annihilated the Takeda cavalry. For the

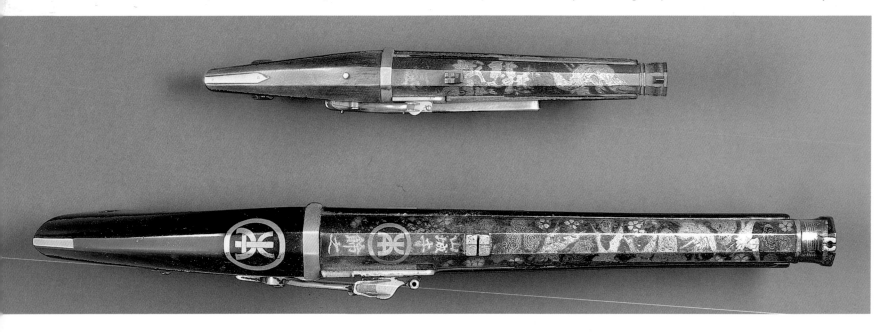

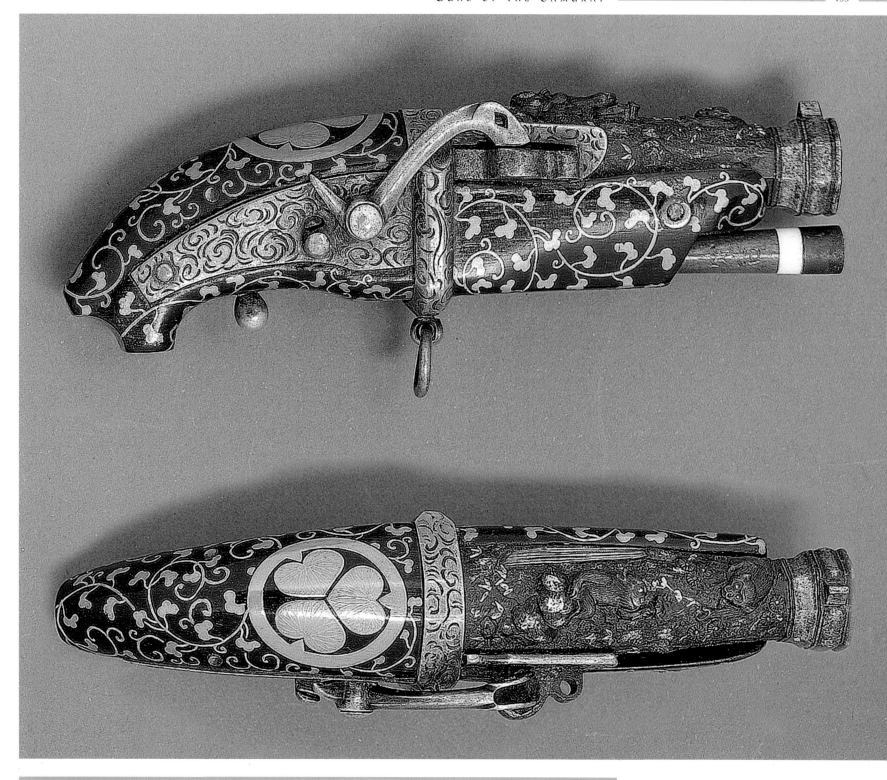

LEFT: The upper matchlock (of two) is only 10 inches (254mm) long and is decorated with silver and gilt. The lower one is richly decorated and is signed "Koshu Kunitomo Tamba Daijo Munetoshi". Both are late Edo period work.

ABOVE LEFT: A very rare Sakai style matchlock with three barrels and signed "Sakai Ju Suketsugu, Kyobei Saku". The barrels are decorated in brass and copper inlay.

ABOVE: A rare miniature *teppo* with an iron barrel boldly carved with two monkeys beside a silver waterfall and signed "Hara Matsuda". The ramrod is of wood, ivory and iron and is signed "Sadayoshi".

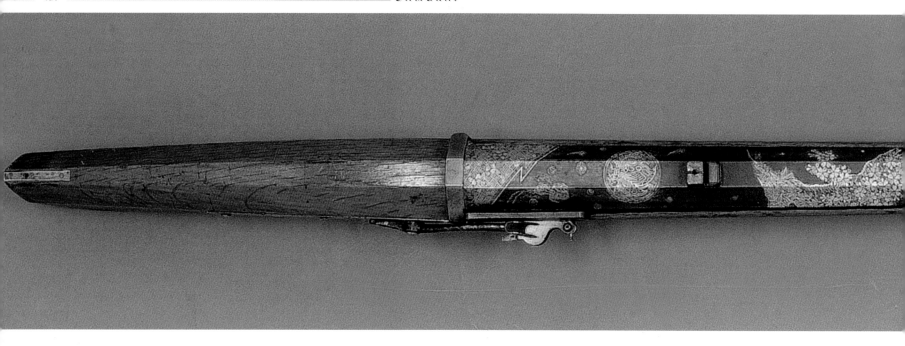

next fifty years or so, the *Tanegashima* or *teppo* was at its height in popularity and most *daimyo* commissioned their swordsmiths to produce as many as possible.

The variations in style of *Tanegashima* were both regional and functional. Satsuma province in the south of Kyushu and the closest mainland province to Tanegashima island is considered to have the style closest to the original Portuguese imports. Those of Hizen province (like Satsuma, a province in Kyushu) and Bizen province, both famous sword-making areas, were renowned for the quality of steel in their barrels. Kishu, Yonezawa and Sendai provide further variations.

Although many gun makers were personally retained by individual *daimyo*, three main groups of gunsmiths produced most of the guns in the country during the later Momoyama period at the end of sixteenth century. The first of these groups were based in Kyushu, assimilating the spread of the technology from Tanegashima into Satsuma, Hizen and Higo provinces. In 1554, a group began production in Sakai near Osaka. This group was known for the quality of their locks and the decorative brass inlay of their guns. They also received commissions from other gun makers or *daimyo* to finish previously made barrels. The third group of gun makers, known as the Kunitomo, were founded in the Kyoto area in 1560. They are said to have supplied the armies of Oda Nobunaga before the battle of Nagashino.

The functional classifications of matchlock guns in Japan, excluding cannon, which were mainly, cast bronze affairs, are as follows:

- *Azama-zutsu*: This may be described as a "loophole" gun for use within a castle or on board a ship. Up to 6 feet 6 inches (2m) in length, they needed a resting place to take aim.
- *Ban-zatusu*: This was a "numbered" gun, an arsenal-issued piece that would be used by low-class *samurai* and would be essentially mass-produced. However, the number, which would be carved onto either

the barrel or the stock, seldom exceeded double figures and the gun was usually 4 foot 3 inches (1.3m) in length.

- *Chyu-zutsu*: This was a "medium sized" gun that would be used as the personal firearm of a reasonably high-ranking *samurai* and was popularly known as the "gun of the *samurai*".
- *Oh-zutsu*: Literally "large" gun, this shot balls ranging from 1 to 3 ½ inches (25 to 89mm) in diameter. It was impossible to shoot without using both hands.
- *Tan-zutsu*: A pistol-style gun that was shot with one hand.
- *Bajou-zutsu*: Essentially a carbine designed for use from horseback, though it was both difficult to load when mounted and to shoot with one hand. Usually it ranged in length from 1 foot 8 inches to 2 feet (50 to 60cm).

The rapid adoption and production of the *teppo* was due to the eagerness of the *samurai* to find ever more efficient ways of killing each other helped by the advanced metal- and wood-working techniques already possessed by Japanese craftsmen. Only three basic skills were required to produce a matchlock: that of a blacksmith to make the barrel, a metal worker to make the lock and a cabinet maker to produce the stock.

The barrel making was relatively straightforward as both the sword makers and armourers of the day had already attained an extremely high level of skill. They wrapped a hot steel slab around another steel bar and sealed it at the seam. If desired, this process could be repeated to produce a "double-wrapped barrel". The central bar was then removed to leave the hollowed barrel. At this stage the sights would be fitted and the fire-pad was welded on.

If the gunsmith was skilled at his job, as most were, the making of a basic gun could be accomplished reasonably quickly, but the finishing work, especially on a high quality custom-made piece, could take as long again. This involved fitting the components together, polishing the outside

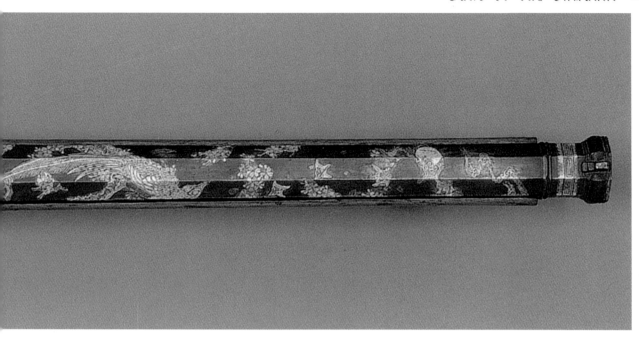

LEFT: The iron octagonal barrel of this piece is inlaid with silver depicting a peacock on a blossoming branch, scrolling clouds and birds in flight. It is signed "Nijubari Oshikaji Shigezaemon Saku".

surfaces and finally polishing the inside of the barrel with a long slender burnishing pin. The stock, which was usually made of hard Japanese oak, was lacquered – a ramrod was often produced from the same piece of oak.

Unlike a Western stock, which would be made to fit into the shoulder, the stock of the *teppo* rested against the cheek and looked somewhat like a pistol grip. It is thought that this might reflect the fact that those early examples brought to Tanegashima by the Portuguese in 1543 might have been sporting guns rather than military weapons, or that the bulky nature of sixteenth-century Japanese armour made placing the stock against the shoulder impossible.

On better quality pieces, the barrel, which was sometimes signed by the maker, might also be decoratively engraved. This engraving and decoration, similar in style to that seen on the *tsuba* of swords, might be simply the *mon* (crest of the clan for which it was made) a dragon or religious characters such as bonji (from Sanskrit). These decorations were usually made soft metals such as copper, brass gold or silver. Sometimes such decorations have been added later to enhance the value of the piece and, where *mon* were used, this would be replicated on other accessories such as powder flasks and ammunition bags.

The actual range and efficiency of *Tanegashima* or *teppo* were quite restricted by modern standards. Although a killing range could be as much as 300 yards (275m) under ideal conditions, the shooter was unlikely to consistently hit a human target at over 50 yards (45m). Weather conditions also had to be favourable, as a matchlock was notoriously difficult to use in the rain or wind as the match used to ignite the primer is easily extinguished. Various covers were made to combat this but their effectiveness could not be relied on.

The use of the *teppo* was considered in the same way as the other traditional martial arts and schools were founded to teach the proper use of the weapon. Several of these schools produced manuals of instruction and

advice. Probably the largest and best known was the Inatomi school whose illustrated book of instructions included invaluable advice such as:
- When facing the sun at dawn or sunset, a target of about 600 yards (550m) appears to be about 650 yards (600m).
- When looking through narrow places, such as the loopholes of castle walls, objects appear to be more distant.
- On water, when shooting from ships, objects appear less distant.

Instructions concerning good manners and gun safety were also set down. For example: "When setting the matchcord in a kneeling position, the muzzle must never be pointed in the direction of others, and excessive movement of the hands or shoulders is forbidden."

The illustrations included in the Inatomi instruction manual show various firing positions. These vary from regular mounted, standing and kneeling positions to the unlikely position of the shooter lying on his back supporting the barrel on his knees. One shows the shooter in the "cross-legged standing position" which is claimed to be effective when standing on an uneven surface. A feature of the manual is that all illustrations depict the shooter dressed only in a loin cloth to show the precise position of legs and arms, unencumbered with clothes that would make this less clear. The Inatomi also gave advice on how to shoot according to the time of day, season, place and environment, all factors which could influence the effectiveness of the powder. In common with other schools, the Inatomi made long-distance shooting as their main discipline, which has led to speculation that the Japanese matchlock was often used as a defensive weapon behind castle walls. Some claims of the effectiveness of weapons over extreme distances are thought impossible in reality, but they might be included to provide the aspiring marksmen with a challenge to his mental and spiritual abilities, and a desire to exceed normal limitations.

In fact, the *teppo* was in military use in Japan for a relatively short time, some seventy years. As well as playing a crucial role at Nagashino, it saw

great use in Toyotomi's Korean invasions. The first invasion in 1592, known as the Bunroku War, lasted eighteen months and the invasion force numbered about 200,000 men with about 60,000 guns, while in the second attempt, the Keicho War of 1597, which lasted about two years, 140,000 men carried 50,000 guns. As the Koreans had no such weapons, the Japanese matchlock wreaked havoc in a somewhat unequal contest. In 1600 when Tokugawa Ieyasu fought the one-day battle at Sekigahara, 140,000 men opposed his force of 100,000. Between them they carried a total of 80,000 guns.

At the winter and summer battles at Osaka castle in 1614-15, both the defenders and attackers made good use of firearms. They had about 100,000 between them. In both the important battles of Nagatuke in 1584 and at Odawara in 1594, significant numbers of firearms were used. The last major battle utilising the matchlock was in the suppression of the so-called Christian Rebellion at the castle of Shimabara in Hizen province (present-day Nagasaki prefecture). This took place in 1638, less than one hundred years after the introduction of the gun in Tanegashima and less than seventy after they were first employed on a grand scale at Nagashino.

After Shimabara, the Tokugawa rule was further tightened and guns became as closely regulated as every other aspect of life. The isolation policy of the *shogunate* government meant that the technology of the West passed the Japanese by for over two hundred years. When eventually faced with the modern post-industrial revolution weapons of the West in the mid-eighteenth century, the Japanese were still armed with matchlocks that were essentially the same as those brought to Tanegashima three hundred years previously and swordsmiths, such as the eighth generation Tadayoshi of Hizen province, were still casting bronze cannon for coastal defences. It must have been quite a shock to the first *samurai* to fire an Enfield or Springfield rifle. He would have immediately realised that the accurate range was ten times better than his ancient smooth-bored matchlock and that the foreign weapon was superior in all aspects. To have to acknowledge just how far behind they had fallen in this and every other aspect of modern warfare must have been a salutary lesson to the proud *samurai*. It was a lesson that they were to learn quickly and thoroughly.

LEFT: A group items displaying the *maru-juji mon* of the powerful Shimazu clan of Satsuma province. It comprises a *jingasa* (war hat), *abumi* (stirrups), a shot flask and a *teppo* simply decorated with the *mon*.

GLOSSARY OF TERMS

ARMOUR

Asa-nagashi: (lit: sweat running hole) – Hole under the chin of a face mask designed to allow perspiration to drain away.

Do: Cuirass of armour.

Do-maru: An armour that wraps completely round the torso and is fastened at the side.

Fukigaeshi: Continuation of the *shikoro* (see), turning back like ears on a *kabuto* (see).

Gunpai-uchiwa: War fan, used for signalling but occasionally as a weapon.

Haidate: Thigh protectors, usually of chain-mail on a cloth backing.

Haramaki: Similar to the *do-maru* (see) but joined at the back.

Hoshi-kabuto: Helmet with standing rivets.

Jimbaori: Surcoat worn over armour.

Kuwagata: Horn-like decorations that adorned the front of many *kabuto* (see).

Kusasari: The "skirt" of the armour.

Kabuto: Helmet.

Kebiki-odoshi: Close lacing (on armour)

Kote: Hand and arm armour (also *gote*).

Kutsu: Shoes.

Kuwari-kabuto: Decorative or unusual helmet.

Maedate: Crest in front part of helmet.

Mempo: Face armour, sometimes called *mengu*.

Nodawa: Throat defence, usually on old style armours.

Saiha: A commander's baton, which ends in paper strips and is used for signalling.

Sashimono: Flag worn on the back of armour for identification purposes.

Shikoro: Neck defence of an armour.

Sode: Shoulder defences.

Sugake-odoshi: Wide-spaced lacing on armour.

Suji-kabuto: Helmet with standing flanges (*suji*).

Suneate: Shin protectors.

Tehen: Ornamental ventilation hole on the top of a *kabuto* (see).

Uchidashi-do: Embossed cuirass.

Yodarekake: Throat defence attached to *mempo* (see).

ARCHERY, POLEARMS AND SWORDS

Aikuchi: A type of *tanto koshirae* where there is no *tsuba* and the handle makes a flush fit with the *koiguchi*.

Ara-nie: Coarse or large *nie* (see *nie*).

Ashi: A feature of the *hamon* (see) that appears like small legs running downtowards the edge of the blade, from the *habuchi*, forming small fracture zones. Also: *tachi* scabbard mounting.

Atari: "Hit" – the term used by a judge when a correct vote is given in *nyusatsu kantei* (sword identification competition).

Ato-bori: *Horimono* or carving made after the original blade was made.

Ayasugi: A wave-like pattern, most common in Gassan blades (see *jihada*).

Bo-hi: Straight groove cut in the blade to lighten or give balance.

Bonji: Sanskrit inscriptions on the surface of a blade.

Boshi: That part of the hardened edge that appears in the point of the sword.

Bushi: See *samurai*.

Chikei: Lines of *nie* similar to *sunagaeshi* (see) but found in the *ji* (see).

Choji-abura: Clove oil used to protect a blade from humidity.

Choji-midare: Irregular clove shaped *hamon*.

Chu: "Middle" – the adjective used in conjunction with various nouns such as *chu-kissaki* (medium point), *chu-itame-hada* (medium-sized wood grain pattern), etc.

Daimei: A substitute signature, where a pupil has signed a master's name with his permission, not considered as a fake but the genuine work of the master.

Daimyo: (lit. – big name) feudal lord of Japan.

Dai-saku: A substitute blade, where a blade is made by the student but is usually signed with the master's name, by the master.

Daisho: Matched pair of swords worn only by those of *samurai* rank.

Fuchi: Usually soft metal or iron decoration at the bottom (nearest the *tsuba*) end of a sword *tsuka* (see), like a collar, usually paired with the *kashira* at the top end of the *tsuka*.

Fudo-Myo: A Buddhist god often the subject of carvings on swords and considered the patron saint of swordsmen.

Fukkoto: Swords made in the *shinshinto* period but in style of the Kamakura and Nambokucho periods.

Fukura: The curve on the cutting edge of the *kissaki* (see).

Fukusa: Silk cloth used when handling sword blades or lacquer.

Futatsu-bi: Double grooves carved parallel in the blade.

Gendaito: Modern swords produced by traditional methods, after 1876.

Gimei: False or fake inscription.

Gombashi-hi: Short double grooves that resemble chopsticks.

Ha: The tempered or quenched hardened edge of a blade.

Habaki: The collar of the blade that ensures a tight fit into the *saya* (see).

Habaki-moto: The area of the blade covered by the *habaki* (see).

Habuchi: Area of transition between the *hamon* (see) and the *ji* (see).

Hagiri: A crack in the *ha* (see) that runs at right angles to the *ha* into the blade.

Ha-machi: The notch on the cutting edge side, where the blade proper meets the *nakago* (see). Also see **mune-machi**.

Hamon: The pattern of the hardened edge.

Han-dachi: (lit. – half *tachi*) A mount that incorporates the *saya* (see) mounts of a *tachi* (see) but is worn like a *katana* (see).

Hakko-gaki: An appraisal brushed onto a box, usually a *tsuba* box. Also see *saya-gaki*.

Ha-saki: Cutting edge.

Hataraki: "Workings" or "activities" on a blade, such as *ashi* (see), *sunagaeshi* (see), etc.

Hi: Groove cut into the surface of a blade.

Hira-tsukuri: Describes a flat-surfaced blade, ie with no ridgeline.

Hizen-to: Swords made in Hizen province; this expression usually refers to the main Tadayoshi school of makers.

Horimono: Carvings on the surface of the blade.

Hoso: Narrow, as in *hoso-suguha hamon* (see).

Ichimonji: A famous group of swordsmiths from the Kamakura period.

Iori-mune: Roof-shaped back edge or *mune* (see) of a blade.

Itame: An elongated wood pattern found in the *jihada* (see) of some swords.

Ito: Thread, used to wrap the *tsuka* (see) of a sword and also part of the *saya* (see) on an *ito-maki tachi* (thread wrapped *tachi*).

Ji: Area of a sword between the *shinogi* (see) and the *hamon* (see). Also see *jihada*.

Jigane: The actual steel that forms the blade, also called *jitetsu*.

Jihada: The woodgrain-like pattern visible in the body of a properly polished and forged blade.

Jiri: Butt end of the *saya* (see), *ko-jiri*, or *nakago* (see), *nakago-jiri*.

Jizo: A shape of *boshi* (see), a characteristic of Mino blades.

Jumonji-yari: Cross-shaped spear, also called *magari-yari*.

Kabuto-gane: The top part of the *tsuka* (see), replacing the *kashira* (see) on *tachi* (see) and *han-dachi katana* (see).

Kaeri: Return of the *boshi* (see) along the *mune* (see) of a blade.

Kantei: Sword appraisal or judging, often as a competition to attempt to name a maker without reference to any inscription.

Kashira: The butt end of the *tsuka* (see). Also see *fuchi*.

Katana: A long sword that is worn with the cutting edge uppermost.

Katana-kake: Sword rack.

Kazu-uichi-mono: Mass-produced blades.

Kinnoto: Swords worn by royalists at the end of the Edo period.

Kinzogan-mei: Gold inlay appraisal, added to shortened blades that may have lost their original inscriptions. *Kinzogan*, or gold-inlay is also a technique used on *tsuba* (see) and other sword mounts.

Kinsuji: An activity in the *hamon* (see); short golden lines.

Kissaki: The point section of a blade.

Kodzuka: The ornate handle of a *ko-gatana* (see).

Ko-gatana: The small auxiliary knife usually found slotted into the *saya* (see) of either *wakizashi* (see) or *tanto* (see).

Kogai: A skewer-like instrument, similarly located to the *ko-gatana* (see) and *kodzuka* (see).

Koi-guchi: The open mouth of the *saya* (see), literally "carp mouth".

Ko-nie: Small *nie* (see).

Koshirae: The entire mount of a sword or polearm, excluding the blade.

Koshi-zori: Curvature on a sword, which is strongest at the waist of the wearer.

Kurikata: The loop on the outside of the *saya* (see) through which the *sageo* (see) passes.

Koto: Old swords made prior to 1596

Nakago: The tang of a blade.

Masame-hada: Straight grain pattern associated with Yamato blades.

Mei: Inscription, usually found on the *nakago* (see); may give smith's name, dates, and other information.

Mekugi-ana: Holes drilled in the *nakago* (see) of a blade to accommodate a *mekugi*-securing peg.

Mekugi-nuki: Tool for removing the *mekugi*.

Menuki: Small decorative hilt ornaments found under the wrapping of a sword *tsuka* (see).

Mitsugashira: The junction of the *shinogi* (see), *yokote* (see) and *ko-shinogi*.

Mokume-hada: A burl-like wood grain (see *jihada*).

Monouchi: First approx one-third of a blade nearest the point, the striking area.

Mumei: Unsigned, no inscription.

Mune: Back edge of a blade.

Mune-machi: The notch on the back edge where the *nakago* (see) meets the blade proper.

Nagasa: Length of blade measured from the *mune-machi* (see) to the tip of the *kissaki* (see), also called the *ha-watari*.

Naginata: Glaive or halberd

Nakago: The tang of a blade.

Nanako: Ground of raised dots on sword fittings, resembling fish-roe.

Nie: Martensite crystals, individually visible to the naked eye, that are a product of the quenching of a blade and that are usually found at the edge of the *hamon* (see) but may appear on other parts of the blade.

Nioi: The same as *nie* (see), but smaller and not individually visible to the naked eye.

Obi: The sash in which the *katana* (see) was thrust.

Omote: The front side of a blade, usually bearing any signature, and facing outwards when worn.

Sageo: A cord attached to the *saya* (see) to help hold the sword in the *obi* (see).

Saidan-mei: Inscription recording a cutting test; also referred to wrongly as a *tameshigiri*.

Samé: Ray skin that is wrapped around the *tsuka* (see); the nodules facilitate the grip of the wrap. Sometimes polished flat and also used on *saya* (see).

Samurai: Warrior class of Japan, often also called *bushi* (see).

Saya: Scabbard.

Sayagaki: Brushed appraisal onto the *shira-saya* (see), usually by a well-known appraiser. Also see *hakko-gaki*.

Sayashi: A maker of *saya* (see).

Sentoku: Alloy found in sword fittings, similar to brass.

Seppa: Spacers or small washers fitted either side of the *tsuba* (see).

Shakudo: Alloy found in sword furniture, usually patinated black.

Shibuichi: Alloy found in sword furniture, often a grey colour.

Shinogi: The central ridgeline found on most sword blades.

Shinogi-ji: The area between the *shinogi* (see) and the *mune* (see) on a sword.

Shira-saya: Plain wood storage mount for a blade. Also cover for a regular *tachi saya* (see) made of bear fur or tiger skin.

Shinto: New swords, made between 1596 and approximately 1780.

Shinshinto: Very new swords made between 1780 and 1877.

Shumei: Lacquered appraisal, usually on the *nakago* (see) of a *mumei* (see) blade.

Sugata: General characteristics of a blade, including shape, curvature, width, size of point, etc.

Suguha: Straight *hamon* (see).

Su-ken: *Horimono* (see) representing a straight sword.

Sunagaeshi: An activity within the *hamon* (see), which resembles drifting sand.

Suriage: Shortened *nakago* (see); *o-suriage*, greatly shortened.

Su-yari: Straight spear.

Tachi: A slung sword worn with the cutting edge down.

Tamahagane: The raw material for making a blade that must be forged into steel.

Tanto: The generic name for a dagger.

Togishi: A polisher of blades.

Tsuba: Hand guard of a sword.

Tsuka: The complete handle.

Tsunagi: Wooden replica of a blade to keep the *koshirae* (see) together after the blade has been polished and put into *shira-saya* (see).

Tsuru: String of a bow.

Ubu: Unaltered, original, used especially in reference to *nakago* (see).

Ubu-ha: "Original edge" – a small, unsharpened section on some blades at the very beginning of the blade near the *nakago* (see). Usually only found in 20th century blades, but occasionally on *shinshinto* (see) swords.

Uchiko: Powder used to remove oil from a blade.

Umabari: "Horse needle" – one-piece straight knife, fitted in place of *kogai* (see).

Utsuri: A shadow of the *hamon* (see), considered an indication of quality, especially in blades from Bizen province.

Wakizashi: The short sword that normally forms part of a *daisho* (see).

Ya: The shaft of an arrow.

Ya-haki: Arrow-maker or fletcher.

Yajiri: Arrow head, later called *yanone*.

Yakidashi: Straightening of the *hamon* (see) towards the *nakago* (see).

Yasurime: The file marks on a *nakago* (see).

Yari: Generic name for spears.

Yokote: The vertical line on *shinogi-zukuri* (see) blades that goes directly to the cutting edge from the *shinogi* and defines the beginning of the *kissaki* (see).

Yumi: The Japanese bow.

Zori: Sometimes written as *sori*, the curvature of the blade.

BIBLIOGRAPHY

I have found all of the following books to be useful.

ENGLISH LANGUAGE

Arai Hakuseki. *Armour Book in Honch-Gunkiko (The)*, edited by H. Russell Robinson

Akamatsu P. *Meiji 1868, Revolution and Counter Revolution in Japan.*

Anderson, L. J. *Japanese Armour*

Arai Hakusei. *Sword and Samé*, translated by Joly and Inada

David Berganini. *Japan's Imperial Conspiracy*

Bottomley, I., and Hopson A. P. *Arms and Armour of the Samurai*

Christie's. *Nippon-to: Art Swords of Japan*, The Walkter Compton Collection

Christie's. *One Hundred Materpieces from the Collection of Dr Walter A. Compton*

Dobree, A. *Japanese Sword Blades*

Fujishiro. *Nihon-to Shinto and Koto Jiten* (translated by H. Watson)

Fuller and Gregory. *Japanese Civil and Military Swords and Dirks*

Harris, Victor, and Ogasawara Nobuo. *Swords of the Samurai* – British Museum exhibition catalogue

Homma Junji. *Masterworks of Japanese Swords by Masamune and his School*

Inami Hakusui. *The Japanese Sword*

Inazuka. *The Technique of Oshigata Making of the Japanese Sword* (partial translation by Sato K.)

Japan Society of New York. *Spectacular Helmets of Japan, 16th-19th Century*

Japan Sword Society of US. *Art and the Sword* (various)

Japan Sword Society of US. *Newsletter* (various)

Kajihara Kotoken. *Nihon-to, Swords of Japan, A Visual Glossary*

Kaplan, D. and Dubro, A. *Yakuza*

Kapp, Leon and Hiroko, Yoshihara Yoshindo. *The Craft of the Japanese Sword*

Kishida T. *Yasukini-to* (translated by Mishina Kenji)

Knutsen, Roald. *Japanese Polearms*

Mabine and Becheret. *The Samurai*

Miyamotot Musashi. *A Book of Five Rings* (*Go Rin No Sho*) (translated by Victor Harris)

Morris, I. *Nobility of Failure*

Nagajima Kokan. *The Connoisseur's Book of the Japanese Sword* (translated by Mishina Kenji)

Nihon Bijutsu Token Hozon Kyokai. *Token Bijutsu*

Ogawa Morihiro. *Japanese Swords & Sword Furniture in the Museum of Fine Arts, Boston*

Perrin, N. *Giving Up the Gun*

Ratti, Oscar, and Westbrook, Adele. *Secrets of the Samurai*

Robertshaw, Roger. *Hizen Tadayoshi*

Robinson, B. W. *Arts of the Japanese Sword*

Sakibara Kozan. *The Manufacture of Armour and Helmets in 16th Century Japan* (edited by H. Russell Robinson)

Sasano Masayuki. *Early Japanese Sword Guards, Sukashi Tsuba*

Sato Kanzan. *The Japanese Sword* (translated by J. Earl)

Storry, R. *A History of Modern Japan*

Sugawa Shigeo. *The Japanese Matchlock* (English and Japanese)

To-ken Society of Great Britain. *Nihon-to Magazine* (various)

To-ken Society of Great Britain. *The Programme* (various)

Turnbull, S. *The Samurai, A Military History*

Warner and Draeger. *Japanese Swordsmanship*

Watson, H. *Nihon-to: Koza* (various, translated)

Yamamoto. *The Hagakure* (translated by Takao)

Yamanaka, Albert. *Nihon-to Newsletter*

Yates, C. *Saigo Takamori: The Man Behind the Myth*

Yumoto, John. *The Samurai Sword*

JAPANESE LANGUAGE

Fujishiro. *Nihon-to Shinto and Koto Jiten*

Fukunaga Suiken. *Hizen-to To Tsuba*

Homma Junji. *Masamune to Sono Mon* (Japanese and English)

Koto, Shinto and Shinshinto Taikan (various authors)

Mino To Taiken (various)

Nihon Bijutsu Token Hozon Kyokai. *Token Bijutsu magazine*

Ogasawara Nobuo. Tokyo National Museum exhibition catalogue

Shibata Matsuo. *Rei Magazine* (various)

Tadayoshi School, The. *Hizen-to Taikan*

Tokeno. *Tokeno Taikan*

Tokyo National Museum publication. *Koshirae*

Yoshikawa. *Catalogue of Excellent Swords* (Nihon Token Hozon Kai publication)

INDEX

A
Akechi Mitsuhide, 14 et seq, 50
Amada Akitsugu, 60
Archery competitions, 123
Archery, 120 et seq
Armour, 26 et seq
Arrows, 120 et seq
Asano Takumi no Kami, Lord, 21
Ashikaga Takaugi, 13, 47
Azama-zutsu (loophole gun), 134
Azuchi-Momoyama period, 15, 50

B
Bajou-zutsu (carbine), 134
Ban-szatusu (numbered gun), 134
Battles,
    Dannoura, 12
    Nagashino, 14, 49, 132
    Nagatuke, 137
    Odawara, 137
    Sekigahara, 17, 50, 114, 137
    Shimabara, 137
    Shizugadake, 112
    Ueono, 24 et seq, 58
Bizen-den (sword style), 43
Blade construction, 60 et seq
Bows and arrows, 40, 120 et seq
Bunroku period, 50
Bushido, 20 et seq

C
Chisai-katana (short/small swords), 85
Chishingura, 22
Choshu, 25
Chyu-zutsu (medium-sized gun), 134

D
Daisho, 15, 19, 47
Dai-to (long swords), 81
Dai-to, 15
Do-maru armour, 26

E
Edo period, 53

F
Face masks, 30
Firearms, 49, 128 et seq

Forty-seven *ronin*, 22 et seq
Fuchi-kashira (metal fittings on sword handle), 76
Fujiwara, 11
Fushimi castle, 20

G
Gassan Sadakuzu, 59
Gempei Wars, 12, 40, 107, 121
Gendaito (modern swords), 58
Genghis Khan, 13
Genji, 12
Genroku period, 24, 56
Go Rin No Sho, 10, 20, 25, 60, 106, 120, 128
Gochim-no-Tajima, 108
Go-Daigo, Emperor, 13, 46, 47
Gokkaden (swordmaking traditions), 49
Gotoba, Emperor, 44
Guns, 128 et seq
Gunto (army sword), 59, 85 et seq

H
Hakagure, 20
Haramki armour, 26
Harima Daijo, 54
Hashimoto Shinsaemon, 53
Heian period, 11, 41, 43, 106
Heiki, 12
Helmets, 26
Hineno Hisanori, 32
Hirohito, Emperor (Showa), 12, 42
Hizen-to, 53
Hogen War, 121
Hori Toshihide, 59
Horikawa Kunihiro, 65
Horimono (carvings), 67
Hoshino Kansaemon, 125

I
Ikkansai Kasama Shigetsugu, 63
Importing swords to Japan, 96

J
Japan Swordsmiths Association, 60
Japanese Art Sword Preservation Society, 60
Japanese Sword Forging Institute, 59
Japanese Sword Forging Society, 59
Japanese Sword Museum, 60
Jimbaori (surcoat), 37

K

Kabuto (helmet), 29 et seq
Kai-gunto (navy sword), 59, 85 et seq
Kamakura period, 13, 44
Kamikaze, 12 et seq
Kanbun period, 55
Kanehira, 63
Kanemichi, 54
Kantei nyusatsu (sword blade examination), 102
Kasama Ikkansai Shigetsugu, 58
Katana, 49
Katana-kake (sword rack), 91
Kato Kiyomasa, 12, 34
Kawanakajima, 14
Kawabi Hachiro Masahide, 57
Kawachi (no) Kami, 54
Keicho period, 50 et seq
Keicho War, 137
Keicho-shinto sugata (sword style), 53
Kemmu no Chuko (Kemmor Restoration), 47
Kira Kozuke no Suke, 21
Kiyomaro (Minamoto Masayuki), 58
Ko-gatana (auxiliary knives), 79, 86
Korea, Invasion of, 17, 50, 114, 137
Kotetsu, 55
Koto (old swords), 40 et seq
Koyama Munetsugu, 58
Kozuka (handles of *ko-gatana*, knives), 79
Kublai Khan, 12 et seq, 45
Kunihiro, 54
Kuroda Nagamasa, 34
Kusajishi (archery competition), 123
Kusonuki Masashige, 13, 47

L

Living National Treasures, 60

M

Makura yari (small polearm), 119
Masamune (swordmaker), 45 et seq
Meiji, Emperor, 24, 59
Meiji Restoration, 24, 57
Mempo, 30
Mengu, 30
Minamoto, 12 et seq
Minamato Tametomo, 121

Minamoto Yoritomo, 24, 43, 121
Minamoto Yoshikazu, 35
Minamoto Yoshitsune, 34, 73, 109
Mino-den (sword style), 47
Miochin Kunimichi, 38
Miochin Munesuke, 38
Miochin Nobuiye, 34 et seq
Miochin Yoshimichi, 34 et seq
Miyamoto Kanenori, 59
Miyamoto Musashi, 18
Momoyama period, 32, 114
Mongols, 13, 45
Mori Nagayoshi, Lord, 132
Mori Ranmaru, 16
Mountings of swords, 70 et seq
Muramasa, 50
Muromachi period, 29, 49 et seq, 110
Musashi, 25

N

Nabeshima clan, 53
Nagashino, 24
Naginata (glaives, halberds), 42, 106 et seq
Nakamura Kansuke Tadatoki, 23
Nambam, 32
Namboku-cho period, 13, 29, 47, 65
Nara period, 11, 40
Nasu no Yoichi, 121
National Treasures, 41
Nihon Bijutsu To-ken Hoson Kyokai (NBTHK), 41, 60
Nihon To Tanren Kai, 59
Niita Yoshisada, 13
Ningen Kokuho (Living National Treasure), 60
Nitta Yoshisada, 47

O

Oda Nobunaga, 11, 14 et seq, 49, 132
Oei Bizen Yasumitsu, 65
Ohnishi Token, 60
Oh-zutsu (large gun), 134
Onin period, 49
Ono (war axe), 114
Origami (sword certificates), 99
Osaka castle, 51, 137
Osumi Yoshitsugu, 60
Otsuchi, 23

Otushi (war mallet), 119
O-yoroi, armour part, 28, 41
Ozawa, Mr. (amour restorer), 35

P
Pacific War (1941-1945), 25, 43, 59
Pearl Harbor, 25
Perry, Commodore, 24, 58
Polearms, 106 et seq

Q
Quivers, 121 et seq

S
Saigo Takamori, 24
Saito-Musashi-bo Benki, 109
Saki-zori, 49
Sasaki Takatsuna, 40
Satsuma clan, 24 et seq
Saya (scabbard), 77 et seq, 88
Sengoku Jidai, 14, 29, 49
Shibata Katsuiye, 16
Shigetaka, 56
Shimabara castle, 137
Shin-gunto (army swords), 85 et seq
Shinsa (sword judging and appraisal), 60, 96 et seq
Shinsakuto (newly made swords), 58 et seq
Shinshinto (new new sword style), 56 et seq
Shinto (new swords), 42, 51 et seq
Shira-saya (storage scabbard), 88
Shizu Saburo Kaneuji, 47
Sho-to (short swords and daggers),15, 86
Showa Mei Zukushi, 44
Showa period, 58 et seq
Society for the Preservation of Japanese Art Swords, 98 et seq
Sode-garami (sleeve entangler), 119
Somen, 30, 31
Soshu-den (sword style), 45 et seq
Spears, 42, 106 et seq
Sword handling etiquette, 90 et seq
Sword restoration and preservation, 94
Swords (parts of), 62 et seq

T
Tachi (slung sword), 16, 83
Tadayoshi, 53, 57

Taira, 12
Takeda Katsuyori, 132
Takeda Shingen, 14, 34, 132
Tamba (no) Kami, 54
Tameshirgiri, 55
Tanegashima (firearms), 128 et seq
Tanto (daggers), 45 et seq, 88 et seq
Tan-zutsu (pistol), 134
Tensho period, 50
Teppo (firearms), 111, 128 et seq
Tetsubo, 25
Tokitaka, Lord, 129
Tokugawa Ieyasu, 17 et seq, 34, 50 et seq, 114, 137
Tokugawa period, 47 et seq, 53
Tokyo National Museum, 35
Tomotaka, 57
Toshihara Yoshindo, 56
Toshiro Mifune, 10
Toyotomi Hideyoshi, 15 et seq, 34, 50, 112
Tsuba (hand guards), 36, 71 et seq
Tsuka (sword handle) 74 et seq

U
Ueda castle, 35
Ueno, Memorial Shrine, 24
Uesugi Kenshin, 14
Uichi-gatana, 49
Uji river, 40, 108
Umahari (horse-needle), 87
Umetada Myoju, 53 et seq
Utushi (copies), 60

W
Wakizashi (companion sword), 86 et seq
Wasa Daihachiro, 125
World War II, 42

Y
Yamada Satake Asaemon, 55
Yamamoto Tsunetomo, 20
Yamano family, 55
Yamashiro-den (sword style), 43
Yamato-den (sword style), 43
Yari (spears), 106 et eq
Yoritomo, 12
Yoshitsune, 10 et seq
Yumi (bow), 120 et seq

PICTURE CREDITS

Japan Sword Co.
p.27, p.28 (right), p.31, p.33 (left), p.34, p.35 (left), p.36 (right), p.38 (and front cover), p.74, p.114, p.123, p.128.

Iida Tomihiko:
p.44, p.46 (right), p.47 (left), p.48 (left), p.50, p.51, p.52, p.56, p.63 (right), p.64, p.65, p.66, p.67 (right), p.68 (left), p.69, p.76, p.80/81, p.82, p.83, p.84, p.85, p.86, p.87 (right and above), p.88 (left), p.93, p.101, p.102, p.103, p.104, p.105, p.110.

Christie's:
p.28 (far left), p.30, p.36 (left), p.55, p.119, p.120, p.124, p.126/7, p.130/131, p.132, p.133, p.134/5, p.137.

Sotheby's:
p.37, p.47 (right), p.53, p. 66 (left), p.71, p. 72, p.73 (top), p.78/79, p.121, p.122, p.129.

British Museum:
p.40, p.43, p.46 (left), p.48 (right and far right), p.70.

Rochester Guildhall Museum and L. J. Anderson:
p.32, p.33 (right), p.39.

R. Knutsen:
p.29, p.106, p.107, p.108.

Tsuchiko Tamio:
p.61, p.73 (bottom), p.75, p.77, p.92.

All other pictures sourced by the author.